NATIONAL INDEX OF PARISH REGISTERS

A Guide to Anglican,
Nonconformist
together with information (
modern copies and M

CU00662140

VOLUME 8

PART 4

CORNWALL

Compiled by

Anthony Wilcox   M.A.   M.Phil.   F.R.S.A.

General Editor

C.R.Webb   M.A.   F.S.G.

SOCIETY OF GENEALOGISTS
14 Charterhouse Buildings
Goswell Road
London EC1M 7BA

1999

Published by
Society of Genealogists
14 Charterhouse Buildings
Goswell Road
London EC1M 7BA

1999 Society of Genealogists

ISBN 1 85951 603 3

Volumes of the National Index of Parish Registers already published

Volume 1   *General Sources of Births, Marriages and Deaths before 1837*
            Parish Registers, Marriage Licences, Monumental Inscriptions,
            Newspapers, Clandestine Marriages, Divorce, Mediaeval Sources,
            Other Records. General Bibliography.

Volume 2   *Sources for Nonconformist Genealogy and Family History*
            The Three Denominations (Presbyterians, Independents
            and Baptists), Society of Friends, Moravians, Methodists,
            Foreign Churches, Other Denominations.

Volume 3   *Sources for Roman Catholic Genealogy and Family History*
            With a short section on Jewish Records contributed by Edgar
            Samuel. Index to Volumes 1, 2 and 3.

Volume 4   *South East England*
            Kent, Surrey and Sussex.
            A revised edition of Surrey has appeared as Volume 4 Part 1.

Volume 5   *South Midlands and Welsh Border*
            Gloucestershire, Herefordshire, Oxfordshire, Shropshire,
            Warwickshire, Worcestershire.

Volume 6   *North and East Midlands*
            Part 1: Staffordshire.
            Part 2: Nottinghamshire.
            Part 3: Leicestershire and Rutland.
            Part 4: Lincolnshire.
            Part 5: Derbyshire.

Volume 7   *East Anglia*
            Cambridgeshire, Norfolk, Suffolk.

Volume 8   *The West of England*
            Part 1 : Berkshire.
            Part 2 : Wiltshire.
            Part 3 : Somerset.
            Part 4 : Cornwall.

Volume 9   *Home Counties (North of the Thames) and South-East Midlands*
            Part 1 : Bedfordshire and Huntingdonshire.
            Part 2 : Northamptonshire.
            Part 3 : Buckinghamshire.
            Part 4 : Essex.
            Part 5 : London and Middlesex.

Volume 10   *North West England*
            Part 1 : Cheshire.
            Part 2 : Lancashire

Volume 11   *North East England*
            Part 1: Durham, Northumberland.
            Part 2: Yorkshire (North and East Ridings and York).
            Part 3: Yorkshire (West Riding).

Volume 12   *Sources for Scottish Genealogy and Family History*
            Historical background, Parish Registers, Ancillary Sources
            Nonconformists, Bibliography.

Volume 13   *Parish Registers of Wales*

Volume 14   *Nonconformist Registers of Wales*

VOLUME 8

PART 4

CONTENTS

CORNWALL

ABBREVIATIONS FOR RECORD REPOSITORIES, LIBRARIES AND SOCIETIES

Researchers are advised to make a preliminary telephone enquiry about
opening times and conditions of admission.

A.   Nationa1

AAB   Archives of the Archbishop of Birmingham
           Cathedral House, St Chad's Ringway, Birmingham B4 6EX

AAW   Archives of the Archbishop of Westminster,
           16a Abingdon Road, Kensington, London W8 6AF

AFCC   Armed Forces Chaplaincy Centre, Amport House, Amport,
           Andover, Hampshire SP11 8BG.   Registers for RAF station
           chaplaincies, when completed,or when station closes.

BL   The British Library, Euston Road, London NW1 2DB
           A reader's ticket is required

Bod   Department of Western Manuscripts, Bodleian Library,
           Broad Street, Oxford OX1 3BG.

BRS   British Record Society, c/o College of Arms, below.

C of A   College of Arms, Queen Victoria Street, London
           EC4V 4BT.   The Library is not open to the public.

GL   Guildhall Library, Aldermanbury, London EC2P 2EJ.

Harl Mss   Harleian Manuscripts, in the Department of Manuscripts,
           The British Library.

MoD   [Army registers] Ministry of Defence Chaplains (Army), Trenchard
           Lines, Upavon, Pewsey, Wiltshire SN9 6BE
           [Naval registers] Central Services (Records Management) Room 1/07,
           3-5 Great Scotland Yard, London SW1A 2HW. Registers will be moved
           to PRO in due course.

Phil Mss   Manuscript copies of parish registers in the possession of
           Phillimore and Co. Ltd, Shopwyke Manor Barn, Chichester,
           West Sussex PO20 6BG. A fee is normally charged.

PRO   Public Record Office, Ruskin Avenue, Kew, Richmond TW9 4DU
           Non-parochial registers in the PRO may be seen on microfilm at:
           Family Records Centre, 1 Myddleton Street, London EC1R 1UW

RCRO   Roman Catholic Records Office, Bishopric of the Forces, AGPDO,
           Middle Hill, Aldershot, Hampshire GU11 1PP.
           Registers of RC chaplaincies to the Royal Navy, Army and RAF, in
           Britain and abroad.

SG   Society of Genealogists, 14 Charterhouse Buildings,
           Goswell Road, London EC1M 7BA.
           The library is open to non-members on payment of hourly, half-daily
           and daily fees.

SLC   The Genealogical Society of Utah, 35 North West
           Temple Street, Salt Lake City, Utah 84150 U.S.A.

B.   Local repositories holding Cornwall records

CFHS   Cornwall Family History Society: Headquarters and Library
             5 Victoria Square, Truro TR1 2RS   Tel: 01872 264044

CRO   Cornwall Record Office, County Hall, Truro TR1 3AY
             Tel: 01872 273698

CSL   Cornish Studies Library, Clinton Road, Redruth   TR15 2QE
             Tel: 01209 216760

DCRS/WSL Collections of the Devon and Cornwall Record Society at
             Westcountry Studies Library, Castle Street, Exeter EX4 3PQ
             Tel: 01392 384216

DRO   Devon Record Office, Castle Street, Exeter EX4 3PU
             Tel: 01392 384253

Morrab   Morrab Library, Morrab Gardens, Penzance TR18 4DA
             Tel: 01736 364474

RIC   Courtney Library, Royal Institution of Cornwall, Royal Cornwall
             Museum, River Street, Truro TR1 2SJ   Tel: 01872 272205

C.   Other local abbreviations

CMI   Cornwall Marriage Index (*see* p.12)

CBI   Cornwall Burial Index   (*see* p.18)

DCRS   Devon and Cornwall Record Society (publications)

Ross   Ross Marriage Index (*see* p.13)

OTHER ABBREVIATIONS USED THROUGHOUT THE SERIES

B	Burials
Bapt	Baptists (never Baptisms)
Boyd	Marriage index complied by late Percival Boyd (*see* p.12)
Boyd Misc	Boyd's Marriage Index: Miscellaneous Volumes
BT	Bishop's Transcript
c.	*circa*
C	Baptisms; christenings; adult baptisms.
Cem	Cemetery
Ch Sec	Church Secretary (see current yearbook of denomination)
CFHS	Catholic Family History Society
CMI	Catholic Marriage Index
Cong	Congregationalist
Cong Fed	Congregational Federation
Cons.	Consecrated
Cop	Modern copies
CRS	Catholic Record Society publication
Cy	Churchyard
D	Deaths
Extr	Extracts

f	Founded
FFHS	Federation of Family History Societies
FIEC	Fellowship of Independent Evangelical Churches
fl.	Flourished
Gen Bapt	General Baptist
Gent.Mag.	*Gentleman's Magazine*
I	Index(ed)
IGI	The International Genealogical Index (*see* p.11)
Inc	Incumbent (i.e. rector, vicar, parish priest etc)
Ind	Independent (Congregationalist)
Lady Hunt Conn	Countess of Huntingdon's Connexion
LBA	London Baptist Association
M	Marriages
Mf	Microfilm
Mfc	Microfiche
M Lic	Marriage Licences
MM	Monthly Meeting (Society of Friends)
Ms	Manuscript
n.d.	No date
NIPR	National Index of Parish Registers
Nonc	Nonconformist
OR	Original Registers
Part Bapt	Particular Baptist
PCC	Prerogative Court of Canterbury
Phil	Phillimore's printed Marriage Series; with volume number
Pres	Presbyterian
Prim Meth	Primitive Methodist
Ptd	Printed
QM	Quarterly Meeting (Society of Friends)
RC	Roman Catholic
S of F	Society of Friends (Quakers)
Ts	Typescript
U Meth	United Methodist Church
UMFC	United Methodist Free Church
URC	United Reformed Church
VCH	Victoria County History
Wes	Wesleyan Methodist
Z	Births
+	Onwards. Normally, up to the present day

ACKNOWLEDGEMENTS

I am particularly grateful for the considerable help given to me in the preparation of this volume by Christine North, County and Diocesan Archivist, and by Colin Edwards at the Cornwall Record Office, Truro. I wish also to express my thanks to Angela Broome, Librarian of the Courtney Library, Royal Institution of Cornwall, Truro; to Terry Knight, Principal Librarian, and to Joanne Hillman, at the Cornish Studies Library, Redruth; to Trudy Martin, Librarian, and Frances Armstong, Secretary, of the Cornwall Family History Society, Truro; to Ian Maxted and Kati Va'mos of the Westcountry Studies Library, Exeter; to John Brunton of Devon Record Office; to Lesley Lowdon of the Morrab Library, Penzance; to Susan Lumas for updated lists of nonconformist registers at the Public Record Office; to Josef Keith of the Society of Friends; to Monnica Stevens, Parish Register Secretary at the Society of Genealogists; to Kay Day of the Roman Catholic Record Office; and to Jack Jacobs of the LDS Family History Centre, Ipswich.

I am no less gratefui to the following incumbents, church secretaries and others for willingly answering my questions about records in their care: Douglas Adams, Brian Anderson, Robert Andrews, Cedric Appleby, Christopher Baker, Michael Bartlett, Peter Berry, Simon Brocklehurst, Roger Elks, Michael Fisher, Geoff Fox, Sue Godfrey, Simon Golding, Timothy Gouldstone, R.A.Greet, John Halkes, Patricia Jackman, Pauline Lambe, Peter Long, David Manning, J.M.Mather, David Miller, Peter Mitchell, Martyn Pinnock, David Rake, P.J.Rodway, David Rose, Gordon Smyth, Andrew Wade, W.B.Vanstone, Andrew Wilson and G.M.Yould,

As always Cliff Webb has given sterling support as General Editor of this series.

Anthony Wilcox
Ipswich
December 1998

THE COUNTY OF CORNWALL

Cornwall is in many respects unique. Covering some 350,000 hectares, and with a population of about 450,000, it lies at the south-western extremity of England, and adjoins only one other county, Devon, the boundary being the River Tamar, historically the border between Cornwall and England. It was stated in a Government publication in 1995 that it was likely that Cornwall had never been legally incorporated into England. Its Celtic name was Kernow. It had its own language, long dead but with a recently revived interest. Cornwall's place-names and church dedications are predominantly Celtic, unlike those of any other part of England. In terms of Celtic geography, Cornwall lies half-way between Wales and Brittany. Christianity had reached Cornwall in Roman times, and was reinforced in the 5th century by an influx of saintly missionaries from Ireland and Wales, notable among whom were Piran and Petroc. Their chapels, hermitages, holy wells and wayside crosses still feature in the Cornish landscape. In 1337 Edward III created the Duchy of Cornwall and gave it to his son, the Black Prince. Today the Duchy, still held by the first-born son of the sovereign, owns about 21,000 acres in Cornwall and 160 miles of its coastal foreshore, but its holdings in other counties are greater. During the Civil War the county was largely on the side of King Charles I, copies of whose letter of thanks to the people (1643), can still be seen in many local churches, praising their *zeal for ye Defence of our Person and ye Just rights of our Crown.* A Cornish regiment was raised on the side of King James at the time of the Duke of Monmouth's rebellion in 1685.

Much of the economic wealth of Cornwall has come from beneath the earth or from the waters around the coast. Mining and fishing were the principal occupations. Tin, copper, lead, and china clay, pilchards and mackerel have all in their time provided occupation and income. Granite and slate have also been quarried. Agriculture was historically less well developed, but in more recent times early fruit and vegetables and spring flowers, flourishing in a mild and humid climate, have loomed large in a market gardening economy. Dairy farming is also important. Tourism is now dominant, with the advantages of picturesque scenery, an attractively rugged coastline and a mild climate. Its development was closely connected with the coming of the railway to the coastal towns. The population of the county in 1801 was 192,281. By 1851 it was 355,558, but subsequent emigration by miners and others, mainly across the Atlantic, contributed to a decline to 322,334 by 1901.

Bodmin is the historic county town, although Launceston had that title until 1838, while the cathedral city of Truro is now effectively the capital and centre of administration. Camborne and Redruth were at the centre of the mining industry. St Austell dominates the area which produces china clay. Falmouth, with the advantage of a large safe harbour, has long been an important port of call for ships going out into the Atlantic. Penzance, an old market town, is the point of departure for the Scilly Isles. Newquay and Bude are predominantly modern seaside resorts. The promontories of Lands End and The Lizard, Tintagel Castle, St Michael's Mount, and the fishing villages and ports such as St Ives, Fowey, Looe, Mevagissey and Polperro all attract many tourists.

The Scilly Isles, of which there are 140, only five being inhabited, lie about 25 miles from Lands End and are technically outside Cornwall. They were owned by the Godolphin family from 1571 to 1830. In 1835 Augustus Smith became the owner, succeeded by Lieut. Dorrien-Smith. The proprietors live on Tresco. St Mary's has the parish church, to which the churches on the other islands are chapels of ease.

ECCLESIASTICAL DIVISIONS

In 931 the Saxon King Athelstan created a Diocese of Cornwall, centred on St Germans. Around 1040 this was combined with Devon, and thereafter the see was first at Crediton, then from 1050 at Exeter. The Diocese of Truro was founded over 800 years later, in 1876, from the Archdeaconry of Cornwall in the Diocese of Exeter. Covering Cornwall, the Scillies and a handful of Devon parishes, it is divided into the Archdeaconries of Bodmin (Deaneries of Trigg Major, Trigg Minor and Bodmin, Stratton, East Wivelshire, West Wivelshire) and of Cornwall (Deaneries of St Austell, Carnmarth South, Kerrier, Penwith, Powder, Pydar). There is a suffragan bishop of St Germans.

ORIGINAL PARISH REGISTERS

There are 208 parishes with registers dating back before 1800, of which 17 start in 1538-40, 88 later in the 16th century, 79 in the 17th, and 24 in the 18th. With very few exceptions they are deposited in the Cornwall Record Office at Truro, together with registers for many 19th and 20th century churches. They are produced for researchers in microfiche form only. Photocopies may be taken from the fiches.

Occasional reference is made in our parish lists to the incumbents' comments made in connection with a survey of registers taken at the time of the 1831 Census. These include evidence of early misdemeanours, as at Menheniot where *pages have been wilfully cut out*; and at Botus Fleming where leaves had been cut out *for fraudulent purposes doubtless*. At Paul *registers anterior to 1595 burnt by the Spaniards when they set fire to the Church*, and at Tresmere *an old Burial Register was taken to Launceston Assizes, and proceedings have been instituted against the Churchwarden to whose care it was entrusted, to compel its restoration.* A somewhat different case is that at St Ewe, where *the parishioners refused to allow 5s for a Register, and none was kept from 1675 to 1677*

A degree of neglect is suggested in a few parishes such as Calstock and Feock where registers, apparently unknown or reported missing in 1831, exist today. In others there are suggestions that record-keeping was haphazard, as at Blisland where the register to 1716 was described as being *composed of fragments of old Registers, imperfect and confused*, or at Quethiock where marriages were deficient 1738-59 *but imperfectly supplied by loose pages preserved by the Clerk*. The parish clerk also features at Duloe, where one volume is described as *probably a private book of the Clerk, from which the Clergyman copied the entries*, and at Towednack where a register *contains loose Papers of Bap.1676-1706; Bur. 1683-1706, copied from a private list of the Parish Clerk*, Other cases where transcription has taken place, with the possibility of inaccurate copying, include Botus Fleming where a volume covering 1548-1801 is described as *a transcript of the earlier Registers now lost*; Trewen where the first register, from 1616, is said to be *a partial transcript*; and Cardynham where the register from 1701 is *a transcript for the first 17 years*. The physical condition of some registers was in 1831 less than satisfactory, as at Gwithian, where 16th and 17th century entries were on loose leaves; at St Anthony in Meneage, where *the Registers consist of a bundle of parchment, commencing A.D.1602 to 1744, interrupted by a Parchment Book 1726-1812"*; at Kenwyn, where the first two volumes were *much injured and partially illegible* and another was *in equally bad condition*; or at Launcells where the marriages from 1642 to 1700 were contained *on eight loose sheets of vellum*. In some parishes a comparison of dates suggests that pages relating to a year or two of entries may have been torn from the beginning or end of a volume.

Early registers had already disappeared by 1831 from St Grade to 1700, Laneast to 1700, Sennen to 1700, St Levan to 1700, St Gennys to 1702, St Petroc Minor to 1706, St Wenn to 1706, Davidstow to 1708, Advent to 1709, Boconnoc to 1709, Forrbaury to 1710, Helland to 1722, Tremaine to 1726 and St Endellion to 1732, Michaelstow baptisms to 1680, and Cubert baptisms and marriages to 1733, At Lewannick marriages to 1755 and burials to 1738 were already missing by 1831, whereas baptisms survived from 1660. At St Keyne no earlier register than 1721 was noted, but there exists a photocopy under ultra-violet light of a faded register from 1538. In all these cases there exist earlier bishop's transcripts, even in the case of chapelries, so that registration did in fact take place. At Colan a register not noted in 1831, but microfilmed in 1959, is apparently lost. Early registers or parts or registers which have apparently disappeared since 1831 include those of St Agnes 1601-53, Antony marriages 1569-1677, Tregony with Cuby 1571-1661, Sithney 1623-64, St Ive 1561-1683, St Blazey 1663-1710, and Philliegh 1544-1733,

BISHOP'S TRANSCRIPTS

A survey of bishop's transcripts for Cornwall parishes was made by Jasper Nicholls of Bideford and printed in the *Journal of the Royal Institution of Cornwall* Vol.19 1912-14. Nicholls noted that these fell into four periods: 1597-c.1640, 1662/63-1673; 1737-40; 1773-1812. In the case of the 27 peculiars of the Bishop of Exeter 'some original bundles, from 1707 to 1736, have entirely disappeared'. Extant returns 'run from 1661 to 1783, with a gap from 1707 to 1736, and again from 1759 to 1783'. He adds that 'especially in the earlier years the record is very defective'. For the five parishes which were peculiars of the Dean and Chapter of Exeter virtually every transcript between 1640 and 1735 had been lost, although the series from 1735-1758 was '*comparatively full*'. After 1758 no transcripts had survived for these peculiars. Nicholls did not search or list any transcripts for 1778-1812, '*on the strong presumption that the series...is complete ...Besides, time and opportunity were denied me*'. He has several pages of unidentified or undated transcripts, quoting surnames from most of them. He notes that '*between the years 1641 and 1663, judging from the paucity of transcripts now extant, the submission of these returns was almost wholly in abeyance*'.

At present the bishop's transcripts for Cornwall parishes are divided between the county record offices at Exeter (c.1600-c.1670, 1735-40, 1772-c.1830s) and Truro (c.1670-1735, 1740-72). Those for the peculiars are at Exeter. Microfilm copies of those at Exeter up to 1812 are available at Truro and at the Cornish Studies Library, Redruth. Apart from Nicholls' contribution, and a manuscript list of 1897 in Cornwall Record Office, the accuracy of neither of which has been tested in recent times, there is at present no fully reliable list of extant BTs showing individual years, although this year (1998) a full check has started at Truro.

In this volume, therefore, with the exception of BTs held at Exeter, after 1812, for which full details are available, we give covering dates rather than individual years, so that in every case it must be noted that, as Nicholls showed, there are gaps, sometimes of considerable length, Thus while for example at Helston we quote CMB 1675-1736, in fact the surviving transcripts are for 1675-76, 1683-87, 1689-98, 1700-01, 1703, 1708, 1710-11, 1713-14, 1716, 1718, 1720-28, 1730-36. Transcripts for early periods were used by the compilers of some of the Phillimore volumes of marriages (see below) to cover the absence of original registers, but the sporadic nature of the surviving collections does not in general make the transcripts a fully adequate substitute for the registers for most periods.

PRINTED COPIES

The registers of Camborne to 1837. Falmouth to 1812 and Truro to 1837 have been published by the Devon and Cornwall Record Society. Those of St Breward to 1900, St Columb Major to 1780, Gulval to 1837, Madron to 1681, and Redruth to 1716 have been published privately.

Marriages, mainly to 1812, for 147 parishes, appear in twenty-six volumes of Phillimore's Marriage series, published between 1900 and 1935. It cannot be said that this series is always completely accurate, and entries should be checked in the original registers. There is editorial confusion in volume 22, where the marriages for Kea are described as those of Kenwyn, and vice-versa. The confusion was carried over into Boyd's Marriage Index (see p 12). The marriages at Week St Mary in volume 25 have recently been described as 'hopelessly inaccurate'. An index by A T Satterford, to volumes 1 to 6, was published in 1915.

The contents of the Phillimore volumes are held on computer by Cornwall FHS, from whom print-outs may be obtained. The Royal Institution of Cornwall has a card-index of the marriages, arranged alphabetically by surname, and within each surname by parishes.

Cornwall Family History Society has published parish volumes of marriages 1813-37 and pre-1813, in their Cornwall Marriage Index series, and burials 1813-37, referred to in our parish lists as CMI and CBI respectively.

OTHER COPIES

Microform, typescript and manuscript copies and transcripts of the registers of a large number of parishes are to be found at The Royal Institution of Cornwall, the Westcountry Studies Library, the Cornish Studies Library, the County Record Office, the Morrab Library and the libraries of the Cornwall Family History Society and the Society of Genealogists. Full details appear in our parish lists.

THE INTERNATIONAL GENEALOGICAL INDEX

Baptisms and marriages of 269 Cornwall churches and chapels, for various periods, extracted from registers and bishops transcripts, are to be found in the International Genealogical Index of the Genealogical Society of Utah, U.S.A., held on computer and published on microfiche, from which printouts may be obtained from Cornwall FHS and elsewhere.. The only pre-1812 parishes not represented for any period are St Breock, Lawhitton, East Looe, Saltash and Trewen. This useful but incomplete source of information should be used with caution, and original registers should always be checked. This is particularly the case with the 1992 edition of the IGI. A key to which parishes are represented, and the years covered, is to be found in the Parish and Vital Records List. Instructions for the 1992 IGI contain the note : '*Changes have been made in the way names are added to the International Genealogical Index. As a result, the Parish and Vital Records List does not coordinate with the current [1992] edition of the International Genealogical Index exactly as it did in the past, the relationship between the two sources will continue to evolve over the next few years... .You can no longer tell by using the Parish and Vital records List whether a name will be listed in the International Genealogical Index. You must look in the index....the Parish and Vital records Index does not indicate gaps in the records.*'

For the purposes of this volume we have used a copy of the PVRL dated July 1997 and have included those entries which are marked with a double asterisk, indicating that 'records in this batch and period are not in the 1988 edition of the IGI'. It may therefore be safer to take the IGI dates given in this volume as indicating the availability in general of genealogical material from a variety of Mormon sources, accessible through the PVRL, rather than the certain presence of entries in the IGI itself.

Some care should be exercised in interpreting in particular the terminal dates of nineteenth century extracts, and especially those deriving from Nonconformist registers held in the Public Record Office. A recent survey has shown that early printed lists of these registers are inaccurate, and it appears that the terminal dates quoted for IGI extracts were taken from those early lists. The same must apply to details given in this volume for the holdings in the Genealogical Society Library at Salt Lake City, Utah, of microfilmed print-outs of parish indexes derived from the IGI.

For the location of copies of the IGI consult the latest edition of:
J.Gibson and M.Walcot Where to find the International Genealogical Index (FFHS, 1985)

The resources of the Family History Library at Salt Lake City are available also to the general public at over 1,600 Family History Centres in 57 countries, where the IGI and microfilm copies of all available records may be ordered and consulted. There are FHCs at

Church of the Latter Day Saints, Clodgey Lane, Helston
Church of the Latter Day Saints, Mannamead Road, Hartley, Plymouth

An appointment should always be made before visiting these centres.

MARRIAGE INDEXES

CMI   ### Cornwall Marriage Index

Cornwall FHS has a card-index by male surname for all marriages in the county from 1813 to 1837. A computer print-out service is also available. The Society has published parish volumes of the marriage index (1813-37) for over 200 parishes, and indexes of pre-1812 marriages for about 150 parishes, of which details are given in the parish lists.

Boyd   ### Boyd's Marriage Index

Marriages for most of the ancient parishes, for various periods, are listed in the Main and Miscellaneous Series. Copies of Boyd are held by Cornwall FHS, the Westcountry Studies Library, the Society of Genealogists, the LDS Family History Centre at Helston, the Genealogical Society of Utah, and the College of Arms.

Covering dates in our parish lists are taken from:
A List of Parishes in Boyd's Marriage Index: Society of Genealogists 1987

Pallot   **Pallot's Marriage Index**

Includes 145 Cornwall parishes, mainly 1790-1812 or 1800-1812. Covering
dates in our parish lists are taken from:
C.Humphery-Smith *The Phillimore Atlas and Index of Parish Registers*
1984 edition.

Institute of Heraldic and Genealogical Studies, Northgate, Canterbury,
Kent CT1 1BA

Ross Marriage Index

A card index by Mr R.Ross, held on 43 reels of microfilm by Cornwall FHS and
the Royal Institution of Cornwall, with marriages for 217 Church of England
parishes, accessed under surname in date blocks of about 25 years. Covering
dates given in this volume are taken from a list held by the Royal
Institution of Cornwall. It is not known how complete is the coverage
between the given dates. There appear to be no entries for the pre-1812
parishes of St Erney, St Juliot, Landrake, Lanteglos by Camelford,
Lawhitton, Lewannick, Lezant, St Mellion, Menheniot, South Petherwin,
Saltash and St Teath. The index also includes Catholic marriages at
Lanherne; Quaker marriages for Marazion and Liskeard; Baptist marriages from
Falmouth; marriage allegations 1660-1700 and licences 1540-1837 from the
Bishop of Exeter; and marriage announcements from the *Royal Cornwall Gazette*
1836-45, 1864-75.

Phillimore   Indexes to Phillimore's Marriage Series (see p.12)

MARRIAGE LICENCES

Devon Record Office has marriage licence records for the Diocese of Exeter
1523-1837, for which there are 20 volumes of calendars and indexes in the
Devon and Cornwall Record Society archives at the Westcountry Studies
Library in the same building. Copies of these volumes covering 1631 to 1762
are held by the Society of Genealogists. Licence records for parishes which
were Peculiars of the Dean and Chapter of Exeter are at Exeter Cathedral
Library.

An index by J.L. Vivian of licences for the years 1523 to 1631 was published
in 1887, with additions for 1598-99 appearing in an article by J.F.Chanter
in *Devon and Cornwall Notes and Queries* 10, 1918-19. The Society of
Genealogists has a list of marriage licences for the Peculiar of St Germans
1704-1719/20.

Licences 1540-1837 and Allegations 1660-1700 are included in Ross's Marriage
Index (see above).

PROBATE RECORDS

Until 1857 most of Cornwall was under the probate jurisdiction of the
Archdeaconry of Cornwall in the Diocese of Exeter. There were also a number
of peculiars subject either to the Bishop of Exeter or to the Dean and
Chapter of Exeter. The Royal Peculiar Deanery of St Buryan was subject to
the Duchy of Cornwall. When a parish did not come under the Archdeaconry,
parish entries in the present volume include a note of the peculiar
jurisdiction.

Most of the records of the courts at Exeter were destroyed by enemy action during the Second World War. Records of the Consistory Court of the Archdeacon of Cornwall, and of the peculiar of St Buryan, are at Cornwall Record Office. Cornish probate records after ecclesiastical jurisdiction ceased in 1858 are at the District Probate Registry, Market Street, Bodmin PL31 2JW.

Access to the wills and administration bonds is facilitated by published and unpublished lists and indexes. As well as an overall *Guide to Cornish Probate Records* (revised 1996), Cornwall Record Office has published an *Index to Cornish Probate Records 1600-1649* in five volumes, and an *Index to Cornish Estate Duty and Deanery of St Buryan Wills*. The British Record Society published in 1929 and 1932 two volumes of the *Archdeaconry of Cornwall Wills and Administrations*, covering 1569-1699 and 1700-1799, both edited by R.M.Glencross (BRS Index Library volumes 56, 59). In 1982 the BRS produced in print and on microfiche *Cornish Probate Records in the Cornwall Record Office 1800-57*, by Brenda Hull. At Cornwall Record Office there are seven manuscript volumes of contemporary indexes to wills and administrations, arranged alphabetically by parish, covering 1570-1649 and 1660-1857.

Wills from the parish of Constantine 1570-1808 are listed in *Subsidy Rolls, Muster and Hearth Tax Rolls and Probate Calendars of the Parish of St Constantine...* (DCRO 1910).

see also:

M. Medlycott *Index to Cornish wills from the Lost Probate Court, Exeter, of which copies or extracts exist in the Society of Genealogists*: 1976

MONUMENTAL INSCRIPTIONS

The Cornwall FHS has an ongoing programme of transcription, and has so far published indexes of the monumental inscriptions of over 120 graveyards and cemeteries. These appear in our parish lists. The Society can also provide computer printouts from their ongoing index of monumental inscriptions.

See also:
A.J.Jewers *Heraldic Church Notes from Cornwall* 1886

F.Wall *Lists of Vicars and Monumental Inscriptions in Twelve Cornwall Churches*: 1942 (Ms SG)

E.H.W.Dunkin *Monumental Brasses of Cornwall*: 1882

O.Beckerlegge *Why do we mourn ? A collection of poetical epitaphs found in Cornish Methodist burial grounds*: Cornish Meth Hist Assn No.23: 1993

OTHER DENOMINATIONS

From the returns made in the 1851 Religious Census it has been estimated that in Cornwall 51% of the population did not attend any church, 32% belonged to one of the branches of Methodism, 13.2 % attended the Church of England, and under 4% belonged to other churches.

Major sources of information about the existence of these chapels include Kelly's Directories, various denominational yearbooks, and a return of registered chapels made to Parliament in 1882, hereafter referred to as [1882 Return]. Although every effort has been made to include in the present volume a reference to every church or chapel that has existed in each parish, it is clear that many ephemeral foundations and some existing modern ones have been inadvertently left out.

Cornwall Record Office has a large collection of registers and other records of nonconformist churches and chapels in the county mainly for the period after 1837. A total of 72 volumes of earlier registers from 64 chapels in Cornwall were surrendered to the Registrar General and are now in the Public Record Office. This total does not include the deposited Quaker registers. Early published lists of these registers contain some inaccurate dates, and for the purposes of this volume corrections have been made to IGI datings, and those of microfilm copies, taken from the earlier lists. For these registers, see:

L.W.L.Edwards *Index to Cornish nonconformist registers deposited at the Public Record Office*: 1976

Roman Catholics

Lanherne, home of the Catholic Arundells, was a Mass centre throughout penal times and a place of refuge for seminary priests, among whom was Cuthbert Mayne, family chaplain to the Tregians of Golden, in Probus, who was martyred at Launceston in 1577. In 1794 Lanherne was given by Lord Arundell of Wardour to a community of English Carmelite nuns, founded at Antwerp in 1619. Registers for the Lanherne mission date back to 1710. In the 18th century Jesuit priests served as chaplains to, among others, the Arundell family at Trevithick and the Couches at Tolfrey near Fowey. There were Franciscan friars at St Ives in the late 18th century. An Exeter Diocese return of Papists in 1767 showed a total of only thirty-six in the county, including John Couche of Fowey and John Hanne at Cardinham, with nineteen at St Mawgan (Lanherne) and ten at St Columb Major. In 1773 it was reported to Rome that there were two secular priests active in Cornwall, caring for about 45 faithful. The Trelawnys at Trelawne were served by French *émigré* priests until 1802. A mission was opened in Falmouth in 1805, but its registers date only from 1819. Those at Trelawne and at Sclerder started in 1833, and those at Penzance, Camborne and Liskeard in the 1850s.

From 1688 Cornish Catholics came under the authority of the Vicars Apostolic of the Western District, until 1850 when the diocese of Plymouth was founded.

Further reading:

Michael Gandy *Catholic Missions and Registers 3: Wales and the West of England*: 1994

Plymouth Diocesan Directory

Journal: *South-Western Catholic History*

Methodists

John Wesley visited Cornwall 32 times between 1743 and 1789. In 1743-64 there was a single Cornwall Circuit. In 1764 this was divided into Cornwall East and Cornwall West. By 1809 the Launceston, Truro and Helston, Camelford, Bodmin and Liskeard Circuits had been formed, and there were a number of later changes.

The Bible Christians, a distinctively south-western branch of Methodism, were founded in Shebbear, Devon, in 1815 by a Cornishman, William O'Bryan, born in Luxulyan in 1778. They were also popularly known as Bryanites, Shouters, Trumpeters or Free Willers, and spread rapidly in Cornwall and Devon.

The relative strengths of the branches of Methodism in the late 19th century may be seen in the return to Parliament made in 1882 of registered nonconformist chapels. Of these 293 were Wesleyan and 147 were Bible Christian, while the United Methodist Free Church had 71 and Primitive Methodists 49. At the time of the 1907 merger of the UMFC with the Bible Christians and the New Connexion there were 380 Wesleyans, 210 Bible Christians, 105 Free Methodists, 40 Primitive Methodist, 10 Wesleyan Reform and 7 Methodist New Connexion.

The Public Record Office has registers of 27 Wesleyan chapels of which the only pre-1800 registers are those of Launceston (1794) and St Agnes (1799). There are two from Primitive Methodist chapels (St Ives and Redruth, 1832) and one Methodist New Connexion (Truro 1832). The earliest Bible Christian registers are those of Kilkhampton (1817).

Cornwall Record Office is the authorised place of deposit for Cornish Methodist records, and has a large collection of registers and other records from all branches of Methodism, of which the earliest is that for the Wesleyan chapel at North Hill (1780).

The *Journal of the Cornish Methodist Historical Association* contains a wealth of local material. see also: S.Foot *Methodist Celebration - A Cornish Contribution* 1988

Baptists

The *Baptist Manual* for 1850 listed sixteen chapels in the county, and gave foundation dates, earliest of which were those at Falmouth (1772), Truro (1789), Redruth (1801) and Penzance (1802).

The Public Record Office has registers for Truro dating from 1760, Helston from 1814, Scilly Isles from 1819 and Padstow for 1836. Cornwall Record Office has those for Falmouth from 1763 and Truro from 1760, and an Independent Baptist register of Feock from 1820.

Independents, Congregationalists, Unitarians

Surrendered registers in the Public Record Office include those of the Independents of Truro from 1769), Launceston (1777), Falmouth (1783), Mevagissey (1786), Looe (1787), St Austell (1789), Penzance (1791), St Columb (1795), Fowey (1798), St Mawes (1798), Penryn (1805), St Agnes (1807), Cawsand (1810), Lostwithiel (1812), Torpoint (1815), Lanreath (1816) and Portscatho (1826). Cornwall Record Office also holds copy registers of the same chapels at Falmouth from 1783, Fowey from 1798, Penryn from 1806 and Truro from 1770, as well as those of Liskeard from 1809 which appear to have escaped surrender. No registers survive, therefore, earlier than 1769.

The *Congregational Yearbook* of 1851 listed some 25 chapels and mission stations. At the present day the United Reformed Church is represented at Falmouth, Looe, Mevagissey, Newquay and Portscatho, the Congregational Federation at Cawsand and Tregony, and the FIEC at Gorran. Unitarian churches existed at Falmouth, Flushing and Penzance, but are now closed.

Society of Friends

George Fox visited Cornwall in 1655, and was imprisoned at Launceston in 1656. From the latter year he gave instruction that registers should be kept, although some extant volumes have earlier, retrospective entries. A general meeting was held at St Austell in 1663, and Cornwall Quarterly Meeting was established in 1668, at first with three Monthly Meetings, Falmouth, St Austell and East Cornwall. Such was the persecution suffered by Quakers that in 1683-84 several quarterly meetings were held in Launceston Prison. Devon and Cornwall Yearly Meeting dated from 1702.

The Public Record Office holds 34 volumes of surrendered Quaker registers, but published 19th century listings of these are sometimes less than accurate in describing their provenance. Digests or indexes of the entries in these registers are available on microfilm at Friends House, London; at the Society of Genealogists; and at Cornwall Record Office. Hugh Peskett provides a useful list of registers in his *Guide to the parish and non-parochial registers of Devon and Cornwall 1538-1837*: DCRS: 1979: pp.222-224.

Cornwall Record Office has a significant collection of Quaker registers and other records from Cornwall Quarterly Meeting. As elsewhere in the country, Birth Notes and Death Notes, the latter with instructions to gravediggers, are a useful complement to, or even a substitute for registers. Where available, these are noted in our lists.

At the present time [1998] meetings exist at St Austell, Falmouth, Kea, Liskeard, Marazion, Penzance, Truro and Wadebridge,

CENSUSES

Pre-1841 census returns with householders' names are held by Cornwall Record Office for St Hilary (1801), Poundstock (1811), Boyton and Veryan (1821), and St Breock (c.1824). The Local Studies Library, Redruth, has a copy of an 1833-34 return for St Endellion.

Microfilms of census returns for Cornwall in 1841, 1851, 1861 and 1871 are available by appointment at Cornwall Record Office; a charge of £1 per reel is made. Films of censuses from 1841 to 1891 are held at the Family Records Centre in London, and for 1851-1891 at Cornwall Family History Society. The Society has indexes to returns for the county for 1851, 1881 and 1891 and can provide computer print-outs by name or by household from the 1871 returns, and microfiche printouts for 1881. It has also published a number of booklets of indexes to various parishes in the 1871 census.

Transcriptions and indexes of the 1851 census for the county are being prepared in an ongoing project by Ray Woodbine. Volumes so far published may be obtained from the Society, as may similar volumes produced by the New Zealand Society of Genealogists.

For further details see:

J.Gibson *Census Returns 1841-1891 on microfilm: a directory of local holdings*: FFHS: 1995
J.Gibson, C.Rogers *Marriage, Census and other Indexes for family historians*: FFHS: 6th edit. 1996
J.Gibson, M. Medlycott *Local Census Listings 1522-1930*: FFHS: 3rd edit.1997

OTHER INDEXES

The following are available through Cornwall Family History Society.

CBI Cornwall Burial Index 1813-37
Computer print-outs are available, and CFHS also publishes indexes of burials for a few parishes, and an index of burials in the county in the period 1-15 July 1837.

General Register Office Indexes 1837-1992
Indexes to the state-registered births, marriages and deaths. For a fee, searches can be made for entries in the indexes, from which certificates may be obtained.

Strays Index
Out-of-county register references to events with Cornish connections.

Ships' passengeer lists
About 7665 names from 250 ships, mainly to Australia and U.S.A.

Ross Military/Mariners Strays Index
Cornish-born soldiers, sailors, customs and excise men, and coastguards, from sources in the United Kingdom and overseas

NEWSPAPERS

The earliest newspaper with news from Cornwall of which copies are still available was the *Sherborne Mercury or Western Flying Post*, covering much of south-west England, for which copies are held at the Cornish Studies Library from before 1750 to 1867. The same library has copies from 1810 of the *West Briton*, and from 1808 of the *Royal Cornwall Gazette*, of which there is also a run from 1801 at the Royal Institution of Cornwall, and from 1811 at the British Library at Colindale, which also has the *West Briton* from 1811.

A variety of more local newspapers were published in the nineteenth century at Camborne, Falmouth, Hayle, Launceston, Liskeard, Newquay, Penryn, Penzance, Redruth, St Austell, St Ives and Truro. Among these, there are files of the *Falmouth Packet* from 1829 to 1848 at the Cornish Studies Library, and of the *Cornubian*, published in Falmouth, from 1830 to 1837 at Colindale and from 1830 to 1832 at the Royal Institution of Cornwall. *Lean's Engine Reporter*, published in Camborne, is found at the Cornish Studies Library from 1812 and at Colindale for 1838-55. The *Launceston Weekly News* is to be found at Colindale from 1866, and the *East Cornwall Times* from 1867, as well as the *Liskeard Gazette* 1856-70 and *Penzance Gazette* 1839-58.

Marriages from the *Royal Cornwall Gazette* 1836-45 and 1864-75 are included in Ross's Marriage Index. see p.13

Jeremy Gibson *Local Newspapers 1750-1920:* FFHS 1987

J.Rowles and I.Maxted *Bibliography of British Newspapers - Cornwall:* 1991

N.Tangye *Cornwall Newspapers: 18th and 19th century finding list:* 1980

DIRECTORIES

Kelly's Directories for the county were published in 1856, 1873, 1883, 1889, 1893, 1897, 1902, 1906, 1910, 1914, 1919, 1923, 1926, 1930, 1935 and 1939.

Pigot's 1830 Directory of Cornwall may be obtained on microfiche from the Society of Genealogists.

For a variety of other county and local directories, of which copies are widely available at libraries in the county and elsewhere, see:

J.E.Norton   *Guide to the National and Provincial Directories of England and Wales...before 1856*: Royal Historical Society: 1950

G.Shaw and A.Tipper   *British Directories 1850-1950*: 1988

L.W.L.Edwards   *Directories and Poll Books in the Library of the Society of Genealogists* 1989

POLL BOOKS AND ELECTORAL REGISTERS

Cornwall Record Office has poll books for the county for 1710, 1772, 1774 and 1790, for Lostwithiel in 1790, and poll sheets for Mitchell 1672-1714. The British Library and Guildhall Library have poll books for Truro in 1832.

Electoral registers for the county are at Guildhall Library for 1837, at the Local Studies Library, Redruth, for 1858-59 and 1865-68, and at the Public Record Office for 1874. The County Record Office has twentieth century registers.

MILITARY HISTORY

The regiment most closely associated with the county was the Duke of Cornwall's Light Infantry, which took its origins in Colonel Edward Fox's Regiment of Marines, raised in 1702, which in 1704 became Colonel Jacob Borr's Regiment of Marines, in 1715 the 32nd Regiment of Foot, from 1782 to 1858 The 32nd (The Cornwall) Regiment of Foot, and from 1858 to 1881 The 32nd (Cornwall) Light Infantry. In 1881 it was linked with the 46th South Devonshire Regiment of Foot, as the Duke of Cornwall's Light Infantry, and saw distinguished service in the two World Wars. Further amalgamations came in 1959, when it joined with the Somerset Light Infantry to become the Somerset and Cornwall Light Infantry, and in 1968 when it became part of The Light Infantry. The Duke of Cornwall's Light Infantry Regimental Museum is at The Keep, Victoria Barracks, Bodmin PL31 1EG. Army service records in general are held in the Public Record Office.

R.F.K.Goldsmith *The Duke of Cornwall's Light Infantry*: 1970
E.Wyrall *The History of the Duke of Cornwall's Light Infantry 1914-19:* 1932

Militia were based at both Pendennis and St Mawes Castles dominating Falmouth harbour, which were also used by the Army in the First and Second World Wars. Militia records held at Cornwall Record Office include ballot lists for Gulval (1761) and North Petherwin (1816); muster lists or rolls for Kerrier Hundred (1781-82), East Hundred (1798) and North Cornwall (1799), and for the Royal Cornwall Regiment (1807-31), the 1st Cornwall (1780-1876), the 2nd Cornwall (1798-99, 1853-56) and the Cornwall Miners (1798-1876). Supplementary and local militia lists are held for the county

(1803-14) and Cornwall miners (1798-1814), and for the 1st-5th Cornwall, Pandennis Artillery, Stany Artillery (1808-16). For further details see:

J. Gibson and M. Medlycott *Militia Lista and Musters 1757-1857*: FFHS: 1990

The Public Record Office and the Cornwall and Devon Record Offices all hold Cornwall muster rolls for the Tudor and Stuart periods, covering the period from 1522 to 1715. Some rolls have been printed, including those for the Hundreds of Penwith and Pydar in 1522, for Constantine in 1568-69, and for the whole county in 1569. For further details see:

J.Gibson and A.Dell *Tudor and Stuart Muster Rolls*: FFHS: 1989

The strong maritime traditions of the county, and the close proximity of the naval base at Plymouth just over the border in Devon, meant that many Cornish men joined the Royal Navy. Shore stations within Cornwall include HMS Raleigh and HMS Fisgard at Torpoint, and the Royal Naval Air Station at Culdrose. Naval service records are held at the Public Record Office.

Many local men served from 1688 to 1852 on the Falmouth packets, control of which was taken over from the Post Office by the Royal Navy in 1822. These ships, based in Falmouth because of its geographical position and its safe harbour, carried mail, naval and military papers, bullion and passengers across the Atlantic and further afield to the colonies, and had a stirring history combating pirates. Some records are held at the Post Office Archives and Record Centre, Freeling House, Mount Pleasant Complex, London EC1A 1BB, and at the Royal Institution of Cornwall. For descriptive accounts of the service see:

David Mudd   *The Falmouth Packets* 1978
A.H.Norway   *History of the Post Office Packet Service 1793-1815*: 1895

In this century Royal Air Force stations have been located at St Mawgan and St Eval. Some modern Royal Navy and R.A.F. chaplaincy registers of baptisms and marriages are available and are noted in our parish lists.

SELECTIVE BIBLIOGRAPHY

Stuart Raymond   *Cornwall* British Genealogical Bibliographies: 1998

Publications of Cornwall Record Office:

Handlist of Pedigrees and Heraldic Documents: 1985
Handlist of Parish Poor Law Records: 1993
Guide to Sources at Cornwall Record Office: 1995
Sources for Cornish Family History: 1997
Maritime Sources at Cornwall Record Office: 1998

Language and names:
P. Beresford Ellis *The Cornish Language and its Literature* 1974
R.M.Nance   *An English-Cornish and Cornish-English Dictionary* 1978
G.Pawley White   *A Handbook of Cornish Surnames*: 1981
C.Bice   *Names for the Cornish: three hundred Cornish christian names* 1970
O.J.Padel   *Cornish Place-Name Elements*: English Place-Name Society 1985

General works on the County:
C.S.Gilbert   *An Historical Survey of the County of Cornwall* 2 vols: 1817-20
J.Polsoe   *Complete Parochial History of the County of Cornwall*: 1867-72
A.L.Salmon   *Cornwall*: Methuen's Little Guides: 1903; revised H.R.Hicks 1950
C.Berry   *Portrait of Cornwall*: 1963
C.Mumford   *Portrait of the Isles of Scilly*: 1967, revised 1972
F.E.Halliday *A History of Cornwall*: 1959; 2nd edit.1975

The Church:
C.Henderson   *The Ecclesiastical History of the Church in Cornwall*: 1962
H.Miles Brown   *What to look for in Cornish Churches*: 1973
N.Pevsner   *Cornwall*: The Buildings of England: 1951
C.Henderson   *Cornish Church Guide*: 1925
C.Stell   *An inventory of nonconformist chapels and meeting houses in South West England*: HMSO: 1991

Journals:
Journal of the Royal Institution of Cornwall   from 1864
Journal of the Cornwall Family History Society   from 1976
Cornish Studies: Journal of the Institute of Cornish Studies from 1973

Towns and villages:
Viv Acton   *A History of Truro vol.I*: 1987
Cyril Bunn   *The Book of St Austell*: 1978
Jonathan Coach   *The History of Polperro*: 1871; reprinted c.1986.
Henry L.Douch   *The Book of Truro*: 1977
Bob Dunstan   *The Book of Falmouth and Penryn*: 1984
Brenda Duxbury   *About Mevagissey*: 1978
Geoffrey Grigson *The Scilly Isles*: 1977
John Keast   *The Story of Fowey*: c.1983
Frank Michell   *Annals of a Cornish Town* [Redruth]: 1978
David Mudd   *Down along Camborne and Redruth*: 1978
                Home along Falmouth and Penryn: 1980
Cyril Noall   *The Story of St Ives*: 1970
                The Book of Penzance: 1983
                The Book of Hayle: 1985
Joan Rendell   *Gateway to England* [Launceston]: 1981
Michael Tangye   *Redruth and its people*: c.1988
Arthur B Venning *Yesterday's Town: Launceston...*: 1988
James Whetter   *The History of Falmouth*: c.1981
James Willmot   *The Book of Bodmin*: 1977

Cornwall Federation of Women's Institutes *Cornwall Village Book*: 1991

PARISH LISTS

Parishes appear in these lists in alphabetical order, the first element
St (Saint) in a parish name being ignored for this purpose. Modern parishes
are grouped with the ancient parish from which they are descended, except
where a former chapelry had early registers of its own. The figure in square
brackets at the head of each parish is its population in 1831.

ADJEWHELLS   *see* CAMBORNE

ADVENT St Adwena [Lesnewth Hundred; Camelford Union] [244] Chapelry in
LANTEGLOS BY CAMELFORD, with which now united
OR C 1709-1987 M 1721-1979 B 1718-1983 (CRO) No earlier registers noted in
1831. *see* LANTEGLOS BY CAMELFORD
BT CMB 1676-1736, 1741-72 (CRO); CMB 1608, 1616, 1623, 1629, 1631, 1638,
1665, 1737-40, 1773-1812, 1838-43 (DRO)
Cop M 1676-1715 from BT, 1721-1801 (Ptd Phillimore:1900); M 1813-37 (CMI);
B 1813-37 (CBI); M 1616-65, 1676-1801 (SG); M 1676-1801 from OR;
M 1608-65 from BT (Boyd); M 1790-1812 (Pallot)
Cop (Mf) CMB 1608-1812 (Mf of BT at DRO: CRO,CSL); M 1798-1809, 1813-77
(Ross); Extr C 1676-1772, 1801-05 M 1676-1801 (IGI); C 1676-1772,
1801-05 (SLC)
MI (Ptd CFHS)

ST AGNES   *see* SCILLY ISLES

ST AGNES St Agnes [Pydar Hundred; Truro Union] [6642] Chapelry in
PERRANZABULOE. Peculiar of Dean and Chapter of Exeter 1846-48. Separate
parish 1846. Rebuilt 1848
OR C 1653-1934 M 1674-1969 B 1674-1865 (CRO)
Noted in 1831: Vol.1 C 1601-1712; Vol.2 C 1715-53 M 1741-54 B 1726-32
BT CMB 1596-1838 (DRO)
Cop M 1598-1812 (Ptd Phillimore: 1911); C 1830-39 B 1820-39 (Ms CRO);
C 1837-80 M 1876-1900 (CFHS); C 1597-1776 MB 1616-1776 (CSL);
CMB 1596-1806 from BT; C 1653-1837 B 1674-1837 (DCRS/WSL); C 1653-1776
MB 1674-1776 (Ts with index, RIC, CRO); M 1837-75 (Ts RIC); M 1813-37
(WSL); M 1813-37 (CMI); M 1596-1812 (Boyd); M 1790-1812 (Pallot);
B 1813-37 (CBI)
Cop (Mf) CMB 1597-1643, 1734-1811 (Mf of BT at DRO: CRO,CSL); M 1813-75
(Ross); Extr C 1597-1837 M 1596-1643, 1736-1806, 1813-37 (IGI);
C 1597-1806 M 1596-1643 (SLC)
MI (Ptd CFHS)

ST AGNES St Peter, Mithian. Parish created 1846 from ST AGNES, KENWYN, KEA, PERRANZABULOE, CHACEWATER. Erected 1861. United with MOUNT HAWKE
OR C 1848-1977 M 1862-1977 B 1861-1977 (CRO)
MI (Ptd CFHS)

ST AGNES St John the Baptist, Mount Hawke. Parish created 1846 from ST AGNES, ILLOGAN. Church purchased from 'dissenters'. New church erected 1878. United with MITHIAN
OR C 1847-1906 M 1878-1975 (CRO)
Cop M 1878-1900 (CFHS)
MI (Ptd CFHS)

ST AGNES (RC) St Agnes 1874-1931, served from Camborne. Modern parish 1958+ served from Perranporth

ST AGNES (Ind) Peterville Chapel f 1779. Closed 1868
OR ZC 1807-37 (PRO)
Cop ZC 1807-37 (SG)
Cop (Mf) ZC 1807-37 (DCRS/WSL); Extr ZC 1807-37 (IGI); ZC 1807-37 (SLC)

ST AGNES (Wes) Circuit
OR C 1837-1903 (CRO)
Cop Newlyn, Truro and St Agnes Methodist baptisms 1837-75 (CFHS)

ST AGNES (Wes) Goonbell [1882 Return]

ST AGNES (Wes) Goonown f 1780; [1882 Return]
OR ZC 1799-1837 (PRO); Sunday School attendance registers 1839-1971 (CRO)
Cop ZC 1799-1837 (SG)
Cop (Mf) ZC 1799-1837 (DCRS/WSL); Extr ZC 1799-1837 (IGI); ZC 1799-1837 (SLC)

ST AGNES (Wes) Blackwater. Erected 1820-24
OR C 1844-1984 M 1934-64, 1967-80 (CRO)

ST AGNES (Wes) Mawla, Mount Hawke. Erected 1820 (demolished 1960). New chapel 1908
OR C 1850-67 (CRO)

ST AGNES (Wes) Mithian. Erected 1800 [1882 Return]; Meth [Kelly 1935]

ST AGNES (Wes) Mingoose. Erected 1851. [1882 Return] Now a cottage

ST AGNES (Wes) Porthtowan. f late 18th century. Erected 1820; rebuilt 1841, 1980

ST AGNES (Wes) Skinner's Bottom
OR C 1920-73 (CRO)

ST AGNES (Wes) Trevellas Downs [1882 Return] Later Trevellas and Crosscombe

ST AGNES (Wes) New Room, Church Town [1882 Return]

ST AGNES (Wes) Silverwell or Silver Well Chapel [1882 Return]; rebuilt 1900-03

ST AGNES (Wes) Beacon [1882 Return]

ST AGNES (Bible Christian) Wheal Rose, Mount Hawke [Kelly 1889]

ST AGNES (Prim Meth) Three Burrows, Mithian f 1846 [1882 return]

ST AGNES (Prim Meth) Silver Well [1882 Return]

ST AGNES (Prim Meth) Croscombe or Cross Combe [1882 Return]

ST AGNES (Prim Meth) Skinner's Bottom [1882 Return]

ST AGNES (UMFC) James Goldsworthy's Chapel, Skinner's Bottom [1882 Return]

ALBERSTON *see* CALSTOCK

ST ALLEN St Alleyne [Powder Hundred; Truro Union] [637] United with KENWYN
OR   C 1680-1857 M 1680-1977 B 1680-1874 (CRO)
BT   CMB 1678-1735, 1741-72 (CRO); CMB 1611-72, 1737-40, 1773-1827, 1829-37
     (DRO)
Cop M 1611-1812 (Ptd Phillimore: 1911); CMB 1611-72 from BT; CB 1680-1837
     (DCRS/WSL); M 1813-37 (CMI); M 1611-1812 from OR,BT (Boyd); M 1790-1812
     (Pallot); B 1813-37 (CBI)
Cop (Mf) C 1680-1959 MB 1680-1958 (RIC); CMB 1611-1812 (Mf of BT at DRO:
         CRO,CSL); M 1813-1910 (Ross); Extr C 1611-1875 (IGI); C 1611-1875
         (SLC)
MI   (Ptd CFHS); cemetery (Ptd CFHS)

ST ALLEN (Wes) Zelah [1882 Return]
OR   C 1922-83 (CRO)

ST ALLEN (Bible Christian) St Allen Lane [1882 Return]

ALTARNON or ALTERNUN or ALTERNON St Nonna [Lesnewth Hundred; Launceston
Union] [1069] Church at Penpoint. United with BOLVENTOR, LANEAST, ST CLETHER
OR   C 1611-1980 M 1610-1973 B 1611-1963 (CRO)
     Noted in 1831: C 1688+ MB 1689+
BT   CMB 1679-1736, 1741-72 (CRO); CMB 1611-73, 1737-40, 1773-1813, 1819-21,
     1830-43 (DRO)
Cop CMB 1611-86 from BT; CMB 1610-1837 (DCRS/WSL); CMB 1611-86 from BT
     (CRO); M 1813-37 (CMI); B 1813-37 (CBI); M 1611-73 (SG); M 1611-73 from
     BT (Boyd)
Cop (Mf) C 1688-1960 MB 1688-1959 (RIC); CMB 1611-1812 (Mf of BT at DRO:
         CRO,CSL); M 1679-1925 (Ross); Extr C 1611-86, 1688-1875
         M 1610-1757, 1787-1874 from BT (IGI); C 1611-86, 1688-1875
         M 1610-1757 from BT (SLC)
MI   (Ptd CFHS)

ALTARNON Holy Trinity, Bolventor. Erected 1848. Parish created 1849 from
ALTARNON, CARDINHAM, ST NEOT. United with ALTARNON, LANEAST, ST CLETHER.
Closed late 1970s. Graveyard still in use
OR   C 1849-1978 M 1849-1977 B 1850-1979 (CRO); later CMB registered at
     ALTARNON
Cop (Mf) C 1849-1959 M 1849-1956 B 1850-1959 (RIC); M 1849-1925 (Ross);
         Extr C 1848-75 M 1849-75 (IGI); C 1848-75 (SLC)
MI   (Ptd CFHS)

ALTARNON (Wes) f c.1748. Erected 1795; rebuilt 1836. New church 1859

ALTARNON (Wes) Bowithwick [1882 Return]

ALTARNON (Bible Christian) [Kelly 1856]

ALTARNON (Bible Christian) Providence, Callas [1882 Return]

ALVERTON   *see* PENZANCE

ANGARRACK   *see* PHILLACK

ST ANTHONY IN MENEAGE St Anthony [Kerrier Hundred; Helston Union] [300]
United with MANACCAN, ST MARTIN IN MENEAGE
OR   C 1608-1981 M 1638-1995 B 1602-1981 (CRO) Noted in 1831: "The Registers
    consist of a bundle of parchment, commencing A.D.1602 to 1744,
    interrupted by a Parchment Book 1726-1812".
BT   CMB 1674-1736, 1741-72 (CRO); CMB 1597-1673, 1737-40, 1773-1832, 1835-36
    (DRO)
Cop M 1726-1812 (Ptd Phillimore: 1912); CMB 1596-1608 from BT; C 1608-1837
    B 1602-1837 (DCRS/WSL); CMB 1597-1726 from BT (CRO); M 1813-37 (CMI);
    B 1813-37 (CBI); M 1597-1725, 1813-36 (CSL); M 1597-1673 (SG);
    M 1726-1812 from OR; M 1597-1673 from BT (Boyd); M 1800-12 (Pallot)
Cop (Mf) C 1608-1959 M 1638-1959 B 1602-1959 (RIC); CMB 1597-1812 (Mf of BT
    at DRO: CRO,CSL); M 1813-1925 (Ross); Extr C 1597-1875 (IGI);
    C 1597-1875 (SLC)
MI   (Ptd CFHS)

ST ANTHONY IN MENEAGE (Bible Christian) [Kelly 1856]; a building, Gilly
Wartha [1882 Return]

ST ANTHONY IN ROSELAND St Anthony [Powder Hundred; Truro Union] [344]
Peculiar of the Bishop of Exeter. United with ST GERRANS
OR   C 1660-1812 M 1668-1983 B 1678-1812 (CRO) Noted in 1831: M defective
    1668-97
BT   CMB 1623-1837, 1820, 1823-27, 1839-30, 1832, 1834, 1836-39, 1841-47
    (DRO)
Cop CMB 1623-77 from BT; C 1660-1812 M 1668-1812 B 1678-1812 (DCRS/WSL);
    CMB 1623-1812 from BT (RIC); C 1660-1812 M 1668-1809 B 1678-1811
    (Ts RIC, Morrab); M 1623-1837 (CRO); M 1813-37 (CMI); B 1813-37 (CBI);
    M 1623-99 (SG); M 1668-1700 from OR; M 1623-38 from BT (Boyd)
Cop (Mf) C 1660-1959 M 1668-1959 B 1678-1956 (RIC); CMB 1623-1812 (Mf of BT
    at DRO: CRO,CSL); M 1668-1809, 1862-76, 1883-1925 (Ross);
    Extr C 1623-36, 1650-1859, 1876-95 M 1623-36, 1660-1721, 1729-30,
    1737-1818, 1874-95 (IGI); C 1623-36, 1660-1859 M 1678-85,
    1697-1718, 1729-30, 1754-1818, 1827-95 (SLC)
MI   Ch,cy (Wall,40-77, Ms SG)

ST ANTHONY IN ROSELAND (Wes) Bohurrow [1882 Return]; St Anthony [Kelly 1897,
1935]

ANTONY or ST ANTONY EAST or ANTONY BY SALTASH St James the Great
[East Hundred; St Germans Union] [3099] United with SHEVIOCK
OR   C 1678-1861 M 1678-1866 B 1677-1925 (CRO) Noted in 1831: Vol.1 with M
    1569-94. Presumably originally continued to 1677 when surviving volume
    begins. Seven leaves transcribed 1934, including two burials 1593.
    Location now unknown; see DCRS/WSL copy below
BT   CMB 1677-1736, 1741-72 (CRO); CMB 1608-74, 1737-40, 1773-1815, 1817-26,
    1828-29, 1831-32, 1834-38, 1841-49 (DRO)
Cop CMB 1608-70 B 1714-25, 1727-28, 1787-89 from BT, C 1678-1807 M 1569-94,
    1678-1755 B 1593, 1677-1714, 1728-87, 1789-90 (DCRS/WSL); C 1861-1995
    M 1866-1995 B 1925-97 (CFHS); M 1813-37 (CMI); B 1813-37 (CBI);
    M 1608-39 (SG); M 1608-64 from BT (Boyd)

ANTONY cont.
Cop (Mf) CMB 1609-1812 (Mf of BT at DRO: CRO,CSL); M 1569-1866 (Ross);
        Extr C 1608-39, 1677-1807 M 1569-1755 (IGI); C 1608-39, 1677-1771
        M 1569-1755 (SLC)
MI Ch (Ptd Jewers 41-60)

ANTONY St James, Torpoint Erected 1819. Chapel-of-ease to ANTONY. Separate
parish 1873
OR C 1819-1968 M 1873-1975 B 1928-52 (CRO) Earlier M B at ANTONY
BT CMB 1828-33, 1838-46, 1848-63, 1871 (DRO) *and see* ANTONY
Cop M 1819-28, 1876-1900 (CFHS)
Cop (Mf) M 1873-75 (Ross)

ANTONY St Philip and St James, Maryfield. Erected 1865. Former estate church
for Antony House. District church 1972

ANTONY Chaplaincy, H.M.S. Raleigh, Torpoint
OR C 1940-91 (MoD); C 1991+ M 1977+ (Chaplain)

ANTONY St Dunstan's Chapel, H.M.S. Fisgard, Torpoint
OR C 1950-83 (MoD)

ANTONY (RC) St Joan of Arc, Torpoint f 1933

ANTONY (RC) Our Lady Star of the Sea, H.M.S. Raleigh, Torpoint
OR C 1951-72 (RCRO)

ANTONY (Ind/Cong) Bethel, Torpoint f 1812 [*Cong.Yearbook* 1850]
OR ZC 1815-37 (PRO)
Cop ZC 1815-37 (SG); C 1948-80 funerals 1950-81 (CFHS)
Cop (Mf) ZC 1815-37 (DCRS/WSL); Extr ZC 1815-37 (IGI); ZC 1815-37 (SLC)

ANTONY (Wes) Quarry Street, Torpoint. Erected 1795

ANTONY (Wes) Fore Street, Torpoint. One Wes at Torpoint [1882 Return]
OR M 1940-87 (CRO)

ANTONY (Wes) Ebenezer, Wilcove. Erected 1806 [1882 Return] Demolished

ANTONY (Bible Christian) Torpoint [Kelly 1889]

ANTONY (Meth)
OR C 1952-81 (Plymouth Record Office, Devon)

ANTONY (Meth) Torpoint
Cop C 1918-70 (CFHS)

ASHTON or ASHTOWN *see* BREAGE

ST AUSTELL Holy Trinity [Powder Hundred; St Austell Union] [8758]
OR C 1564-1961 M 1564-1941 B 1564-1972 (CRO)
BT CMB 1678-1736, 1741-72 (CRO); CMB 1611-72, 1737-40, 1773-1812, 1820,
      1831-34, 1836, 1838, 1841 (DRO)
Cop M 1813-37 (CMI); B 1813-37 (CBI); C 1564-1713 M 1565-1840 B 1564-1695
      (SG); M 1600-27 from OR; M 1611-72 from BT (Boyd)
Cop (Mf) CM 1564-1969 B 1564-1932 (RIC); M 1564-1900 (Ross); CMB 1611-1812
      (Mf of BT at DRO: CRO,CSL); Extr C 1696-1875 (IGI); C 1696-1875
      (SLC)

ST AUSTELL All Saints, Pentewan. Mission church in parish of St Austell. Erected 1821; little used, closed, used as carpenter's workshop. Re-opened 1878
OR M 1985+ (Inc)

ST AUSTELL St Levan, Porthpean. Mission church erected 1885

ST AUSTELL Boscoppa. Bishop Bronescombe C of E Primary School. Designated worship centre

ST AUSTELL St Paul, Charlestown. Formerly Porthmeor or West Polmear. Parish created 1846 from ST AUSTELL. Consecrated 1851
OR C 1847-1944 M 1851-1973 B 1851-1974 (CRO)
Cop C 1847-75 (CFHS)
Cop (Mf) M 1851-75 (Ross)
MI (Ptd CFHS)

ST AUSTELL St Peter the Apostle, Treverbyn. Erected 1850. Parish created 1854 from ST AUSTELL
OR C 1854-1979 M 1850-1976 B 1853-1959 (CRO)
Cop (Mf) M 1850-75 (Ross): M 1850-1900 (CFHS)
MI (Ptd CFHS)

ST AUSTELL (RC) Mission f 1857. Served from Bodmin 1857-58, 1893-95; Plymouth 1858-60; Sclerder 1860-61; Lanherne 1861-64; Liskeard 1864-88, 1895-1902; Par 1888-93 [1882 Return] Modern parish of St Augustine of Hippo, Woodland Road f 1913
OR M 1983-88 (CRO)

ST AUSTELL (Bapt) Ebenezer, West Hill f 1833 in church purchased from Meth. New church erected 1853; [1882 Return] Rebuilt 1899
OR M 1845 ? -1946 ? (missing from church, 1998); dedications 1932-37:
      10 entries; membership lists, 20th century (Ch Sec)
MI (Ptd CFHS)

ST AUSTELL (Ind) South Street (Kiln Lane) f 1788. Closed
OR ZC 1789-1835 (PRO)
Cop ZC 1789-1835 (SG)
Cop (Mf) ZC 1789-1835 (DCRS/WSL); Extr ZC 1739-1835 (IGI); ZC 1789-1835
      (SLC)

ST AUSTELL (Ind/Cong) Victoria Place. Erected 1850 [1882 Return]

ST AUSTELL (Wes) Circuit
OR ZC 1803-36 (PRO); C 1837-1987 (CRO)
Cop ZC 1803-36 (SG)
Cop (Mf) ZC 1803-36 (DCRS/WSL); Extr ZC 1803-36 (IGI); ZC 1803-36 (SLC)

ST AUSTELL (Wes) Bodmin Road, now St John's. Erected 1828
OR C 1934-89 (CRO)

ST AUSTELL (Wes) Mount Charles, Victoria Road [1882 Return]
OR C 1846-1975 M 1960-85 (CRO)

ST AUSTELL (Wes) Charlestown. Erected 1827 [1882 Return]

ST AUSTELL (Wes) Pentewan. Erected 1880 [1882 Return] [Kelly 1889]
OR C 1919-79 (CRO)

ST AUSTELL (Wes) Trenarren
OR   C 1913-79 (CRO)

ST AUSTELL (Wes) Trethurgy [1882 Return]
OR   C 1839-1983 (CRO)

ST AUSTELL (Wes) Stenalees. Erected 1861. Bodmin Circuit; Stenalees section
[Kelly 1889]
OR   C 1893-1960 (CRO)

ST AUSTELL (Prim Meth) Circuit
OR   C 1829-1932 (CRO)

ST AUSTELL (Prim Meth) High Street [1882 Return]

ST AUSTELL (Prim Meth) Clifden Road
OR   M 1967-72 (CRO)

ST AUSTELL (Prim Meth) Rescorla. Erected 1873 [Kelly 1889]
OR   C 1932-63 (CRO)

ST AUSTELL (Prim Meth) Mollionis [1882 Return]

ST AUSTELL (Prim Meth) St Austell Downs [1882 Return]

ST AUSTELL (Prim Meth) Tregreghan Mills [1882 Return]

ST AUSTELL (Prim Meth) South Street, Mount Charles [Kelly 1889]

ST AUSTELL (Bible Christian) Circuit
OR   C 1839-1903 (CRO)

ST AUSTELL (Bible Christian/U Meth) Bethel. f 1819 in a barn. Chapel erected
1822, rebuilt 1836 [Kelly 1889] Now two cottages
OR   C 1921-66 (CRO)
MI   Methodist (Ptd CFHS)

ST AUSTELL (Bible Christian/U Meth) Zion [1882 Return]
OR   C 1921-94 M 1945-94 (CRO)

ST AUSTELL (Bible Christian/U Meth) Fore Street, Bugle. Erected 1858 ?
[1882 Return]
OR   C 1920-23 (CRO)

ST AUSTELL (Bible Christian) Bethel Chapel, Fat Work, Boscoppa Down
[1882 Return]

ST AUSTELL (Bible Christian) Pentewan [1882 Return] 2 chapels, one erected
c.1820, the other 1889 [Kelly 1889]

ST AUSTELL (Bible Christian) Carclaze [1882 Return]

ST AUSTELL (Bible Christian) Carthew [1882 Return] [Kelly 1889]

ST AUSTELL (Bible Christian) Tregonissey Road [Kelly 1889]

ST AUSTELL (UMFC) Eastern Hill [1882 Return]

ST AUSTELL (UMFC/U Meth) Mount Charles Bridge [1882 Return]
OR C 1923-72 (CRO)

ST AUSTELL (U Meth) Bodmin Circuit, Bugle section
OR C 1911-38 (CRO)

ST AUSTELL (UMFC) Kiln Lane [1882 Return]

ST AUSTELL (UMFC/U Meth) Greensplat [Kelly 1889]
OR C 1887-1994, membership records 1920-37 (CRO)

ST AUSTELL (Latter Day Saints) Kingfisher Drive

ST AUSTELL (S of F) Austell (Tregangeeves) Monthly Meeting f 1668; became
East Cornwall MM 1787-1903
OR C 1634-1781 M 1663-1780 B 1664-1782 in CORNWALL QM register RG 6/1578;
    Z 1634-1796 M 1658-1780, 1782-87, 1798-1835 B 1664-1799 in EAST
    CORNWALL MM registers RG 6/174,185,949,950,1314,1518,1519 (PRO);
    Membership lists 1813-1903; burial note-books (St Austell) 1839-42,
    1848-78, (Liskeard) 1838-1904 (CRO)
Cop Z 1634-1781 M 1663-1780 B 1664-1782 in 1828 copy of old register book of
    Cornwall QM (CRO); B 1694-1783 extracted from MM registers 1838 (CRO)

ST AUSTELL (S of F) St Austell or Tregangeeves Meeting f 1656. Meeting house
High Cross Street erected 1690; rebuilt 1788, 1829: still [1998] in use
OR B notes 1837, 1839-40, 1842-46, 1848, 1851; B notes with D certs
    St Austell and Tregangeeves 1839-94; B notes Tregangeeves 1837, 1839-42,
    1844-45; B counterfoils 1862-1904; St Austell B notes and certs 1905-07;
    list of DB St Austell 1835-73, Tregangeeves 1820-72; list of subscribers
    for St Austell meeting house n.d. (CRO)
Cop Z 1590-1783 M 1741 Tregangeeves and Milton meetings, extracted from MM
    registers 1838 (CRO); B at Tregangeeves 1664-1917: 20th century extract
    (CRO)

BAKESON CHAPEL   see WEEK ST MARY

BALDHU   parish formed from KEA q.v., KENWYN, CHACEWATER

BALNOON   see LELANT

BALNOON   see ST IVES

BALWEST   see GERMOE

BANGORS   see POUNDSTOCK

BARRIPPER   see CAMBORNE

BEACON   see ST AGNES

BEALBURGH   or BEALBURY see ST MELLION

BELOWDA   see ROCHE

BENNICO   see BOYTON

BERIPPER   see GUNWALLOE

BISSICK   see LADOCK

BLACK ROCK   see CROWAN

BLACKCROSS   see ST COLUMB MAJOR

BLACKWATER   see ST AGNES

ST BLAZEY St Blaise [Powder Hundred; St Austell Union] [2155] Chapelry in
ST AUSTELL. Separate parish 1844
OR C 1710-1970 M 1710-1968 B 1710-1945 (CRO)
Noted in 1831: Vol.1: C 1675-1710 M 1663-1700 B 1663-1709
BT CMB 1681-1736, 1741-72 (CRO); CMB 1608-73, 1737-40, 1773-1837, 1841-43
      (DRO)
Cop CMB 1608-1741 from BT; CMB 1710-1837 (DCRS/WSL); M 1813-37 (CMI);
      B 1813-37 (CBI); M 1608-74 (SG); M 1608-73 from BT (Boyd)
Cop (Mf) CMB 1710-1959 (RIC); M 1698-1925 (Ross); CMB 1608-1812 (Mf of BT at
      DRO: CRO,CSL); Extr C 1608-1875 M 1608-1837 (IGI); C 1608-1875
      M 1608-1837 (SLC)
MI (Ptd CFHS)

ST BLAZEY St Mary the Virgin, Par. Parish created 1846 from ST BLAZEY,
TYWARDREATH, ST AUSTELL. Erected 1848-49
OR C 1849-1959 M 1850-1974 B 1857-1961 (CRO)
Cop M 1851-1925 (CFHS)
Cop (Mf) C 1849-1959 M 1850-1959 B 1857-1959 (RIC); M 1850-1925 (Ross);
      Extr C 1849-75 (IGI); C 1849-75 (SLC)
MI (Ptd CFHS)

ST BLAZEY Good Shepherd, Par. Chapel-of-ease erected 1896

ST BLAZEY (RC) Christ the King, Par f 1936

ST BLAZEY (Wes) Mount Pleasant
OR C 1839-1989 (CRO)
Cop C 1839-1946 (CFHS)

ST BLAZEY (Wes) St Blazey Gate [1882 Return]

ST BLAZEY (Wes) Leek Seed (Leekseed) Chapel. Erected 1824
Cop C 1839-84 M 1912-96 B 1896-1993 (CFHS)
MI (Ptd CFHS)

ST BLAZEY (Wes) Par, St Mary. Erected 1862 [Kelly 1889]
OR M cert counterfoils 1918-74 (CRO)
Cop C 1854-1929 (CRO,CFHS)

ST BLAZEY (Prim Meth) Tregrehan
OR Members' list 1889-90 (CRO)

ST BLAZEY (Prim Meth) Par. Erected 1875 [Kelly 1889]

ST BLAZEY (Bible Christian/U Meth) Ebenezer, Blazey Gate. Erected 1862
[1882 Return]
OR C 1920-30 (CRO)

ST BLAZEY (UMFC) Foundry Street [1882 Return]

ST BLAZEY (Meth) Central Hall
OR M 1983-89 (CRO)

BLISLAND St Protus and St Hyacinth [Trigg Hundred; Bodmin Union] [644]
United 1972 with TEMPLE. Now united with ST BREWARD
OR C 1563-1859 M 1539-1974 B 1539-1901 (CRO)
  Noted in 1831: vols. 1 and 2, to 1716, "composed of fragments of old
  Registers, imperfect and confused"
BT CMB 1682-1736, 1741-72 (CRO); CMB 1608-73, 1737-40, 1773-1812, 1831,
  1836-45 (DRO)
Cop M 1539-1912 (Ptd Phillimore: 1903); People from other parishes married
  at Blisland 1654-1837 (CFHS); M 1813-37 (CMI); B 1813-37 (CBI);
  C 1563-1837 B 1539-1837 (SG); M 1539-1812 (Boyd); M 1790-1812 (Pallot)
Cop (Mf) C 1563-1959 M 1539-1921 B 1539-1901: pre-1813 transcript (RIC);
    CMB 1608-1812 (Mf of BT at DRO: CRO,CSL); M 1813-1921 (Ross);
    Extr C 1563-1859 M 1539-1753, 1755-1875 (IGI); C 1563-1859 (SLC)
MI (Ptd CFHS)

BLISLAND (Wes) Erected 1798; rebuilt 1812. Closed. Now an hotel annexe

BLISLAND (Bible Christian) Ebenezer. Erected 1879. Derelict by 1969

BLISLAND (Bible Christian) Temple. Erected 1875. Disused by 1979

BOCONNOC Dedication unknown [West Hundred; Liskeard Union] [259] Peculiar of
the Dean and Chapter of Exeter
OR C 1709-1918 M 1709-1839 B 1709-1812 (CRO) No earlier register noted in
  1831
BT CMB 1608-1809 with Bradock (DRO)
Cop CMB 1709-1850 (DCRS/WSL); M 1712-1839 (Ts RIC, CRO); M 1712-1812
  B 1838-1980 (CFHS); M 1813-37 (CMI); B 1813-37 (CBI); M 1608-36,
  1712-1837 (SG); M 1608-64 from BT (Boyd)
Cop (Mf) M 1712-1850 (Ross); Extr C 1709-1850 M 1712-1850 from BT (IGI);
    C 1709-1850 M 1712-1850 from BT (SLC)
MI (Ptd CFHS)

BOCONNOC (Wes) [Kelly 1856]; Couches Mill [1882 Return]

BOCONNOC (Bible Christian) [Kelly 1889]

BODINNICK *see* LANTEGLOS BY FOWEY

BODMIN St Petroc [Trigg Hundred; Bodmin Union] [Borough 3375; parish 407]
United with LANHYDROCK, LANIVET
OR C 1558-1963 M 1564-1653, 1660-1983 B 1558-1983 (CRO)
BT CMB 1683-1736, 1741-72 (CRO); CMB 1608-70, 1737-40, 1773-1812, 1831-32,
  1834-36 (DRO)
Cop M 1559-1812 (Ptd Phillimore:1907); C 1747-1820 M 1768-1813 B 1767-1820,
  1558-1812 (Ms CRO); C 1558-1737 (CSL); M 1813-37 (CMI); B 1813-37 (CBI);
  CB 1558-1812 (SG); M 1559-1812 (Boyd); M 1790-1812 (Pallot)
Cop (Mf) C 1558-1959 M 1668-1958 B 1558-1951 (RIC); CMB 1609-1812 (Mf of BT
    at DRO: CRO,CSL); M 1559-1812 (SG); M 1813-1900 (Ross);
    Extr C 1558-1875 M 1558-1876 (IGI); C 1558-1875 M 1558-1876 (SLC)
MI (Ptd CFHS); ch,cy 1959 (Ts SG)

BODMIN St Leonard. Chapel-of-ease; restored 1884

BODMIN Bodmin Prison, Berrycombe. Chapel
Cop: executions from 1785 (Ptd A Brunton *Bodmin Gaol, Cornwall*: 1992}

BODMIN County Lunatic Asylum. Chapel erected 1859-61

BODMIN (RC) St Mary's Abbey f 1846. Served from Plymouth 1858-61, from
Liskeard 1862-81
OR C 1881+ M 1875+ Confirmations 1892+ DB 1916+ (Inc); Confirmations 1882,
   1892-1933 (Plymouth Diocesan Archives)

BODMIN (Bapt) Town Wall f 1984

BODMIN (Ind/Lady Hunt Conn) Providence Chapel f.1804 [Cong.Yearbook 1850];
Fore Street. Rebuilt 1871 [1882 Return]
OR ZC 1826-37 (PRO)
Cop ZC 1826-37 (SG)
Cop (Mf) ZC 1826-37 (DCRS/WSL); Extr C 1826-37 (IGI); C 1826-37 (SLC)

BODMIN (Presb) Licensed 1672; closed by 1772

BODMIN (Wes) Fore Street. Erected 1803; rebuilt 1839
OR ZC 1804-37 (PRO)
Cop ZC 1804-37 (SG)
Cop (Mf) ZC 1804-37 (DCRS/WSL); Extr C 1804-37 (IGI); C 1804-37 (SLC)

BODMIN (Wes) Circuit
OR C 1837-1936 (CRO) see also LOSTWITHIEL, STENALEES

BODMIN (Wes) A building, St Lawrence [1882 Return]

BODMIN (Bible Christian) Circuit (Luxulyan Circuit pre-1850s)
OR C 1837-1907 (CRO)

BODMIN (Bible Christian) Bore Street. Erected 1851 [Kelly 1889]

BODMIN (Wes Meth Ass/UMFC/U Meth) Pool Street. Erected 1842 [Kelly 1889]
OR C 1934-63 (CRO)

BODMIN (UMFC) Circuit
OR see LOSTWITHIEL

BODMIN (UMFC) Back Street [1882 Return]

BODMIN (U Meth) Circuit
OR C 1907-32; southern section C 1907-21; Bugle section C 1911-38 (CRO)

BODMIN (U Meth) Circuit
OR see LOSTWITHIEL

BODMIN (Meth) Circuit, formerly U Meth
OR C 1932-63 (CRO)

BODMIN (Meth) Circuit, formerly Wes, Lostwithiel section
OR C 1932-59 (CRO)

BODMIN (Meth) Circuit, Bugle section
OR C 1938-66 (CRO)

BODMIN (Meth) Circuit
OR C 1952-77 (CRO)

BODMIN LANDS see ST IVE

BODWAY   see MENHENIOT

BOFARNEL   *see* ST WINNOW

BOHURROW   *see* ST ANTHONY IN ROSELAND

BOJEWYAN   *see* ST JUST IN PENWITH

BOLLINGEY   *see* PERRANZABULOE

BOLVENTOR   *see* ALTARNON

BONYTHON   or BONITHIN *see* CURY

BOOT   *see* WHITSTONE

BORAH   *see* ST BURYAN

BOSCASTLE in FORRABURY q.v. and MINSTER. Parish of BOSCASTLE WITH DAVIDSTOW now includes DAVIDSTOW, FORRABURY, ST JULIOT, LESNEWTH, MINSTER, OTTERHAM, TREVALGA

BOSCASWELL   *see* ST JUST IN PENWITH

BOSCOPPA DOWN   *see* ST AUSTELL

BOSKYNWEN DOWN   *see* WENDRON

BOSSINEY   *see* TINTAGEL

BOSWARTHEN   *see* MADRON

BOSWINGER   *see* GORRAN

BOTALLACK   *see* ST JUST IN PENWITH

BOTUS FLEMING St Mary [East Hundred; St Germans Union] [279] United with
LANDRAKE, ST ERNEY
OR C 1548-1968 M 1550-1982 B 1548-1992 (CRO)
    Noted in 1831: Vol.1 (1548-1801) described as "a transcript of the
    earlier Registers now lost". M 1549-1754 certain leaves cut out "for
    fradulent purposes doubtless..the last act of this kind is in 1767".
BT CMB 1675-1736, 1741-72 (CRO); CMB 1608-73, 1738-40, 1773-1812, 1814-24,
    1828, 1831, 1835, 1837-43 (DRO)
Cop M 1550-1812 (Ptd Phillimore: 1912); CB 1548-1837 M 1560-1837 (DCRS/WSL);
    M 1549-1812 (Ts CRO,CFHS,RIC,SG); M 1813-37 (CMI); B 1813-37 (CBI);
    M 1550-1812 (Boyd); M 1800-12 (Pallot)
Cop (Mf) CMB 1608-1812 (Mf of BT at DRO: CRO,CSL); M 1813-37 (Ross);
        Extr C 1547-1837 (IGI); C 1547-1837 (SLC)
MI (Ptd CFHS); Ch (Ptd Jewers 156-61)

BOTUS FLEMING (Wes) Erected 1854; [1882 Return]

BOWGYHERE   *see* ST MAWGAN IN MENEAGE

BOWITHWICK   *see* ALTARNON

BOYTON Holy Name [Part Stratton Hundred (Cornwall), part Black Torrington Hundred (Devon); Launceston Union] [557] United with NORTH TAMERTON, and with Werrington, St Giles in the Heath and Virginstow [Devon]
OR   C 1568-1870 M 1568-1837 B 1568-1970 (CRO)
BT   CMB 1679-1736, 1741-72 (CRO); CMB 1611-73, 1737-40, 1772-1812, 1818,
     1822, 1825, 1829-31, 1833-34, 1836 (DRO)
Cop M 1568-1812 (Ptd Phillimore: 1910); M 1672-76, 1754-1812 (Ptd
     Phillimore: 1911); M 1813-37 (DCRS/WSL); M 1813-37 (CMI); B 1813-37
     (CBI); M 1568-1812 (Boyd); M 1790-1812 (Pallot)
Cop (Mf) C 1568-1870 MB 1568-1960 (RIC); CMB 1611-1813 (Mf of BT at DRO:
          CRO, CSL); M 1813-1900 (Ross); Extr C 1568-1870 M 1568-1751,
          1756-1876 (IGI); C 1568-1870 M 1568-1751, 1756-1876 (SLC)
MI   (Ptd CFHS)

BOYTON (Wes ?) f 1889 ?
MI   (Ptd CFHS)

BOYTON (Bible Christian) Bennico [1882 Return]

BOYTON (UMFC) Boyton Town [1882 Return]

BRADOCK or BROADOAK Blessed Virgin Mary [West Hundred; Liskeard Union] [301] Peculiar of the Dean and Chapter of Exeter. United with LISKEARD, ST KEYNE, ST PINNOCK, MORVAL
OR   C 1578-1947 M 1600-1979 B 1555-1980 (CRO)
BT   CMB 1611-1817, 1819-36 (DRO)
Cop C 1578-1850 M 1600-1850 B 1555-1850 (DCRS/WSL); M 1600-1837 (Ts with
     index, CRO,RIC,SG); M 1600-1812 (CFHS); M 1813-37 (CMI); B 1813-37
     (CBI); M 1611-33 from BT (Boyd)
Cop (Mf) CMB 1608-1809 (Mf of BT at DRO: CRO,CSL); M 1600-1875 (Ross);
          Extr C 1578-1850 M 1600-1850 (IGI); C 1578-1850 M 1600-1850 (SLC)
MI   (Ptd CFHS)

BRADOCK (Wes) [Kelly 1856]; [1882 Return]; West Taphouse f 1828 rebuilt 1883 [Kelly 1889]

BRANE MOOR   see SANCREED

BRAYS SHOP   see STOKE CLIMSLAND

BRAZACOTT   see PETHERWIN, NORTH

BREA   see CAMBORNE

BREAGE or ST BREOCK IN KERRIER St Breaca [Kerrier Hundred; Helston Union] [5149] United with GERMOE. see also CURY, GUNWALLOE
OR   C 1603-1918 M 1559-1982 B 1559-1966 (CRO) Noted in 1831: C deficient
     1757-78, 1683-1700, M deficient 1656-78 B deficient 1564-69.
BT   CMB 1597-1673, 1737-40, 1773-1812, 1814-15, 1817, 1820-24, 1826-27,
     1834, 1836-38 (DRO)
Cop M 1559-1812 (Ptd Phillimore: 1903); CMB 1597-1602 from BT; C 1603-1837
     MB 1559-1837 (DCRS/WSL); M 1813-37 (CMI); B 1813-37 (CBI); C 1597-1700
     B 1559-1694 (SG); M 1559-1812 (Boyd); M 1800-12 (Pallot)
Cop (Mf) C 1603-1959 M 1559-1958 B 1559-1959 (RIC); CMB 1597-1812 (Mf of BT
          at DRO: CRO,CSL); M 1813-1900 (Ross); Extr C 1597-1875 M 1559-1875
          (IGI); C 1597-1763 M 1559-1754 (SLC)
MI   (Ptd CFHS)

BREAGE The Annunciation, Ashton. Licensed mission church

BREAGE St John the Baptist, Godolphin Cross. Parish formed 1846 from BREAGE.
Erected 1851. United with CROWAN
OR C 1846-97 M 1851-1982 B 1851-1926 (CRO)
MI (Ptd CFHS)

BREAGE (Wes) Trenwheal [1882 Return]
OR C 1866-1960 (CRO)

BREAGE (Wes) Erected 1833

BREAGE (Wes) Carleen. f 1762; new chapel 1833 [1882 Return]

BREAGE (Wes) Kenneggy Downs. Erected 1841 [1882 Return]

BREAGE (Wes) Truscoe [1882 Return]

BREAGE (Wes) Ashton [1882 Return]

BREAGE (Wes) Troon [1882 Return]

BREAGE (Wes) Hendra [Kelly 1883]

BREAGE (Bible Christian) f 1824
OR ZC 1821-37 (PRO)
Cop ZC 1821-37 (SG)
Cop (Mf) ZC 1821-37 (DCRS/WSL)

BREAGE (Bible Christian) Church Town [1882 Return]

BREAGE (Bible Christian) Harland Cross [1882 Return]

BREAGE (U Meth/UMFC) Ashton. Erected 1842 [1882 Return]
OR C 1963-66 (CRO)

BREAGE (UMFC) Church Town [1882 Return]

BREAGE (UMFC) Trescaw [1882 Return]

BREAGE (UMFC) Association Chapel, Rinsey [1882 Return]

BREAGE (S of F) Erected 1731, part of PENZANCE MM

ST BREOCK IN KERRIER   *see* BREAGE

ST BREOCK or PAWTON or NANSANT St Breoke [Pydar Hundred; St Columb Major
Union] [1450] Peculiar of the Bishop of Exeter. United with EGLOSHAYLE as
parish of St Breock and Egloshayle in Wadebridge. see also WADEBRIDGE
OR C 1563-1905 M 1561-1962 B 1561-1905 (CRO)
BT CMB 1813-19, 1838-49 (DRO)
Cop M 1561-1812 (Ptd Phillimore: 1911); C 1563-1812 MB 1561-1811 (CSL);
     M 1561-1714 B 1561-1731 (CRO); C 1563-1637 B 1561-1665 (Ms RIC);
     C 1715-1840 (I, SG); C 1851-1906 M 1837-1945 surname indexes (CFHS);
     M 1561-1714 (Ms CRO); M 1813-37 (CMI); B 1813-37 (CBI); M 1561-1812
     (Boyd)
Cop (Mf) CMB 1609-1813 (Mf of BT at DRO: CRO,CSL); M 1813-75 (Ross)
MI (Ptd CFHS)

ST BREOCK (Bible Christian) Whitecross Street [1882 Return]

ST BREWARD or SIMONWARD St Breward [Trigg Hundred; Camelford Union] [627]
United with BLISLAND
OR C 1558-1917 M 1558-1850 B 1558-1832, 1850-1969 (CRO) C 1832-50 at
    ST TEATH; B 1832-50 at BLISLAND
BT CMB 1676-1735, 1741-72 (CRO); CMB 1608-73, 1737-40, 1773-1816 (DRO)
Cop CMB 1558-1900 (Ptd T.Taylor *The Parish Registers of St Breward in*
    Cornwall: 1900); M 1558-1812 (Ptd Phillimore: 1900); CMB 1900-92
    (Ms RIC); M 1813-37 (CMI); M 1558-1812 (Boyd); M 1813-37 (Pallot);
    B 1813-37 (CBI)
Cop **(Mf)** CMB 1558-1960 (RIC); CMB 1608-1812 (Mf of BT at DRO: CRO,CSL);
        M 1813-1900 (Ross); Extr C 1558-1875 M 1558-1766, 1808-12 (IGI);
        C 1558-1875 (SLC)
MI (Ptd CFHS)

ST BREWARD (Wes) [Kelly 1856]

ST BREWARD (Bible Christian/U Meth) Providence Chapel, Limehead [Kelly 1897]

ST BREWARD (Free Meth) Lower Lanke [Kelly 1897]

BRIDGE   hamlet in ILLOGAN

BRIDGEND   *see* ST WINNOW

BRIDGERULE Devon parish in Diocese of Truro. *see* NIPR Devon

BRIGHTOR   *see* LANDRAKE

BROAD LANE *see* ILLOGAN

BROADOAK   *see* BRADOC

BROCKHILL   *see* ST GENNYS

BRYHER   *see* SCILLY ISLES

BUDE HAVEN *see* STRATTON

BUDOCK St Budock [Kerrier Hundred; Falmouth Union] [1797] Chapelry in
ST GLUVIAS, Separate parish 1890. Peculiar of the Bishop of Exeter.
see also FALMOUTH
OR C 1652-1960 M 1653-1966 B 1653-1954 (CRO) Noted in 1831: CMB 1603+
BT CMB 1610-1845 (DRO)
Cop M 1653-1812 (Ptd Phillimore: 1908); C 1654-1982 M 1654-1966 B 1654-1954
    (CSL); C 1654-1944 M 1654-1926 B 1654-1953 (CFHS); C 1653-1929
    M 1653-1877 B 1653-1846 (CRO); CB 1649-1837 (DCRS/WSL); C 1654-1840
    M 1654-1837 B 1654-1846 (Ts RIC); M 1813-37 (CMI); B 1653-1797 (CSL);
    B 1813-37 (CBI); C 1610-1812 (SG); M 1653-1812 from OR; M 1610-73 from
    BT (Boyd); M 1800-12 (Pallot)
Cop **(Mf)** CB 1653-1959 M 1654-1959 (RIC); CMB 1610-1766, 1772-1812 (Mf of BT
        at DRO: CRO,CSL); M 1813-1925 (Ross); Extr C 1649-1875 M 1653-1875
        (IGI); C 1649-1875 M 1653-1754 (SLC)
MI Ch (Wall,1-5, Ms SG)

BUDOCK St Michael and All Angels, Penwerris. Parish created 1848 from BUDOCK
OR C 1848-1988 M 1848-1984 (CRO)
Cop M 1848-1900 (CFHS)

BUDOCK The Holy Spirit, Penwerris. Licensed mission church

BUDOCK (Wes) Budock Water. Erected 1843. Rebuilt 1897
OR C 1930-85 M 1955-89 (CRO)

BUDOCK (Wes) Treverva. Erected 1843 [1882 Return] New chapel 1880s.
Old chapel now two cottages.

BUDOCK (S of F) pre-1668-c.1682. Part of FALMOUTH MM
OR Z 1654-84 M 1661-76 B 1658-75 in CORNWALL QM register RG 6/1578 (PRO); B
    counterfoils 1906-50 (CRO)
Cop Z 1654-1772 B 1658-1775 in 1828 copy of old register book of Cornwall QM
    (CRO)
MI (Ptd CFHS)

BUGLE   see ST AUSTELL

BURHOS   see WENDRON

BURITON   see PENZANCE

BURLAWN   or BURLORNE, hamlet in EGLOSHAYLE q.v. and ST BREOCK

BURNT HOUSE   see MABE

BURRATON   see ST STEPHENS BY SALTASH

ST BURYAN St Buriana [Penwith Hundred; Penzance Union] [1707] Peculiar of
the Rural Deanery of St Buryan until 1430; Royal Peculiar 1430-1848.
see also ST LEVAN. Now with ST LEVAN, SENNEN
OR C 1653-1940 M 1654-1970 B 1653-1992 (CRO)
BT CMB 1691-1847 (CRO)
Cop M 1654-1812 (Ptd Phillimore: 1903); CB 1653-1812 (DCRS/WSL,Morrab,SG);
     C 1653-1789 B 1653-1812 (CSL); C 1848-75 M 1876-1900 (CFHS);
     CMB 1653-1812 (Ms card index, RIC); M 1813-37 (CMI); M 1654-1812 (Boyd);
     M 1790-1812 (Pallot); B 1813-37 (CBI)
Cop (Mf) CB 1653-1812 (RIC); M 1813-75 (Ross); Extr C 1653-1847 M 1654-1812
         (IGI); C 1653-1847 (SLC)
MI (Ptd CFHS)

ST BURYAN (Wes) Erected 1783; rebuilt 1832, 1981
OR C 1890-1917 (CRO)

ST BURYAN (Wes) Borah. Erected 1817 [1882 Return]

ST BURYAN (Wes) Boscarne, Crows-an-Wra. Erected 1831 [1882 Return]
MI (Ptd CFHS)

ST BURYAN (Bible Christian) Church Town. Erected pre-1851 [1882 Return]

BUSH   in STRATTON q.v. and POUGHILL

BUSVEAL   see GWENNAP

CADGWITH   in RUAN MINOR and GRADE qq.v

CAERHAYS   see ST MICHAEL CAERHAYS

CALENDRA   see VERYAN

CALLESTOCK   see PERRANZABULOE

CALLINGTON St Mary [East Hundred; Liskeard Union] [1388] Borough in SOUTH
HILL. Formerly Killington, Kellington or Calvington. Now with SOUTH HILL
OR C 1558-1979 M 1558-1983 B 1558-1960 (CRO)
BT CMB 1676-1736, 1741-72 (CRO); CMB 1597-1673, 1738-40, 1773-1839, 1841,
    1843 (DRO)
Cop CMB 1558-1603 (CRO); M 1813-37 (CMI); B 1813-37 (CBI); M 1598-1673 (SG);
    M 1597-1673 from BT (Boyd)
Cop (Mf) CMB 1597-1812 (Mf of BT at DRO: CRO,CSL); M 1597-1837 (Ross);
        Extr C 1676-1773 from BT (IGI); C 1676-1773 from BT (SLC)
MI (Ptd CFHS)

CALLINGTON (RC) Our Lady of Victories f 1931

CALLINGTON (Ind/Cong) f 1810. Purchased by Wes 1835
OR None known

CALLINGTON (Wes) Circuit
Cop C 1843-96 (CRO,CFHS)

CALLINGTON (Wes) Haye Road. Erected 1845 [1882 Return]; [Kelly 1935]

CALLINGTON (Prim Meth) Chapel Street [1882 Return]

CALLINGTON (Prim Meth)
Cop C 1856-78: Callington entries from Liskeard Prim Meth register (CFHS)

CALLINGTON (Bible Christian) Circuit
Cop C 1863-70 (CRO,CFHS)

CALLINGTON (Bible Christian) A building [1882 Return]

CALLINGTON (Meth) Newport
OR M 1955-69 (CRO)

CALLINGTON (Plymouth Brethren) Building known by name of "Christian
Brethren", Liskeard Road [1882 Return]
MI (Ptd CFHS)

CALLINGTON (S of F) f by 1697. Part of East Cornwall MM

CALSTOCK St Andrew [East Hundred; Tavistock Union] [2328]
OR C 1658-1969 M 1656-1987 B 1658-1915 (CRO) Noted in 1831: registers from
    1716 only
BT CMB 1684-1736, 1741-72 (CRO); CMB 1602-73, 1737-40, 1773-1812, 1818-25,
    1827-29, 1832-34, 1838-39 (DRO)
Cop M 1602, 1614, 1622-25, 1632-43, 1656-1812 Banns 1805-08 (Ts with index,
    RIC,CFHS,SG); M 1602-1837 (CRO); M 1876-86, 1889-99 (CFHS); CMB 1602-34
    from BT (CSL); M 1813-37 (CMI); B 1813-37 (CBI); M 1602-73 from BT
    (Boyd)
Cop (Mf) CMB 1602-1812 (Mf of BT at DRO: CRO,CSL); M 1604-1875 (Ross);
        Extr C 1684-1772 from BT (IGI); C 1684-1772 from BT (SLC)

CALSTOCK St Anne, Gunnislake. Chapel-of-ease to Calstock. Erected 1880
OR None

CALSTOCK All Saints, Harrowbarrow. Chapel-of-ease to Calstock. Erected 1871
OR None

CALSTOCK St Michael and All Angels, Latchley. Chapel-of-ease to Calstock.
Erected 1883. Closed. Now a house
OR None

CALSTOCK Cotehele House. 15th century chapel of Edgecumbe family
OR None

CALSTOCK (RC) St Joseph, Gunnislake f 1927

CALSTOCK (Bapt) (1815) [*Bapt. Manual* 1850; *Handbook* 1881] became Pentecostal
MI (Ptd CFHS)

CALSTOCK (Bapt) Metherel f.1818

CALSTOCK (Bapt) Gunnislake: sold to Anglicans by 1851

CALSTOCK (Bapt) Harrowbarrow [Bapt.Handbook 1881]

CALSTOCK (Presb) Metherel fl 1715-late 18th century

CALSTOCK (Wes) Calstock Circuit
Cop C 1846-95 (CFHS)

CALSTOCK (Wes) Harewood Road
OR M 1904-57 (CRO)

CALSTOCK (Wes) Gunnislake Circuit
Cop C 1885-95 (CRO)

CALSTOCK (Wes) Gunnislake [Kelly 1856] [1882 Return]

CALSTOCK (Wes) Latchley. Erected 1865; closed 1970

CALSTOCK (Bible Christian) Harrowbarrow. Erected 1842 [1882 Return]

CALSTOCK (Bible Christian) Fore Street, Gunnislake [Kelly 1856] [1882
Return]

CALSTOCK (Bible Christian) Alberston [1882 Return]

CALSTOCK (Bible Christian) Metherill [Kelly 1889]

CALSTOCK (Free Meth) Gunnislake. Erected mid-19th century. [1882 Return]
Later used by Salvation Army

CALSTOCK (S of F) f pre-1668. Part of East Cornwall MM. Two meeting houses
existed 1821

CALVINGTON *see* CALLINGTON

CAMBORNE St Martin and St Meriadoc [Penwith Hundred; Redruth Union] [7699]
OR C 1591-1944 M 1538-1946 B 1538-1937 (CRO)
     Noted in 1831: Vol.1 CMB 1538-1706 defective to 1653
BT CMB 1676-1736, 1741-72 (CRO); CMB 1610-73, 1738-40, 1773-1849 (DRO)
Cop CMB 1538-1837 (Ptd DCRS: 1945); M 1538-1812 (Ptd Phillimore: 1911);
     C 1576-1676 B 1634-98 (CFHS); M 1538-1812 (Boyd); M 1800-12 (Pallot);
     M 1813-37 (CMI); M 1837-75 (CFHS)

CAMBORNE cont.
Cop (Mf) CMB 1538-1837 (RIC); M 1539-1837 (SG); CMB 1610-1812 (Mf of BT at
DRO: CRO,CSL); M 1813-75 (Ross); Extr C 1558-80, 1591-1837
M 1538-1837 (IGI); C 1558-80, 1591-1837 M 1538-1745 (SLC)
MI (Ptd CFHS)

CAMBORNE St John the Evangelist, Treslothan Erected 1841, chapel to
Pendarves House. Parish created 1845 from Camborne
OR C 1845-1991 M 1845-1988 B 1845-1951 (CRO)
MI (Ptd CFHS)

CAMBORNE The Good Shepherd, Troon, Treslothan. Erected 1899

CAMBORNE All Saints, Tuckingmill. Erected and parish created 1844 from
CAMBORNE, ILLOGAN
OR C 1845-1989 Banns 1944-95 M 1845-1988 B 1845-1966 (CRO)
Cop C 1845-75 (CFHS)
Cop (Mf) M 1845-75 (Ross)

CAMBORNE Holy Trinity, Penponds. Erected 1844. Parish created 1847 from
CAMBORNE
OR 1857+ (CRO)
MI (Ptd CFHS)

CAMBORNE (RC) St John the Baptist, Beacon Hill f 1851
OR CM 1852+ Confirmations 1854+ B 1853+ (Inc); Confirmations 1856-1933
(Plymouth Diocesan Archives)
Cop Confirmations 1852-81 (CFHS)

CAMBORNE (RC) The Assumption f 1936

CAMBORNE (Wes) Circuit f 1828
OR ZC 1828-37 (PRO)
Cop ZC 1828-37 (SG)
Cop (Mf) ZC 1828-37 (DCRS/WSL); Extr C 1828-37 (IGI); C 1828-37 (SLC)

CAMBORNE (Wes) Wesley, Chapel Street. Erected 1828 [1882 Return]
OR C 1925-89 M 1901-88 (CRO)

CAMBORNE (Wes) Centenary Street. Erected 1839 [1882 Return]
Cop B 1849-1931 (CRO)
MI (Ptd CFHS)

CAMBORNE (Wes) Condurrow Lower [Kelly 1889]
OR C 1954-85 (CRO)

CAMBORNE (Wes) Kehelland. [1882 Return] Erected 1891
OR C 1936-71 (CRO)

CAMBORNE (Wes) Pengegon [1882 Return]
OR C 1940-83 M 1968-79 (CRO)

CAMBORNE (Wes) Plantation [Kelly 1889]
OR C 1970-73 (CRO)

CAMBORNE (Wes) Adjewhells, Barripper. Erected mid-19th century. Closed.

CAMBORNE (Wes) Bolenowe [Kelly 1889]

CAMBORNE (Wes) Treswithian [Kelly 1889]
OR C 1935-79 (CRO)

CAMBORNE (Wes) Penponds [1882 Return]

CAMBORNE (Wes) Troon [1882 Return]; Troon St John's
OR C 1910-67 M 1968-85 (CRO)

CAMBORNE (Wes) Beacon
OR C 1936-91 M 1966-87 (CRO)

CAMBORNE (Wes) Roseworthy. Erected 1825. [1882 Return] Now a house

CAMBORNE (Wes) Tuckingmill Circuit
OR C 1839-59 (CRO)

CAMBORNE (Wes) Tuckingmill. Erected 1843. [1882 Return] Demolished post-1973
OR C 1905-95 M 1901-92 (CRO)

CAMBORNE (Prim Meth) Circuit
OR C 1916-38 (CRO)

CAMBORNE (Prim Meth) Trevenson Street. Erected 1850. [1882 Return]
Demolished post-1973
OR C 1939-74 (CRO)

CAMBORNE (Prim Meth) Condurrow [1882 Return]

CAMBORNE (Prim Meth) Tuckingmill [Kelly 1889]

CAMBORNE (Bible Christian/U Meth) Penponds. Erected 1844 [1882 Return]
OR C 1910-81 (CRO)

CAMBORNE (Bible Christian) Brea [1882 Return]

CAMBORNE (Bible Christian) Trelowarren Street. Rebuilt 1871 [1882 Return]

CAMBORNE (Meth New Conn/U Meth) Trelowarren Street
OR C 1889-1990 M 1964-95 (CRO)

CAMBORNE (UMFC) Tuckingmill [1882 Return]

CAMBORNE (UMFC/U Meth) North Parade. Erected 1860
OR C 1855-1978 M 1964-75, 1978 (CRO)

CAMBORNE (UMFC/U Meth) Lower Bolenowe
OR C 1893-1948 (CRO)

CAMBORNE (UMFC/U Meth) Troon Chapel Square [1882 Return]
OR C 1884-1967 M 1946-68 (CRO)

CAMBORNE (UMFC/U Meth) Higher Kehelland [Kelly 1889]
OR C 1880-1955 (CRO)

CAMBORNE (Teetotal Wes Meth Conn) North Parade. Erected 1842

CAMBORNE (Free Church) [1882 Return]

CAMBORNE (UMFC/U Meth) Near Albert Street [1882 Return]

CAMBORNE (UMFC/UM) Barripper [1882 Return]
OR C 1886-1941 (CRO)

CAMBORNE (Free Meth) Tuckingmill [Kelly 1889]

CAMBORNE (Salvation Army) Vyvyan Street

CAMBORNE (S of F) Erected c.1821. Part of FALMOUTH MM. Bassett Street [1882 Return]

CAMELFORD   see LANTEGLOS BY CAMELFORD

CANONS TOWN   see LUDGVAN

CANWORTHY WATER   see WARBSTOW

CARADON   see ST CLEER

CARADON   see LINKINHORNE

CARBIS BAY   see LELANT

CARBIS WATER   see LELANT

CARGLAZE   see ST AUSTELL

CARDEAST   see CARDINHAM

CARDINHAM or CARDYNHAM St Meubred [West Hundred; Bodmin Union] [728]
see also ALTARNON Holy Trinity Bolventor
OR C 1701-1933 M 1701-1979 B 1701-1890 (CRO)
Noted in 1831: CMB 1701-57 "a transcript for the first 17 years".
BT CMB 1675-1736, 1741-72 (CRO); CMB 1613-73, 1737-40, 1773-1812, 1815,
     1817-21, 1824-27, 1832-33, 1835-36, 1838, 1841-44 (DRO)
Cop M 1675-1812 (Ptd Phillimore: 1903); M 1613-1837 (Ts with index,
     CRO,RIC); M 1813-37 (CMI); B 1813-37 (CBI); CB 1701-1812 M 1613-1812
     (SG); M 1675-1812 from OR; M 1613-73 from BT (Boyd); M 1790-1812
     (Pallot)
Cop (Mf) CMB 1701-1960 (RIC); CMB 1613-1813 (Mf of BT at DRO: CRO,CSL);
          M 1813-1925 (Ross); Extr CM 1675-1875 (IGI); C 1675-1875
          M 1675-1700 (SLC)
MI (Ptd CFHS)

CARDINHAM (Wes) [Kelly 1856]; Cardeast [1882 Return]

CARDINHAM (UMFC/U Meth) Fletcher's Bridge
OR C 1896-1970 (CRO)

CARDINHAM (UMFC) Millpool [1882 Return]

CARFURY   see GULVAL

CARGREEN   see LANDULPH

CARHARRACK   see GWENNAP

CARLEEN   see BREAGE

CARLIDNACK   see MAWNAN

CARN BREA   *see* ILLOGAN

CARNE HILL   *see* ST DENNIS

CARNHELL GREEN   *see* GWINEAR

CARNKIE   *see* MADRON

CARNKIE   *see* ILLOGAN

CARNKIE COMMON   *see* WENDRON

CARNMARTH   *see* REDRUTH

CARNMENELLIS   *see* WENDRON

CARNON DOWNS   *see* FEOCK

CARTHEW   *see* ST AUSTELL

CARZANTIC   *see* LAWHITTON

CASTEL AN DINAS   *see* LUDGVAN

CAWSAND   or CAUSAND *see* RAME

CHACEWATER   *see* KENWYN

CHAPEL AMBLE   *see* ST KEW

CHARLESTOWN   *see* ST AUSTELL

CHEESWRING   *see* LINKINHORNE

CHERITON CROSS   *see* ST IVE

CHYANCHY   *see* ST IVES

CHYANGWHEAL   *see* LELANT

CHYCOWLING DOWNS   *see* KEA

CHYGNIDDEN   *see* ST LEVAN

CHYNHALE   *see* SITHNEY

ST CLEER St Clarus [West Hundred; Liskeard Union] [982]
OR C 1678-1993 M 1678-1968 B 1675-1992 (CRO)
BT CMB 1699-1717, 1747-59 (CRO); CMB 1597-1673, 1737-40, 1773-1837, 1839-48
    (DRO)
Cop M 1678-1812 (Ptd Phillimore: 1905); CB 1675-1812 (CRO); CMB 1597-1673
    from BT; CMB 1678-1837 (DCRS/WSL); M 1813-37 (CMI); B 1813-37 (CBI);
    C 1676-1812 M 1597-1812 B 1675-1812 (SG); M 1678-1812 from OR;
    M 1597-1673 from BT (Boyd); M 1790-1812 (Pallot); M 1837-1900 (CFHS)
Cop (Mf) CMB 1597-1812 (Mf of BT at DRO: CRO,CSL); M 1813-37 (Ross);
        Extr C 1597-1837 (IGI); C 1597-1837 (SLC)
MI (Ptd CFHS)

44

ST CLEER (Wes) Crow's Nest (also known as Caradon to 1903). 2 Wes chapels
and 2 Wes Assn [Kelly 1856]; Caradon [1882 Return]
OR C 1856-1959 (CRO)

ST CLEER (Wes) Tremar [1882 Return]

ST CLEER (Bible Christian) Hocking's House. Erected 1846. Bible Christian
Chapel [1882 Return]

ST CLEER (Bible Christian) Railway Terrace [Kelly 1889]

ST CLEER (Prim Meth) Tremar Coombe [Kelly 1889]

ST CLEER (UMFC/U Meth) Free Wesleyan Chapel, Common Moor [1882 Return]
OR C 1868-88 (CRO)

ST CLEER (Wes Reform) Tremar Coombe [1882 Return]

ST CLEMENT St Clement [Powder Hundred; Truro Union] [2885] United with TRURO
St Paul
OR C 1543-1939 M 1539-1993 B 1538-1978 (CRO)
BT CMB 1681-1735, 1741-72 (CRO); CMB 1608-72, 1737-40, 1773-1835, 1837-39,
     1841-50, 1852-54, 1856-60, 1862-63, 1865, 1867, 1871 (DRO)
Cop M 1538-1837 (Ptd Phillimore: 1935); C 1543-1837 B 1538-1837 (DCRS/WSL);
     C 1730-1840 M 1730-1838 B 1730-1812 (Ms RIC); C 1545-94 M 1551-94
     B 1539-89 (RIC); C 1837-75 M 1876-1900 (CFHS); M 1539-1837 (CSL);
     M 1813-37 (CMI); M 1608-72 from BT (Boyd); M 1790-1837 (Pallot);
     B 1813-37 (CBI)
Cop (Mf) CMB 1608-1812 (Mf of BT at DRO: CRO,CSL); M 1543-1875 (Ross);
          Extr C 1543-1837 (IGI); C 1543-1837 (SLC)
MI (Ptd CFHS)

ST CLEMENT St Andrew, Malpas. Mission church erected 1887
OR C see ST CLEMENT. No MB

ST CLEMENT (Bible Christian) [Kelly 1897]

ST CLEMENT (S of F) Malpas [Kelly 1887]

ST CLETHER St Clederus [Lesnewth Hundred; Camelford Union] [171] United with
ALTARNON, BOLVENTOR, LANEAST
OR CMB 1640-1979 (CRO)
BT CMB 1676-1736, 1741-72 (CRO); CMB 1610-73, 1737-40, 1773-1846 (DRO)
Cop M 1640-1812 (Ptd Phillimore: 1900); C 1610-1812 (SG); M 1813-37 (CMI);
     M 1640-1811 from OR; M 1610-73 from BT (Boyd); M 1790-1812 (Pallot);
     M 1837-1904 (CFHS); B 1813-37 (CBI)
Cop (Mf) C 1640-1958 MB 1640-1960 (RIC); CMB 1610-1812 (Mf of BT at DRO:
          CRO, CSL); M 1813-1900 (Ross); Extr C 1640-1875 M 1640-1811 (IGI);
          C 1640-1875 (SLC)
MI (Ptd CFHS)

ST CLETHER (Wes) 2 Meth chapels [Kelly 1935]

ST CLETHER (Bible Christian) Coldnorthcott [1882 Return]

CLIMSLAND   see STOKE CLIMSLAND

COADS GREEN   see HILL, NORTH

COCKWELLS   *see* LUDGVAN

ST COLAN or LITTLE COLAN St Colan [Pydar Hundred; St Columb Major Union]
[261] United with ST COLUMB MINOR
OR C 1747-1949 M 1754-1990 B 1747-1990 (CRO) For a register 1665+ filmed in
   1959 but now lost, *see* Cop (Mf) below. (RIC)
BT CMB 1678-1736, 1741-72 (CRO); CMB 1597-1673, 1737-40, 1773-1815, 1818,
   1826, 1838-50, 1852-57 (DRO)
Cop M 1665-1812 (Ptd Phillimore: 1908); CMB 1597-1674 from BT (DCRS/WSL);
   CB 1597-1763 (Ms from BT, RIC); CB 1665-1820 M 1600-1813 (CRO);
   M 1813-37 (CMI); B 1813-37 (CBI); M 1600-1812 (SG); M 1665-1812 from OR;
   M 1600-73 from BT (Boyd); M 1800-12 (Pallot)
Cop (Mf) CB 1665-1959 M 1665-1957 (RIC); CMB 1597-1812 (Mf of BT at DRO:
   CRO, CSL); M 1813-1925 (Ross); Extr C 1597-1875 M 1600-34,
   1665-1875 from OR and BT (IGI); C 1597-1875 M 1600-34, 1665-1738
   (SLC)
MI (Ptd CFHS)

ST COLAN (Wes) [Kelly 1856]

ST COLAN (Wes) Mountjoy [1882 Return]

ST COLAN (Bible Christian) [Kelly 1856]

COLBIGGAN   *see* ROCHE

COLDHARBOUR   *see* TOWEDNACK

COLDNORTHCOTT *see* ST CLETHER

ST COLUMB Poor Law Union
OR D 1914-30 (CRO)

ST COLUMB MAJOR St Columba [Pydar Hundred; St Columb Major Union] [2790]
United with ST WENN
OR C 1540-1964 M 1544-1970 B 1539-1965 (CRO)
BT CMB 1682-1736, 1741-72 (CRO); CMB 1614-73, 1737-40, 1773-1812, 1815-17,
   1819-30, 1836 (DRO)
Cop CMB 1539-1780 (Ptd A.Jewers *The Registers of the Parish of St Columb
   Major...*: 1881); M 1781-1812 (Ptd Phillimore: 1909); CMB 1813-37 (CRO);
   C 1715-27 B 1718-19 (CSL); M 1813-80 (Ts RIC); Cemetery sexton's burial
   book (CFHS); Extr M 1800-80 B 1813-67 (Ts RIC); M 1813-37 (CMI);
   M 1837-1900 (CFHS); M 1539-1812 (Boyd); M 1800-12 (Pallot); B 1813-37
   (CBI)
Cop (Mf) CMB 1614-1812 (Mf of BT at DRO: CRO,CSL); M 1813-75 (Ross);
      Extr C 1540-1780 (IGI); C 1540-1780 (SLC)
MI (Ptd CFHS)

ST COLUMB MAJOR St Francis, Indian Queens. Mission church erected 1884,
now in parish of ST ENODER

ST COLUMB MAJOR (Ind) Bethesda Chapel f 1794; associated with Trevarren
Chapel (1822) Closed 1941
OR ZC 1795-1837 (PRO)
Cop ZC 1795-1837 (SG)
Cop (Mf) ZC 1795-1837 (DCRS/WSL); Extr ZC 1785-1837 (IGI); ZC 1795-1837
      (SLC)

ST COLUMB MAJOR (Cong) Fore Street. Erected 1795. Closed 1939

ST COLUMB MAJOR (Cong) School house, Quoits [1882 Return]

ST COLUMB MAJOR (Wes) St Columb Circuit
OR C 1839-1908 (CRO); North Cornwall Mission, St Columb section C 1908-32
(CRO)

ST COLUMB MAJOR (Wes/Bible Christian/U Meth) Fore Street. Erected 1812
[1882 Return]
OR C 1914-62 M 1937-60 (CRO)

ST COLUMB MAJOR (Wes) Wesley
OR C 1899-1973 (CRO)

ST COLUMB MAJOR (Wes) Indian Queens. Erected 1887
OR C 1902-36 (CRO)

ST COLUMB MAJOR (Wes) Trebuddannon, a building, the property of John Rowse
[1882 Return]

ST COLUMB MAJOR (Bible Christian) St Columb Circuit
OR C 1838-1916 (CRO)

ST COLUMB MAJOR (Bible Christian) Fore Street. Erected 1801 [Kelly 1889]
OR C 1838-1916 (CRO)

ST COLUMB MAJOR (Bible Christian) Talskiddy. Erected 1834 [1882 Return]

ST COLUMB MAJOR (Bible Christian) Blackcross [1882 Return]

ST COLUMB MAJOR (UMFC) St Columb Circuit. Continued as U Meth, below
OR C 1875-1909 (CRO)

ST COLUMB MAJOR (UMFC/U Meth) Emmanuel, Indian Queens [1882 Return]
OR C 1948-89 (CRO)

ST COLUMB MAJOR (UMFC) Victoria Street [1882 Return]

ST COLUMB MAJOR (U Meth) St Columb Circuit
OR C 1909-35 (CRO)

ST COLUMB MAJOR (U Meth) Blackcross
OR C 1951-85 (CRO)

ST COLUMB MAJOR (Meth) St Columb and Padstow Circuit, formerly Wes
OR C 1932-48 (CRO)

ST COLUMB MAJOR (Meth) St Columb and Padstow Circuit, Indian Queens section
OR C 1936-51 (CRO)

ST COLUMB MAJOR Burial ground
OR B 1856-79 (CRO)

ST COLUMB MINOR St Columba [Pydar Hundred; St Columb Major Union] [1406]
United with ST COLAN
OR C 1559-1960 M 1560-1950 B 1564-1957 (CRO)
BT CMB 1676-1736, 1741-72 (CRO); CMB 1597-1673, 1737-40, 1773-1840 (DRO)
Cop M 1560-1812 (Ptd Phillimore: 1909); CMB 1597-1673, 1715-27 from BT
    (DCRS/WSL); C 1560-1783 B 1560-1772 (Ms CRO,RIC); C 1560-67 (CSL);
    M 1813-37 (CMI); B 1813-37 (CBI); C 1560-1689, 1715-27 B 1718-19 (SG);
    C 1715-27 B 1718-19 (Morrab); M 1560-1812 (Boyd); M 1781-1812 (Pallot)
Cop (Mf) C 1560-1925 M 1560-1956 B 1560-1957 (RIC); CMB 1597-1812 (Mf of BT
       at DRO: CRO,CSL); M 1813-1900 (Ross); Extr C 1560-1783, 1813-75
       M 1560-1875 (IGI); C 1560-1783, 1813-75 (SLC)
MI (Ptd CFHS)

ST COLUMB MINOR St Michael, Newquay. Chapelry in St Columb Minor. Erected
1857. New church 1909-11
OR CM 1882+ Banns 1963+ Confirmations 1942+ B 1911+ (Inc)
MI Old cemetery (Ptd CFHS)

ST COLUMB MINOR St George, Trencreek. Mission chapel erected 1906, replacing
wooden building [Kelly 1935]

ST COLUMB MINOR (RC) The Tower, Newquay, erected c.1835. Seat of Dowager
Lady Molesworth [Kelly 1897] Private chapel

ST COLUMB MINOR (RC) Most Holy Trinity, Newquay f 1901

ST COLUMB MINOR (Bapt) Ebenezer, Newquay f 1822 [Kelly 1897]

ST COLUMB MINOR (Cong, now URC) Bank Street, Newquay f 1867
OR 1925+ (Ch Sec)

ST COLUMB MINOR (Ind) Beach Road, Newquay f 1822. Closed
OR None known

ST COLUMB MINOR (Cong) Fore Street, Newquay f 1888 [Kelly 1897]

ST COLUMB MINOR (Wes) Lane
OR C 1882-1959 (CRO)

ST COLUMB MINOR (Wes) Newquay. Erected 1850 [f 1852 Kelly 1897]; on part of
Osborne's garden [1882 Return]
OR C 1857-1902 (CRO)
Cop C 1903-23 (CRO)

ST COLUMB MINOR (Bible Christian) Church Town [1882 Return]

ST COLUMB MINOR (Bible Christian) Deer Park, Newquay [Kelly 1897]

ST COLUMB MINOR (UMFC) Newquay. Erected 1866 [1882 Return]; [Kelly 1897]
Now a house
OR C 1882-1959 (CRO)

ST COLUMB MINOR (UMFC) Shop Chapel [1882 Return]

ST COLUMB MINOR (U Meth) Claremont, Newquay
OR C 1908-46 (CRO)

ST COLUMB MINOR (Meth) Quintrell Downs
OR C 1938-68, 1976 (CRO)

ST COLUMB MINOR (Salvation Army) Crantock Street

ST COLUMB MINOR (S of F) f.1696, part of ST AUSTELL MM; fl c.1731

COME TO GOOD   see KEA

CONDURROW   see CAMBORNE

CONNON   see ST PINNOCK

CONNOR DOWNS   see GWINEAR

CONSTANTINE St Constantine [Kerrier Hundred; Falmouth Union] [2004]
OR C 1571-1943 M 1571-1974 B 1562-1911 (CRO)
BT CMB 1674-1736, 1741-72 (CRO); CMB 1597-1673, 1737-39, 1773-1814,
    1838-48, 1850-51 (DRO)
Cop M 1571-1812 (Ptd Phillimore: 1909); CM 1571-1837 B 1562-1837 (DCRS/WSL);
    M 1813-37 (CMI); B 1813-37 (CBI); M 1571-1812 (Boyd); M 1800-12 (Pallot)
Cop (Mf) CM 1571-1959 B 1562-1959 (RIC); CMB 1597-1812 (Mf of BT at DRO:
         CRO,CSL); M 1571-1675 (SG); M 1813-1925 (Ross); Extr C 1572-1875
         M 1571-1875 (IGI); C 1572-1745 M 1571-1759 (SLC)
MI (Ptd CFHS)

CONSTANTINE Gweek Mission Church Erected 1880s as village school.
OR None

CONSTANTINE (Wes) [Kelly 1856]; Church Town [1882 Return]

CONSTANTINE (Bible Christian) Trebarvah [1882 Return]

CONSTANTINE (Bible Christian) Ponjaravah [1882 Return]

CONSTANTINE (Bible Christian) Port Navas

CONSTANTINE (Prim Meth) [Kelly 1856]

CONSTANTINE (Meth) Helston Circuit, Constantine section
OR C 1946-51 (CRO)

CONSTANTINE (S of F) Gweek. f by 1685; rebuilt 1731. Part of FALMOUTH MM

COOMBE   see ST STEPHEN IN BRANNEL

COPPERHOUSE   see PHILLACK

COPTHORNE   see PETHERWIN, NORTH

CORNELLY or GROGOTH St Cornelius [Powder Hundred; Truro Union] [170] United
with CUBY, TREGONY
OR C 1563-1947 M 1679-1897 B 1561-1956; faded and almost illegible to 1567,
    but see Cop and Cop(Mf) below (CRO)
BT CMB 1685-1736, 1741-72 (CRO); CMB 1608-73, 1737-40, 1773-1812, 1839,
    1841 (DRO)

CORNELLY cont.
Cop M 1679-1812 (Ptd Phillimore: 1915); C 1559-1837 M 1679-1833 B 1562-1837
(DCRS/WSL); CB 1559-1841 M 1559-1678, 1813-41 (C of A); M 1813-37 (CMI);
B 1813-37 (CBI); M 1612-23 (SG); M 1679-1812 from OR; M 1612-73 from BT
(Boyd); M 1800-12 (Pallot)
Cop (Mf) CMB 1563-1959 (RIC); CMB 1612-1812 (Mf of BT at DRO: CRO,CSL);
M 1813-1925 (Ross); Extr C 1561-1875 M 1679-1871 (IGI); C 1561-1875
M 1679-1871 (SLC)
MI (Ptd CFHS)

CORNWALL (S of F) Quarterly Meeting f 1668; amalgamated 1870 with Devonshire
QM; 1967 became Devon and Cornwall General Meeting
OR Z 1609-1781, 1785-1837 M 1659-1780, 1796-1836 B 1659-1782, 1793-1837
(PRO)
Cop Z 1609-1837 M 1647-1837 B 1647-1837 (Digest indexes, CRO); ZMB 1609-1843
(CRO); M 1813-37 (CMI)
Cop (Mf) Digests Z 1609-37 and 1647-1805 M 1657-1836 and 1659-78 B 1656-1837
and 1659-1777 (SG)

CORNWALL, EAST (S of F) East Cornwall or East Division Monthly Meeting f
1668. Included ST AUSTELL MM from 1786
OR Z 1659-1729 B 1690-1775 in CORNWALL QM register RG 6/1578 (PRO);
Z 1609-1837 M 1658-1835 B 1664-1837: RG 6/174,185,219,220,949,950,1020,
1181, 1314,1339,1518,1519 (PRO); Z 1859-1903 (CRO)
Cop Z 1659-1773 B 1690-1775 in 1828 copy of old register book of Cornwall QM
(CRO)
Cop (Mf) M 1663-1836 (Ross)

CORNWALL, WEST (S of F) West Cornwall or West Division MM 1783-1903.
Formerly FALMOUTH MM. From 1904 CORNWALL MM
OR Z 1653-1837 M 1657-1836 B 1653-1837: RG 6/186,221,222,260,261,262,343,
951,1218,1233,1503,1582 (PRO); M 1839-94; Z notes 1837-97, B notes
1903-45; membership lists 1828-1903 (CRO)
Cop Z 1783-92 B 1783-1828: extracted from MM registers 1838 (CRO)

COTEHELE   see CALSTOCK

COUCHES MILL   see BOCONNOC

COVERACK   see ST KEVERNE

CRAFTHOLE   see SHEVIOCK

CRANTOCK St Carantoc [Pydar Hundred; St Columb Major Union] [458]
OR C 1622-1903 M 1559-1983 B 1559-1970 (CRO)
Noted in 1831: Vol.1: C 1615-1721 M 1559-1712 B 1559-1721
BT CMB 1678-1736, 1741-72 (CRO); CMB 1597-1675, 1737-40, 1773-1813, 1836-37
(DRO)
Cop M 1559-1812 (Ptd Phillimore: 1909); CMB 1603-74 from BT (DCRS/WSL);
M 1813-37 (CMI); B 1813-37 (CBI); C 1597-1721 B 1559-1721 (SG);
M 1559-1812 (Boyd); M 1800-12 (Pallot)
Cop (Mf) CMB 1608-1812 (Mf of BT at DRO: CRO,CSL); M 1813-75 (Ross);
Extr C 1608-73, 1682-1772 from BT, M 1559-1812 (IGI); C 1608-73,
1682-1772 from BT (SLC)
MI (Ptd CFHS)

CRANTOCK (Wes) Church Town [1882 Return]

CRANTOCK (Meth)
MI (Ptd CFHS)

CREED WITH GRAMPOUND St Crida [Powder Hundred; St Austell Union]
[Creed parish 258; Grampound Borough 715] Renamed 1974 Grampound with Creed.
United with PROBUS, LADOCK, ST ERME
OR C 1653-1895 M 1654-1978 B 1653-1950 (CRO)
BT CMB 1684-1735, 1741-72 (CRO); CMB 1602-68, 1737-40, 1773-1812, 1828,
1831-39 (DRO)
Cop M 1611-1837 (Ptd Phillimore: 1935); CMB 1602-30 from BT; CB 1653-1837
(DCRS/WSL); CB 1653-99 M 1654-1710 (RIC); M 1813-37 (CMI); B 1813-37
(CBI); M 1611-37 (CSL); M 1602-1837 (SG); M 1602-68 from BT (Boyd);
M 1790-1837 (Pallot)
Cop (Mf) CMB 1602-1812 (Mf of BT at DRO: CRO,CSL); M 1611-1875 (Ross);
Extr C 1603-1837 (IGI); C 1603-1837 (SLC)
MI (Ptd CFHS)

CREED St Nun, Grampound. Chapel-of-ease 1869. United with PROBUS, LADOCK,
CREED, ST ERME
OR see CREED and PROBUS

CREED (Bapt) Grampound f 1804 [*Bapt. Manual* 1850; *Handbook* 1881]

CREED (Presb) fl.1672-90

CREED (Ind) f 1784
OR Membership list 1820-21 (CRO)

CREED (Cong) Grampound [*Cong.Yearbook* 1850] [Kelly 1889]
OR Membership list 1820 (CRO)

CREED (Wes) Grampound [Kelly 1889]

CREED (Bible Christian) Grampound [Kelly 1889]

CREEGBRAWSE   or CRIEGBRAWS *see* KENWYN

CRELLY   *see* WENDRON

CROFTHANDY   *see* GWENNAP

CROSS COMBE   *see* ST AGNES

CROSSWYN   *see* ST EWE

CROW'S NEST   *see* ST CLEER

CROWAN St Crewenna [Penwith Hundred; Helston Union] [4332] United with
GODOLPHIN
OR C 1691-1869 M 1691-1979 B 1697-1947 (CRO)
BT CMB 1674-1736, 1741-72 (CRO); CMB 1614-73, 1737-40, 1773-1812 ?, 1814,
1819-28, 1831-32, 1834 (DRO)
Cop M 1674-1812 (Ptd Phillimore: 1900); C 1614-1861 M 1614-1837 B 1614-1845
(CSL); CMB 1691-1743 (CRO); CB 1691-1845 M 1691-1837 (CRO);
CMB 1691-1845 (Ts with index, RIC,CFHS); M 1813-37 (CMI); M 1614-1812
(SG); M 1674-1812 from OR; M 1614-81 from BT (Boyd); M 1790-1812
(Pallot); B 1813-37 (CBI)

CROWAN cont.
Cop (Mf) CB 1691-1959 M 1691-1955 (RIC); CMB 1614-1812 (Mf of BT at DRO:
        CRO, CSL); M 1813-1925 (Ross); Extr C 1674-1869, 1876-85
        M 1691-1895 (IGI); C 1674-1772, 1795-1869 M 1674-87 (SLC)

CROWAN St James, Leedstown. Mission church erected 1882

CROWAN (Wes) Black Rock [1882 Return]
OR C 1872-1976 (CRO)

CROWAN (Wes) Leedstown. Erected 1862 [1882 Return]

CROWAN (Wes) Praze an Beeble. Erected 1828 [1882 Return]

CROWAN (Wes) Horsedowns
OR C 1845-77, 1953-81 (CRO)

CROWAN (Wes) Nancegollan [1882 Return] Cemetery
OR C 1846-1968 (CRO)
MI (Ptd CFHS)

CROWAN (Wes) Praze
OR C 1864-83 M 1913-71 (CRO)

CROWAN (Wes) Releath f 1861 ?; [1882 Return]
OR C 1940-94 M 1984-94 (CRO)

CROWAN (Wes) Townshend. Erected 1871 [1882 Return]
OR C 1932-85 B 1892-1979 (CRO)
MI (Ptd CFHS)

CROWAN (Prim Meth)
OR [Kelly 1856]

CROWAN (Bible Christian) Leedstown. Erected 1837 [1882 Return] Closed

CROWAN (UMFC/U Meth) Praze
OR C 1892-1960 (CRO)

CROWAN (Free Meth) Gew [Kelly 1889]

CROWLAS   see LUDGVAN

CROWN TOWN   see SITHNEY

CROWSA DOWNS   see ST KEVERNE

CROWSANWRAY   or CROWS AN WRA see ST BURYAN

CRUMPLEHORN   see LANSALLOS

CUBERT or ST CUTHBERT St Cubert [Pydar Hundred; St Columb Major Union] [487]
OR C 1733-1864 M 1733-1837 B 1653-1960 (CRO) No earlier volume noted in
    1831
BT CMB 1678-1736, 1741-72 (CRO); CMB 1608-73, 1737-40, 1772-1840, 1843-45
    (DRO)

CUBERT cont.

Cop M 1608-1812 (Ptd Phillimore: 1909); CMB 1608-69 from BT; CB 1653-1812 (DCRS/WSL); C 1727-1812 B 1653-1812 (Morrab); M 1813-37 (CMI); B 1813-37 (CBI); C 1678-1812 B 1653-1812 (SG); M 1608-1812 (Boyd); M 1800-12 (Pallot); M 1850-1925 (CFHS)

Cop (Mf) C 1608-1959 M 1734-1959 B 1653-1960 (RIC); CMB 1608-1812 (Mf of BT at DRO: CRO,CSL); M 1813-1925 (Ross);Extr C 1608-17, 1632-36, 1663-1885 M 1608-1668, 1682-1895 (IGI); C 1608-17, 1632-36, 1663-1743 M 1608-1612 (SLC)

MI (Ptd CFHS)

CUBERT (Wes) Erected 1765. Replaced 1848; Church Town [1882 Return] Now a café

Cop C 1849-1924 (CRO,CFHS)

MI (Ptd CFHS)

CUBERT (Wes) Circuit

Cop C 1885-9? (CFHS)

CUBY WITH TREGONY St Cuby [Powder Hundred; Truro Union] [Cuby parish 455; Tregony Borough 1127] Tregony parish united with Cuby when church (St James) flooded; no separate registers. United with CORNELLY

OR C 1661-1961 M 1661-1837 B 1662-1903 (CRO)
  Noted in 1831 under Tregony (with Cuby) Vol.1: CB 1571-1690 imperfect.
  Vols.2, 3: CB 1697-1812 M 1697-1753

BT CMB 1678-1735, 1741-72 (CRO); CMB 1611-73, 1737-40, 1773-1812, 1814, 1816, 1829-30, 1835, 1847-50, 1857-62 (DRO) Tregony: CMB 1813, 1817-18, 1823, 1828, 1836 (DRO)

Cop M 1661-1812 Tregony with Cuby (Ptd Phillimore: 1914); CMB 1611-1779 from BT; CB 1661-1812 (DCRS/WSL); CB 1611-95, 1780-1812 (Ts RIC); M 1813-37 (CMI); M 1837-1925 (CFHS); B 1813-37 (CBI); M 1661-1812 from OR; M 1611-73 from BT (Boyd); M 1800-12 (Pallot)

Cop (Mf) C 1611-1959 MB 1661-1959 (RIC); CMB 1611-1812 (Mf of BT at DRO: CRO,CSL); CB 1611-1837 (SG); M 1813-1925 (Ross); Extr C 1611-1859 M 1661-1875 (IGI); C 1611-1859 M 1661-96 (SLC)

MI (Ptd CFHS); Ch (Wall,79-80, Ms SG)

CUBY (Ind/Cong, later Cong Fed) Fore Street, Tregony f 1776. Rebuilt 1824 [1882 Return]

OR None at church

CUBY (Bapt) Tregony f 1861 [*Bapt.Handbook* 1869,1881]

CUBY (Wes) Fore Street, Tregony. Erected 1847

OR C 1938-48 (CRO)

Cop C 1938-49 (CFHS)

CUBY (Bible Christian) Tregony [Kelly 1856]

CULDROSE *see* HELSTON

CURY St Corentine [Kerrier Hundred; Helston Union] [523] Chapelry in BREAGE. United with GUNWALLOE 1836. Now also with ST MAWGAN IN MENEAGE

OR C 1690-1875 M 1692-1837 B 1690-1954 (CRO)

BT CMB 1676-1736, 1741-72 (CRO); CMB 1608-73, 1737-40, 1773-1813, 1816-17, 1820-21, 1825, 1827-28, 1830-33, 1835-36 (DRO)

CURY cont.
Cop C 1608-1849 M 1608-1837 B 1608-1845 (CSL); M 1608-1812 (CRO);
CMB 1608-1837 (DCRS/WSL); M 1813-37 (CMI); B 1813-37 (CBI); M 1608-74
(SG); M 1608-1837 (CSL); M 1690-1837 from OR; M 1608-73 from BT (Boyd)
CMB 1690-1845 (CFHS)
Cop (Mf) C 1690-1960 M 1691-1956 B 1690-1959 (RIC); CMB 1608-1812 (Mf of BT
at DRO: CRO,CSL); M 1608-1925 (Ross);Extr C 1676-1875 M 1676-87,
1691-1875 (IGI); C 1676-87 (SLC)
MI Ch,cy,cemetery (Ptd CFHS)

CURY Holy Family, Bonython. Consecrated 1978 in former stable
OR *see* CURY

CURY (Wes) Erected early 19th cent. [1882 Return] Rebuilt 1890

CURY (Wes Association) [Kelly 1856]

CURY (UMFC) Cury Cross [1882 Return]

CURY (UMFC) Whitecross [1882 Return]

DARLEY *see* LINKINHORNE

DAVIDSTOW or DEWSTOW St David [Lesnewth Hundred; Camelford Union] [389]
see also BOSCASTLE
OR C 1708-1977 M 1709-1971 B 1708-1980 (CRO) No earlier register noted in
1831
BT CMB 1676-1736, 1741-71 (CRO); CMB 1608-73, 1737-40, 1773-1835 (DRO)
Cop M 1676-1812 (Ptd Phillimore: 1900); M 1813-37 (CMI); M 1614-1812 (SG);
M 1676-1811 from OR; M 1608-73 from BT (Boyd); M 1790-1811 (Pallot);
M 1876-1914 (CFHS); B 1813-37 (CBI)
Cop (Mf) CMB 1773-1812 (Mf of BT at DRO: CRO,CSL); M 1813-75 (Ross);
Extr C 1676-1773, 1804-05 M 1676-1811 (IGI); C 1676-1773, 1804-05
(SLC)
MI (Ptd CFHS)

DAVIDSTOW (Bible Christian/U Meth) Trewassa [1882 Return]
OR C 1940-78 (CRO)

DAVIDSTOW (UMFC) Tremaill. Erected 1838. Building used as a chapel, the
property of Digory Hayne [1882 Return]
MI (Ptd CFHS)

ST DAY *see* GWENNAP

DEGIBNA *see* HELSTON

DELABOLE *see* ST TEATH

ST DENNIS St Denys [Powder Hundred; St Austell Union] [721] Chapelry in
ST MICHAEL CAERHAYS. Separate parish 1850
OR CMB 1687-1985 (CRO)
BT CMB 1678-1736, 1741-72 (CRO); CMB 1610-73, 1737-40, 1773-1812 (DRO)
Cop M 1610-1812 (Ptd Phillimore: 1912); CMB 1610-14, 1633-34, 1664-73;
M 1773-1812 (CRO); CB 1687-1812 M 1687-1760 (Ts RIC); M 1813-37 (CMI);
CB 1687-1812 (SG); M 1610-1812 (Boyd); M 1800-12 (Pallot); B 1813-37
(CBI)

ST DENNIS cont.
Cop (Mf) CM 1687-1959 B 1687-1958 (RIC); CMB 1610-1812 (Mf of BT at DRO:
        CRO,CSL); M 1677-1925 (Ross); Extr C 1697-1875 (IGI); C 1687-1875
        (SLC)
MI (Ptd CFHS)

ST DENNIS (Wes) [Kelly 1856]

ST DENNIS (Bible Christian/U Meth) Carne Hill
OR C 1927-64 (CRO)

ST DENNIS (Bible Christian) [1882 Return]; [Kelly 1889]

ST DENNIS (Bible Christian) Whitemoor [1882 Return]

ST DENNIS (Bible Christian) Enniseaven [Kelly 1889]

ST DENNIS (UMFC/UM) Providence. Erected 1836. Closed. Now a store
OR C 1876-1969 (CRO)

CEVERAL   see GWINEAR

DEVORAN   see FEOCK

DEWSTOW   see DAVIDSTOW

DIMMA   see POUNDSTOCK

DOBWALLS   see LISKEARD

ST DOMINICK St Dominica [East Hundred; Liskeard Union] [726] United with
LANDULPH, ST MELLION, PILLATON
OR C 1559-1935 M 1559-1978 B 1559-1976 (CRO)
BT CMB 1677-1736, 1741-72 (CRO); CMB 1607-72, 1737-40, 1773-1836 (DRO)
Cop CMB 1559-1837 (DCRS/WSL); M 1669-1812 (Ts RIC); M 1559-1837 (CSL);
        M 1813-37 (CMI); B 1813-37 (CBI); M 1559-1812 (CRO,CFHS); M 1837-1900
        (CFHS); M 1559-1812 Banns 1754-1812 (Ts SG); M 1607-72 from BT (Boyd)
Cop (Mf) CB 1559-1960 M 1559-1959 (RIC); M 1588-1900 (Ross);
        Extr C 1559-1875 M 1602-1718 (IGI); C 1559-1875 M 1602-1718 (SLC)
MI (Ptd CFHS); Ch (Ptd Jewers 166-79)

ST DOMINICK St Indract's Chapel, Halton Quay

ST DOMINICK (Wes) [Kelly 1856]; St Dominick Lower [1882 Return]; New
Wesleyan Chapel [1882 Return]

DOWNDERRY   see ST GERMANS

DOWNGATE   hamlet in STOKE CLIMSLAND q.v. and LINKINHORNE

DOWNHOUSE   see STOKE CLIMSLAND

DOWRAN   see ST JUST IN PENWITH

DULOE St Cuby [West Hundred; Liskeard Union] [928] United with HERODSFOOT
OR C 1668-1984 M 1668-1965 B 1668-1954 (CRO) Noted in 1831: Vol.5:
"probably a private book of the Clerk, from which the Clergyman copied
the entries; it contains Memoranda Bap. Bur. Marr. 1704-77".
BT CMB 1676-1736, 1741-72 (CRO); CMB 1607-72, 1737-40, 1773-1813, 1820,
1831-34, 1838-48 (DRO)
Cop CMB 1607-68 from BT; CMB 1668-1837 (DCRS/WSL, CRO); M 1686-1837 (CSL);
C 1607-35, 1664-1837 M 1607-1837 B 1608-1837 (Ts RIC, CRO, SG);
M 1813-37 (CMI); B 1813-37 (CBI); M 1607-73 from BT (Boyd)
Cop (Mf) M 1607-1837 (Ross); Extr CM 1607-1837 (IGI); CM 1607-1837 (SLC)
MI (Ptd CFHS)

DULOE All Saints, Herodsfoot, Erected 1850. Parish created 1851 from DULOE,
LANNREATH, ST PINNOCK. United with DULOE
OR M 1851-1968 (CRO)
Cop (Mf) M 1851-75 (Ross)

DULOE (Wes) Providence [1882 Return]

DULOE (Bible Christian) Herodsfoot [1882 Return]

DULOE (Wes Meth Assoc) Erected c.1840

DULOE (UMFC/U Meth)

DULOE (S of F) f by 1661. Moved to EAST LOOE 1690. Part of East Cornwall MM
OR Z 1661-89 B 1673-88 in CORNWALL QM register RG 6/1578; Z 1661-1727
M 1663-1718 B 1673-1742: RG 6/1249 (PRO)
Cop Z 1671-96 B 1673-88 in 1828 copy of old register book of Cornwall QM
(CRO)

DUNHEVED   *see* LAUNCESTON

DURGAN   *see* MAWNAN

EAST ANTONY   *see* ANTONY

EAST CORNWALL   (S of F) *see* CORNWALL, EAST

EAST LOOE   *see* LOOE, EAST

EAST NEWLYN   *see* NEWLYN, EAST

EASTCOTT   *see* MORWENSTOW

EDEN CROSS   *see* JACOBSTOW

EDGCOMBE   *see* WENDRON

EDGECUMBE   *see* MABE

EGLOS ROSE   *see* PHILLEIGH

EGLOSCROOK   *see* ST ISSEY

EGLOSHAYLE St Petroc, formerly St Paul [Trigg Hundred; Bodmin Union] [1335]
Peculiar of the Bishop of Exeter. United with ST BREOCK as parish of
St Breock and Egloshayle in Wadebridge. *see also* WADEBRIDGE
OR C 1600-1989 M 1600-1924 B 1600-1881 (CRO)
BT CMB 1608-1812, 1817-18, 1820-30, 1839-45 (DRO)
Cop M 1600-1812 (Ptd Phillimore: 1904); M 1813-37 (CMI); B 1813-37 (CBI);
      M 1600-1812 (Boyd); M 1790-1812 (Pallot)
Cop (Mf) CMB 1600-1960 (RIC); CMB 1608-1812 (Mf of BT at DRO: CRO,CSL);
        M 1813-1910 (Ross); Extr C 1600-1875 M 1600-1837 (IGI); C 1600-1875
        M 1600-1754(SLC)
MI (Ptd CFHS)

EGLOSHAYLE St Conan, Washaway, Erected 1882. Chapel-of-ease to EGLOSHAYLE
OR M 1952+ (Inc)
MI (Ptd CFHS)

EGLOSHAYLE (Wes) Erected 1817; rebuilt 1824 [Kelly 1856, 1889]

EGLOSHAYLE (Wes) Burlawn or Borlorne. Erected 1821, rebuilt 1877 ? [1882
Return] [Kelly 1935]; a building in the occupation of James Hewett Mason,
Dissenting Minister, Burlawn-Egloss [1882 Return]

EGLOSHAYLE (Wes) A building, Polbrock [1882 Return]

EGLOSHAYLE (Wes) Washaway. Erected 1836 [1882 Return]

EGLOSHAYLE (Wes Assn) [Kelly 1856]

EGLOSHAYLE (UMFC) Sladesbridge [1882 Return]

EGLOSKERRY St Petrock and St Keri [East Hundred; Launceston Union] [535]
United with NORTH PETHERWIN, TREMAINE, TRESMERE
OR C 1576-1874 M 1574-1837 B 1573-1909 (CRO)
BT CMB 1676-1736, 1741-72 (CRO); CMB 1610-73, 1737-40, 1773-1836 (DRO)
Cop M 1574-1812 (Ptd Phillimore: 1902); M 1813-37 (CMI); B 1813-37 (CBI);
      M 1574-1812 (Boyd); M 1790-1812 (Pallot)
Cop (Mf) C 1576-1960 M 1574-1959 B 1573-1960 (RIC); CMB 1615-1812 (Mf of BT
        at DRO: CRO,CSL); M 1813-1925 (Ross); Extr C 1576-1875 M 1574-1875
        (IGI); C 1576-1813 M 1574-1875 (SLC)

EGLOSKERRY (Wes) Egoskerry [1882 Return]

EGLOSKERRY (Wes) Tremaine [1882 Return]

ELERKY   *see* VERYAN

ST ENDELLION St Endelienta [Trigg Hundred; Bodmin Union] [1218] United with
PORT ISAAC, ST KEW
OR C 1732-1967 M 1735-1988 B 1749-1968 (CRO) No earlier registers noted in
      1831
BT CMB 1684-1736, 1741-72 (CRO); CMB 1614-73, 1737-40, 1773-1840 (DRO)
Cop M 1684-1812 (Ptd Phillimore: 1903); M 1813-37 (CMI); B 1813-37 (CBI);
      C 1732-1812 B 1738-1811 (SG); M 1684-1812 from OR; M 1614-73 from BT
      (Boyd)
Cop (Mf) CMB 1614-1812 (Mf of BT at DRO: CRO,CSL); M 1813-75 (Ross);
        Extr CM 1684-1812 (IGI); C 1684-1812 (SLC)
MI (Ptd CFHS)

ST ENDELLION St Peter, Port Isaac. Erected 1882. Parish created 1913 from
ST ENDELLION. United with ST ENDELLION, ST KEW
OR C 1913+ M 1940+ B 1914+ (Inc); for B after 1980 *see* ST ENDELLION
MI (Ptd CFHS)

ST ENDELLION (Wes) f 1806 [Kelly 1889]

ST ENDELLION (Wes) Port Isaac. Erected 1805; rebuilt 1885 [1882 Return]
[Kelly 1935]

ST ENDELLION (Bible Christian) f c.1858 [Kelly 1889]

ST ENDELLION (Bible Christian/UMFC) Trelights [1882 Return] rebuilt 1887
[Kelly 1935]

ST ENDELLION (Bible Christian) Port Quin f c.1833

ST ENDELLION (UMFC/U Meth) Roscarrack Hill f 1846 ?
OR C 1868-1925 (CRO)

ST ENDELLION (Wes Meth Assn) Erected 1837. Rebuilt 1869

ST ENDELLION (S of F) Port Isaac. *see* ST MINVER

ST ENODER St Enoder [Part Powder Hundred, part Pydar Hundred; St Columb
Major Union] [1124]
OR C 1570-1931 M 1571-1974 B 1570-1945 (CRO)
BT CMB 1682-1736, 1741-72 (CRO); CMB 1609-67, 1737-40, 1773-1823, 1825,
     1827-32, 1838-53 (DRO)
Cop M 1571-1812 (Ptd Phillimore: 1912); M 1813-37 (CMI); B 1813-37 (CBI);
     M 1571-1812 (Boyd); M 1800-12 (Pallot); B 1813-37 (CBI)
Cop (Mf) C 1570-1931 M 1571-1959 B 1570-1969 (RIC); CMB 1614-1812 (Mf of BT
         at DRO: CRO,CSL); M 1813-1900 (Ross); Extr C 1571-1863 (IGI);
         C 1571-1863 (SLC)
MI (Ptd CFHS)

ST ENODER (Presb) Goenrounson f 1662, closed by late 18th century

ST ENODER (Wes) Wesley, Summercourt [Kelly 1856]; [1882 Return]
OR C 1934-81 (CRO)

ST ENODER (Bible Christian) Summercourt. Erected c.1800 [1882 Return]

ST ENODER (Bible Christian) Fraddon. Erected 1857; rebuilt 1877
[1882 Return]

ST ENODER (U Meth) Retew
OR C 1951-65 (CRO)

ST ENODER (Wes) Mitchell [Kelly 1856] [1882 Return]
OR C 1882-1988 (CRO)

ST ENODOC   *see* ST MINVER

ST ERME St Hermes [Powder Hundred; Truro Union] [586] United with PROBUS, LADOCK, GRAMPOUND, CREED
OR C 1671-1874 M 1671-1967 B 1671-1916 (CRO) Noted in 1831: CM deficient 1686-93 B deficient 1687-95
BT CMB 1694-1735, 1741-73 (CRO); CMB 1614-38, 1737-40, 1774-1835 (DRO)
Cop M 1614-1812 (Ptd Phillimore: 1912); M 1614-15, 1622-24, 1634, 1636, 1638, 1671-1812 Banns 1754-1812 (Ts CRO,RIC,CFHS,SG); CB 1671-1837 M 1813-37 (CRO,RIC,SG); M 1813-37 (CMI); M 1837-1925 (CFHS); B 1813-37 (CBI); M 1614-1812 (Boyd); M 1800-12 (Pallot); B 1813-37 (CBI)
Cop (Mf) CM 1671-1959 B 1671-1958 (RIC); CMB 1614-1813 (Mf of BT at DRO: CRO,CSL); M 1813-1925 (Ross); Extr C 1671-1875 (IGI)
MI (Ptd CFHS); Ch (Ptd *Gent.Mag.*1808: II 585-86)

ST ERME (Wes) Trispen. Erected 1846 [1882 Return]; [Kelly 1897]

ST ERME (Wes) Trisillian [Kelly 1897]

ST ERNEY St Erney [East Hundred; St Germans Union] Chapelry of LANDRAKE. Peculiar of the Bishop of Exeter. United with LANDRAKE and BOTUS FLEMING
OR C 1555-1811 M 1555-1978 B 1559-1812 (CRO) *and see* LANDRAKE
BT CMB 1673-99, 1746-1812 (DRO); and see LANDRAKE
Cop M 1555-1812 (Ptd Phillimore: 1912); CM 1555-1812 B 1559-1812 (DCRS/WSL); M 1555-1758, 1769-1812 (Ts CRO,RIC,CFHS,SG); M 1555-1812 (Boyd); M 1800-12 (Pallot)
Cop (Mf) CMB 1672-1812 (Mf of BT at DRO: CRO,CSL); Extr C 1555-1811 M 1555-1807 from BT (IGI); C 1555-1811 M 1555-1807 from BT (SLC)
MI (Ptd CFHS)

ST ERTH St Erth [Penwith Hundred; Penzance Union] [1922] Now part of GODREVY Team Mission
OR C 1563-1918 M 1563-64, 1578-1980 B 1563-1906 (CRO)
BT CMB 1676-1736, 1741-72 (CRO); CMB 1607-73, 1737-40, 1773-1812; CMB 1813-14, 1835, 1838-50, unfit for production (DRO)
Cop M 1563-64, 1578-1812 (Ptd Phillimore: 1912); CMB 1607-69 from BT; CB 1563-1750 M 1578-1750 (DCRS/WSL); C 1717-47, 1773-1812 B 1565-1750, 1773-1812 (CSL); M 1813-37 (CMI); M 1563-1812 (SG); M 1563-1812 (Boyd); M 1800-12 (Pallot); B 1813-37 (CBI)
Cop (Mf) C 1563-1959 M 1564-1969 B 1567-1960 (RIC); CMB 1607-1813 (Mf of BT at DRO: CRO,CSL); M 1813-1910 (Ross); Extr C 1563-1875 M 1607-64 (IGI); C 1563-1838 M 1607-64 (SLC)
MI (Ptd CFHS)

ST ERTH (Bapt/Presb/Ind) Praze f 1820
OR None known

ST ERTH (Ind) Church Town; erected c.1820; fl.c.1851. Also used by Bible Christians

ST ERTH (Wes) Erected 1826-27; Church Town [1882 Return]
OR C 1881-1978 (CRO)

ST ERTH (Wes) Praze. f.1800

ST ERTH (Bible Christian) A building [1882 Return]

ST ERTH (Prim Meth) Erected 1839

ST ERVAN St Ervan [Pydar Hundred; St Columb Major Union] [453] Peculiar of
the Bishop of Exeter. United with ST MAWGAN IN PYDAR, ST EVAL
OR C 1677-1917 M 1674-1994 B 1677-1993 (CRO)
BT CMB 1602-1839 (DRO)
Cop M 1602-1812 (Ptd Phillimore: 1909); CMB 1602-1738 from BT (DCRS/WSL);
   C 1602-99 (Ms from BT, RIC,SG); M 1674-1812 (Ms RIC); M 1813-37 (CMI);
   M 1602-1812 (Boyd); M 1800-12 (Pallot); B 1813-37 (CBI)
Cop (Mf) C 1677-1959 M 1674-1959 B 1677-1958 (RIC); CMB 1603-1812 (Mf of BT
        at DRO: CRO,CSL); M 1813-1925 (Ross); Extr C 1602-25, 1663-1875
        M 1602-19, 1663, 1674-1874 (IGI); C 1602-25, 1663-1875 M 1674-1874
        (SLC)
MI (Ptd CFHS)

ST ERVAN (Wes) Rumford. Erected early 19th century [1882 Return] New church
1907

ST ERVAN (Bible Christian) f 1820
OR ZC 1820-37 (PRO); *and see* PADSTOW
Cop ZC 1820-37 (Surnames only Ptd M.Tangye: CFHSJ 31: 1984); ZC 1820-37
   (SG,CFHS)
Cop (Mf) ZC 1820-37 (DCRS/WSL); Extr ZC 1820-37 (IGI); ZC 1820-37 (SLC)
MI (Ptd CFHS)

ST ERVAN (Bible Christian/Meth) Penrose. Erected 1861

ESCALLS *see* SENNEN

ETHY *see* ST WINNOW

ST EVAL St Uvelas [Pydar Hundred; St Columb Major Union] [354] Peculiar of
the Bishop of Exeter. United with ST MAWGAN IN PYDAR, ST ERVAN
OR C 1695-1980 M 1695-1994 B 1695-1951 (CRO)
BT CMB 1612-1843 (DRO)
Cop M 1631-1812 (Ptd Phillimore: 1909); CMB 1612-1756 from BT (DCRS/WSL);
   M 1813-37 (CMI); M 1631-1812 from OR; M 1612-67 from BT (Boyd);
   M 1800-12 (Pallot); B 1813-37 (CBI)
Cop (Mf) C 1696-1960 MB 1695-1959 (RIC); CMB 1612-1812 (Mf of BT at DRO:
        CRO,CSL); CMB 1778-1885 (I,SG); M 1813-1903 (Ross);
        Extr C 1612-1875 M 1695-1885 (IGI); C 1612-1875 M 1695-1885 (SLC)
MI (Ptd CFHS)

ST EVAL R.A.F. Chaplaincy, St Eval
OR C 1946-58 (AFCC)

ST EVAL (RC) R.A.F.Chaplaincy, St Eval

ST EVAL (Wes/Free Meth) Tregona. Erected 1838 [1882 Return]

ST EVAL (Wes) [Kelly 1856]

ST EVAL (Bible Christian) [Kelly 1856]

ST EVAL (UMFC/U Meth) = ? Tregona [1882 Return]
OR C 1886-1976 (CRO)

ST EVE *see* ST IVE

ST EWE All Saints [Powder Hundred; St Austell Union] [1699] United with MEVAGISSEY
OR C 1560-1993 M 1560-1973 B 1559-1993 (CRO)
Noted in 1831: "The parishioners refused to allow 5s for a Register, and none was kept from 1675 to 1677"
BT CMB 1681-1736, 1741-72 (CRO); CMB 1611-73, 1737-40, 1773-1844 (DRO)
Cop M 1560-1812 (Ptd Phillimore: 1906); C 1728-1840 (I, SG); M 1813-37 (CMI); M 1560-1812 (Boyd); M 1800-12 (Pallot); B 1813-37 (CBI)
Cop (Mf) CM 1560-1959 B 1559-1959 (RIC); CMB 1611-1812 (Mf of BT at DRO: CRO,CSL); M 1813-1925 (Ross); Extr C 1560-1875 (IGI); C 1560-1875 (SLC)
MI (Ptd CFHS); ch (Ptd E.A.Beynon *Saint Ewe, the Church and Parish*: 1937)

ST EWE (Ind) Crosswyn f 1815; a branch of MEVAGISSEY
OR *see* MEVAGISSEY

ST EWE (Wes) = ? Tuscoyse [Kelly 1889]
OR C 1840-45 (CRO)

ST EWE (Bible Christian/U Meth) Paramore Chapel, Pentrasoe Common [1882 Return]
OR C 1937-92 (CRO)

ST EWE (Bible Christian/U Meth) Polmassick. f by 1836 [1882 Return]

ST EWE (Bible Christian) Kistle [1882 Return]

FALMOUTH King Charles the Martyr. Formerly Smithwick or Penny-come-quick [Kerrier Hundred; Falmouth Union] [Town 4761, parish 2523] Parish created 1664 from BUDOCK chapelry of St Gluvias. Peculiar of the Bishop of Exeter. Church dedicated 1665
OR C 1663+ MB 1664+ (Inc)
BT CMB 1663-1840, 1843-49, 1854-55 (DRO)
Cop CMB 1663-1812 (Ptd DCRS: 2 vols: 1914-15); CMB 1813-46 (DCRS/WSL); C 1813-39 M 1813-37 B 1813-46 (Ts with index, RIC); M 1813-37 (CMI); M 1664-1812 from OR; M 1663-66 from BT (Boyd); M 1790-1812 (Pallot); B 1813-37 (CBI)
Cop (Mf) CMB 1663-1900 (CRO); CMB 1663-1812 (Mf of BT at DRO: CRO,CSL); M 1813-37 (Ross); Extr C 1663-1839 M 1664-1837 (IGI); C 1663-1839 M 1664-1837 (SLC)
MI Old cy (Ptd CFHS); Ch (Ptd J.L.Kempthorne *Falmouth Parish Church*: 1928); Ch,cy (Wall,5-19, Ms SG)

FALMOUTH All Saints, Killigrew Street Erected 1887. Became a parish 1924 ?
OR C 1890-1951 M 1909-70 B 1924-27 (CRO)

FALMOUTH (RC) St Mary Immaculate, Killigrew Street f 1819
OR C 1819+ M 1846+ B 1822+ (Inc); Confirmations 1857, 1865, 1871, 1874, 1878, 1884, 1890-1933 (Plymouth Diocesan Archives)

FALMOUTH (Bapt) Emmanuel f 1662. Webber Street erected c.1814-19. Closed 1877, moved to Market Street. Superseded 1939 by Western Terrace
OR Z 1764-1837 C 1814-18 M 1763-1806, 1924-94 Membership lists 1828-70 (CRO) No registers at church
Cop (Mf) M 1763-1839 (Ross)

FALMOUTH (Bapt) Trinity f 1983

FALMOUTH (Bapt) Mawnan Road [*Bapt.Handbook* 1881]

FALMOUTH (Bapt) Back Hill Road [*Bapt.Handbook* 1881]

FALMOUTH (Presb, Ind/Cong now URC) f 1662 High Street. Rebuilt 1715. Became
Ind. c.1782. Rebuilt 1853. Moved to Berkeley Vale (former Bible Christian
chapel)
OR ZC 1783-1833 B 1808-37 (PRO); Z 1783-1853 C 1853-1907, 1924-28
  M 1861-1907, 1924-28 B 1808-89, 1894-1907, 1925-28 (CRO); C 1955+
  M 1946+ (Ch Sec)
Cop ZC 1783-1833 B 1808-37 (SG)
Cop (Mf) ZC 1783-1833 B 1808-37 (DCRS/WSL); Extr ZC 1783-1837 (IGI);
      C 1783-1837 (SLC)

FALMOUTH (Presb/Unit) f in late 18th century by secession from above.
Former theatre converted into chapel 1818. Closed c.1854

FALMOUTH (Wes) Falmouth Circuit
OR C 1813-1978 mainly PENRYN (CRO); C 1889-91 (CRO)

FALMOUTH (Wes) Killigrew Street f 1791; rebuilt 1874 [1882 Return]
OR ZC 1813-37 (PRO)
Cop ZC 1813-37 (SG)
Cop (Mf) ZC 1813-37 (DCRS/WSL,SG); Extr ZC 1813-37 (IGI); ZC 1813-37 (SLC)

FALMOUTH (Wes) Pike's Hill. Erected 1866 [1882 Return]
OR C 1871-1979 M 1899-1978 (CRO)

FALMOUTH (Wes) The Moor [1882 Return]

FALMOUTH (Bible Christian) Falmouth, Redruth and Camborne Circuit
OR ZC 1822-37 (PRO); C 1837-76 (CRO) *see also* REDRUTH
Cop ZC 1822-37 (SG)
Cop (Mf) ZC 1822-37 (DCRS/WSL); Extr ZC 1822-37 (IGI); ZC 1822-37 (SLC)

FALMOUTH (Bible Christian/U Meth) Smithwick Hill, erected 1830. Moved 1867-
68 to Berkeley Vale [1882 Return]
OR M 1931-56 (CRO)

FALMOUTH (Meth) Circuit, mainly Penryn
OR C 1932-78 (CRO)

FALMOUTH (Prim Meth) Chapel Row. Erected 1869 [1882 Return]

FALMOUTH Seamen's Bethel, Quay Hill. Erected 1848

FALMOUTH (S of F) Falmouth Monthly Meeting f 1668; became WEST CORNWALL MM
q.v. 1783; Cornwall MM 1904
OR Z 1685-1778 B 1682-1708 in CORNWALL QM register RG 6/1578; Z 1677-94
  M 1685-1759, 1777-94 B 1667-1745, 1788-94 in Cornwall West Division
  registers: RG 6/260,262,343,1503 (PRO); M 1839-94 Falmouth, Truro,
  Redruth and Penzance (CRO)
Cop Z 1654-1772 B 1658-1775 in 1828 copy of old register book of Cornwall QM
  (CRO); Z 1674-1780 M 1770-94 B 1676-1782 'Penryn and falmouth MM':
  extracted from MM registers 1838 (CRO)

FALMOUTH (S of F) Falmouth Preparative Meeting; part of Falmouth MM f by
1656. Meeting house at New Street erected 1803; Quay Hill [1882 Return];
Gyllyng Street 1873. Now at All Saints Centre, Albany Place
OR Penryn and Falmouth Z 1654-1788 M 1661-1798 B 1658-1788 in Cornwall West
   Division register RG 6/1218 (PRO); Z notes (West Division) mainly
   Falmouth 1861-97; B notes 1837-1908, 1910-32 (CRO)
Cop M 1682-1759 Falmouth and Penryn (CFHS)
MI New Street Burial Ground 1811-89: RG 37/53 (PRO)

FALMOUTH (Jews) Synagogue 1740-1892. Hamblyn's or Dunstan's Court 1766;
Porham Hill 1808 [1882 Return] Cemetery
MI 1791-1837 (Mocatta Library, University College, London ?)

FALMOUTH Poor Law Union
OR Z 1866-1914 (CRO)

FEOCK St Feock [Powder Hundred; Truro Union] [1210]
OR C 1671-1887 M 1671-1971 B 1671-1955 (CRO)
BT CMB 1676-1736, 1741-72 (CRO); CMB 1597-1672, 1737-40, 1773-1813, 1815-
   28, 1830-38 (DRO)
Cop CMB 1597-1670 from BT; CMB 1671-1837 (DCRS/WSL); CMB 1671-1812 (CRO);
   C 1597-1812, 1845-51 M 1597-1812, 1837-91 B 1597-1850 (Ms RIC);
   C 1814-28, 1830-38 from BT (CFHS); M 1597-1823 (CSL); M 1813-37 (CMI);
   CMB 1671-1812 (SG); M 1597-1672 (Boyd); B 1813-37 (CBI)
Cop (Mf) CMB 1671-1959 (RIC); CMB 1598-1812 (Mf of BT at DRO: CRO,CSL);
      M 1597-1925 (Ross); Extr C 1597-1812, 1843-75 M 1597-1760,
      1768-1812 (IGI); C 1597-1812, 1843-75 M 1597-1670, 1768-1812 (SLC)
MI (Ptd CFHS)

FEOCK St John the Evangelist and St Petroc, Devoran. Erected 1855-56. Parish
created 1873 from FEOCK
OR C 1873-1947 M 1873-1969 B 1873-1951 (CRO)
Cop (Mf) M 1873-75 (Ross)
MI (Ptd CFHS)

FEOCK (Independent Bapt) Townsend f 1820-21
OR Z 1820-39 C 1821-38 (CRO)

FEOCK (Bapt) Penpoll f 1802

FEOCK (Ind/Cong) Penpoll f 1791. Closed
OR None known

FEOCK (Wes) Devoran [Kelly 1856]; [1882 Return]

FEOCK (Wes) Carnon Downs. Erected 1825. A building in the occupation of John
Mitchell [1882 Return]

FEOCK (Wes) Gunpiper. Erected 1866 [1882 Return]

FEOCK (S of F) f by 1681. Part of FALMOUTH MM. Moved to KEA (Come-to-Good)
1697.
OR Z note 1723, William Stephens (CRO)

FILLEIGH   *see* PHILLEIGH

FLETCHER'S BRIDGE   *see* CARDINHAM

FLUSHING   *see* MYLOR

FOREST   *see* ILLOGAN

FORRABURY St Symphorian [Lesnewth Hundred; Camelford Union] [358] United
with MINSTER 1958. see also BOSCASTLE
OR C 1710-1987 M 1710-1975 B 1710-1930 (CRO)   No earlier register noted in
     1831
BT CMB 1676-1736, 1741-72 (CRO); CMB 1611-73, 1737-40, 1773-1812, 1820,
     1823-26, 1828-29, 1831-34, 1836-47 (DRO)
Cop M 1676-1812 (Ptd Phillimore: 1900); C 1710-1846 M 1710-1837 B 1710-1845
     (Ts RIC,CFHS); M 1813-37 (CMI); B 1813-37 (CBI); M 1601-1812 (SG);
     M 1611-73, 1676-1812 BT (Boyd); M 1790-1812 (Pallot); M 1876-1842 (CFHS)
Cop (Mf) CMB 1611-1812 (Mf of BT at DRO: CRO,CSL); M 1813-75 (Ross);
        Extr C 1692-1804 M 1702-1812 (IGI); C 1692-1804 (SLC)
MI (Ptd CFHS); ch,cy c.1927 (Ts SG)

FORRABURY (Wes/Wes Meth Assn) Boscastle. Erected 1807. One Wes chapel in
Boscastle in [1882 Return]

FORRABURY (Wes) Ebenezer, Boscastle. Erected 1837. Later a Post Office

FORRABURY (Bible Christian) Trevored, Erected 1838

FORRABURY (Bible Christian) Siloam, Boscastle. Erected 1859 [1882 Return]

FORRABURY (Free Meth) Boscastle. Erected 1825 [Kelly 1889]

FORRABURY (S of F) Boscastle. f pre-1668; joined ST MINVER c.1694
OR C 1694-1758 B 1669-1754 in CORNWALL QM register RG 6/1578 (PRO);
     Z 1609-1704 M 1798-1835 B 1669-1712 in EAST CORNWALL MM registers
     RG 6/185,1314 (PRO)
Cop St Minver and Boscastle Z 1609-1758; St Minver B 1669-1754 in 1828 copy
     of old register book of Cornwall QM (CRO)

FOUNDRY   *see* PHILLACK

FOUR LANES   *see* WENDRON

FOWEY St Fimbarrus [Powder Hundred; St Austell Union] [1767]
OR C 1543-1967 M 1568-1973 B 1603-1970 (CRO)
BT CMB 1678-1736, 1741-72 (CRO); CMB 1609-73, 1737-40, 1773-1812, 1816,
     1819, 1821-22, 1824-26, 1829, 1831, 1833-35, 1837-49 (DRO)
Cop M 1568-1812 (Ptd Phillimore: 1905); CMB 1750-1836 with index (CRO);
     C 1813-40 M 1813-36 B 1813-38 (Ts with index, RIC); CMB 1813-36 (CFHS);
     M 1813-37 (CMI); CB 1750-1836 (SG); M 1568-1812 (Boyd); M 1790-1812
     (Pallot); B 1813-37 (CBI)
Cop (Mf) CMB 1609-1812 (Mf of BT at DRO: CRO,CSL); M 1813-75 (Ross);
        Extr C 1543-1804 M 1568-1776 (IGI); C 1681-1804 (SLC)
MI (Ptd CFHS)

FOWEY (RC) St Monica f 1913

FOWEY (Ind/Cong) Mount Zion f 1797 [*Cong.Yearbook* 1850]   Rebuilt 1887
OR ZC 1798-1836 (PRO); ZC 1798-1825 (CRO)
Cop ZC 1798-1836 (SG)
Cop (Mf) ZC 1798-1836 (DCRS/WSL); Extr ZC 1798-1836 (IGI); ZC 1798-1836
        (SLC)

FOWEY (Presb) f 1662 ? closed mid-18th century

FOWEY (Wes) North Street. Erected 1801 [1882 Return]
OR C 1838-1961 (CRO)

FOWEY (Bible Christian) Erected 1883 [Kelly 1889]

FOWEY (Meth/URC) United
OR M 1977-85 (CRO)

FOWEY (S of F) fl c.1737, part of ST AUSTELL MM
OR M 1977-85 (CRO)

FOXHOLE   see ST STEPHEN IN BRANNEL

FRADDON   see ST ENODER

FREWORWALL   see LESNEWTH

FROGPOOL   see GWENNAP

GARRAS   see ST MAWGAN IN MENEAGE

GEAR   see GULVAL

ST GENNYS St Gennys [Lesnewth Hundred; Stratton Union] [761] United with
JACOBSTOW, WARBSTOW, TRENEGLOS
OR C 1702-1879 M 1702-1901 B 1702-1885 (CRO) Noted in 1831: "no other
     registers can be found"
BT CMB 1676-1735, 1741-72 (CRO); CMB 1612-73, 1737-39, 1773-1812, 1815-36
     (DRO)
Cop M 1813-37 (CMI); M 1612-74 (SG); M 1612-73 from BT (Boyd); B 1813-37
     (CBI)
Cop (Mf) C 1702-1879 M 1703-1837 B 1702-1885 (RIC); CMB 1612-1812 (Mf of BT
          at DRO: CRO,CSL); M 1612-1875 (Ross); Extr C 1687-1875 M 1687-1837
          (IGI); C 1687-1701 M 1687-1761 (SLC)
MI (Ptd CFHS)

ST GENNYS (Wes Meth Assn/Free Meth) Brockhill. Erected 1842 [Kelly 1889]

ST GENNYS (Bible Christian) Erected 1863 [Kelly 1889]

GEORGIA   see TOWEDNACK

ST GERMANS St Germanus of Auxerre [East Hundred; St Germans Union] [2586]
Peculiar of the Bishop of Exeter
OR C 1590-1880 M 1590-1992 B 1590-1906 (CRO)
BT CMB 1608-1825, 1827-39, 1841-45, 1847-48 (DRO)
Cop CMB 1590-1837 (DCRS/WSL); C 1590-1694 M 1608-75, 1786-1837 B 1590-1695
     (SG); M 1590-1812 (CRO); M 1590-1837 (Ts RIC); M 1813-37 (CMI);
     M 1608-75 from BT (Boyd); B 1813-37 (CBI)
Cop (Mf) CMB 1608-1759, 1771-1812 (Mf of BT at DRO: CRO,CSL); M 1654-1837,
          1840, 1862-86 (Ross); Extr CM 1590-1837 (IGI); CM 1590-1837 (SLC)
MI (Ptd CFHS); Ch (Ptd Jewers 65-78)

ST GERMANS St Nicholas, now St Anne, Hessenford. Erected 1832. Parish
created 1852 from St Germans. Rebuilt 1871
OR C 1834-1992 M 1852-1978 B 1834-1992 (CRO)
BT CMB 1834-36, 1873-76, 1878-84 (DRO)

ST GERMANS St Luke, Tideford. Erected 1845. Parish created 1847 from
ST GERMANS
OR C 1845+ M 1852+ B 1866+ (Inc)

ST GERMANS St Nicholas, Downderry. Mission church

ST GERMANS (Presb) f 1662; closed late 18th century

ST GERMANS (Wes/Wes Reform Union) Bethany f 1753; rebuilt 1825 ?; (Free Wes)
Bethany Chapel, Pennywin Farm [1882 Return]
OR Membership roll 1939-48 (CRO)

ST GERMANS (Wes) Hessenford

ST GERMANS (Wes/Wes Reform Union) The Refuge, Polbathick [1882 Return]

ST GERMANS (Wes) Tideford. Erected 1838 [1882 Return] [Kelly 1889]

ST GERMANS (Free Wes) Salem, Tideford [1882 Return]

ST GERMANS (Wes) Minard Cross, Hessenford. Erected 1860 [1882 Return]
[Kelly 1889]

ST GERMANS (Meth) Fore Street

ST GERMANS (S of F) Rowle. Part of East Cornwall MM. Moved from QUETHIOCK
1697. Later at Tideford [1882 Return] Sold 1905 to Wes
OR Z 1727-73 M 1659-1771 in CORNWALL QM register RG 6/1578; M 1798-1836 in
    Cornwall East Division register RG 6/185, Devon QM register RG 6/192 and
    Devon West Division register RG6/194 (PRO); B notes Tideford 1837, 1839,
    1841-42, 1849 (CRO)

GERMOE St Germoe [Kerrier Hundred; Helston Union] [1175] Chapelry in BREAGE,
with which united
OR C 1679-1991 M 1682-1985 B 1682-1991 (CRO) Noted in 1831: M deficient
    1705-18, 1739-44
BT CMB 1674-1736, 1741-72 (CRO); CMB 1610-73, 1737-40, 1773-1812, 1834-37
    (DRO)
Cop M 1674-1812 (Ptd Phillimore: 1903); CMB 1610-81 from BT; CMB 1668-1837
    (DCRS/WSL); C 1740-1840 M 1813-40 B 1740-1837 (Ms RIC); M 1813-37 (CMI);
    B 1813-37 (CBI); CB 1813-37 M 1610-1837 (SG); M 1674-1812 from OR;
    M 1610-73 from BT (Boyd); M 1800-12 (Pallot)
Cop (Mf) C 1682-1958 MB 1682-1959 (RIC); CMB 1610-1812 (Mf of BT at DRO:
    CRO,CSL); M 1813-37 (SG); M 1813-1925 (Ross); Extr C 1610-1875
    M 1610-73, 1684-89, 1762-66, 1838-95 (IGI); C 1610-1875 M 1610-73
    (SLC)
MI (Ptd CFHS)

GERMOE (RC) The Holy Family. Succeeded by St Mary, Praa Sands. Served from
HAYLE

GERMOE (Wes) Balwest. Erected 1829 [1882 Return]
MI (Ptd CFHS)

GERMOE (Wes) Keneggie Common [Kelly 1889]

GERMOE (S of F) f at Rejarden 1668. Part of PENZANCE MM. Rebuilt 1731

ST GERRANS St Gerrans [Powder Hundred; Truro Union] [766] Peculiar of the Bishop of Exeter. United with ST ANTHONY IN ROSELAND
OR C 1538-1970 M 1538-1969 B 1538-1925 (CRO)
BT CMB 1608-1813, 1815-18, 1821-24, 1828-29, 1832, 1834, 1837, 1839-45, 1849-51 (DRO)
Cop M 1538-1837 (Ptd Phillimore: 1935); CB 1538-1837 (DCRS/WSL); M 1538-1837 (CSL); M 1538-1812 (CRO,Morrab); C 1813-37 B 1813-55 (Ms RIC); CB 1813-37 M 1838-75 (CFHS); M 1813-37 (CMI); B 1813-37 (CBI); C 1813-37 (SG); M 1617-75 from BT (Boyd); M 1790-1837 (Pallot)
Cop (Mf) CMB 1538-1959 (RIC); CMB 1608-1812 (Mf of BT at DRO: CRO,CSL); M 1538-1916 (Ross); Extr C 1538-1875 M 1838-95 (IGI); C 1538-1812 (SLC)
MI Ch,cy 1978 (Ts SG)

ST GERRANS (Ind/Cong) Portscatho f 1822 [*Cong.Yearbook* 1850]
OR C 1826-36 (PRO)
Cop C 1826-36 (SG)
Cop (Mf) C 1826-36 (DCRS/WSL); Extr C 1826-36 (IGI); C 1826-36 (SLC)
MI (Ptd CFHS)

ST GERRANS (Wes) [Kelly 1856]; Church Town [1882 Return]

ST GERRANS (Bible Christian [Kelly 1856]; Zion [1882 Return]

ST GILES IN THE HEATH Devon parish in Diocese of Truro. *see* NIPR Devon

GLOWETH *see* KENWYN

ST GLUVIAS St Gluvias [Kerrier Hundred; Falmouth Union] [Parish 969; Borough of Penryn 3521] Peculiar of the Bishop of Exeter
OR C 1598-1975 M 1599-1605, 1645-1977 B 1601-1975 (CRO)
BT CMB 1608-1816, 1818, 1820-37, 1839-41 (DRO)
Cop M 1599-1812 (Ptd Phillimore: 1908); CB 1599-1837 (DCRS/WSL); C 1712-43 B 1599-1690 (CFHS); M 1813-37 (CMI); M 1599-1812 (Boyd); M 1800-12 (Pallot); B 1813-37 (CBI)
Cop (Mf) C 1598-1959 M 1599-1959 B 1601-1959 (RIC); CMB 1607-1812 (Mf of BT at DRO: CRO,CSL); M 1813-1908 (Ross); Extr C 1599-1876 M 1599-1754, 1837-52, 1869-76 (IGI); C 1599-1875 M 1599-1746, 1837-52 (SLC)
MI (Ptd CFHS); Ch (Wall,27-30, Ms SG)

ST GLUVIAS St Michael and All Angels, Ponsanooth. Mission church erected 1880. Now with MABE
OR M 1996+ (Inc); no CB

ST GLUVIAS (RC) Convent Chapel, Tremough, Penryn 1846-51; served from FALMOUTH
OR *see* FALMOUTH

ST GLUVIAS (Ind/Cong) New Street Chapel, Penryn f 1805. Closed 1934
OR C 1805-37 B 1806-12 (PRO); C 1806-1917 M 1846-54, 1909, 1910 B 1808-59, 1869-1901 (CRO)
Cop ZC 1805-37 B 1806-12 (SG)
Cop (Mf) C 1805-37 B 1808-34 (DCRS/WSL); Extr C 1805-37 (IGI); C 1805-37 (SLC)

ST GLUVIAS (Wes) Chapel Hill, Ponsanooth. f 1812. Erected 1843 [1882 Return]
OR ZCB 1813-36 (PRO)
Cop ZCB 1813-36 (SG); C 1847-1989 B 1846-1989 (CFHS)
Cop (Mf) ZCB 1813-36 (DCRS/WSL)

ST GLUVIAS (Wes) Penryn f 1813; Chapel Row [1882 Return]
OR C 1813-37 (PRO); and see FALMOUTH
Cop ZC 1813-37 (SG); M 1893-99 (CRO)
Cop (Mf) C 1813-37 (DCRS/WSL); Extr C 1813-37 (IGI); C 1813-37 (SLC)

ST GLUVIAS (Wes) Treluswell [1882 Return]

ST GLUVIAS (Wes) Laity Moor f 1910 ?

ST GLUVIAS (Prim Meth) [1882 Return]

ST GLUVIAS (Prim Meth) Summercourt, Penryn. Erected 1878 ? [1882 Return]
[Kelly 1889]

ST GLUVIAS (Bible Christian/U Meth) West Street, Penryn. Erected 1866
[Kelly 1889]
OR C 1928-57 (CRO)

ST GLUVIAS (Meth) Penryn Circuit
OR see FALMOUTH

ST GLUVIAS (S of F) Penryn. f pre-1668, part of FALMOUTH MM
OR Penryn and Falmouth Z 1654-1788 M 1661-1798 B 1658-1788 in Cornwall West
    Division registers RG 6/1218,1503 (PRO)

GOADS GREEN   see TRENEGLOS

GODOLPHIN CROSS   see BREAGE

GODREVY Modern team mission in HAYLE area including HAYLE, ST ERTH,
PHILLACK, GWITHIAN, GWINEAR

GOENROUNSON   see ST ENODER

GOLANT   see ST SAMPSON

GOLBERDON   see HILL, SOUTH

GOLDSITHNEY   see PERRANUTHNOE

GOODNOWN, GOONOWN see ST AGNES

GOONBELL   see ST AGNES

GOONHAVERN   see PERRANZABULOE

GOOSHAM MILL   see MORWENSTOW

GORRAN or ST GORAN St Goranus [Powder Hundred; St Austell Union] [1205]
United with ST MICHAEL CAERHAYS
OR C 1661-1989 M 1668-1975 B 1661-1989 (CRO)
BT CMB 1674-1736, 1741-72 (CRO); CMB 1607-73, 1737-40, 1773-1813, 1816,
  1820, 1823-32, 1837-55 (DRO)
Cop M 1668-1812 (Ptd Phillimore: 1907); CB 1661-1837 M 1668-1837 (DCRS/WSL);
  C 1661-1838 M 1668-1838 B 1661-1840 (RIC,SG); M 1813-37 (CMI); B 1813-37
  (CBI); M 1668-1812 from OR; M 1607-73 from BT (Boyd)
Cop (Mf) CMB 1609-1812 (Mf of BT at DRO: CRO,CSL); M 1668-1812 (SG);
  M 1813-37 (Ross); Extr C 1661-1837 M 1668-1837 from BT (IGI);
  C 1661-1812 M 1668-1837 from BT (SLC)
MI (Ptd CFHS)

GORRAN St Just, Gorran Haven. 15th century chapel, long disused until
restored 1885. Daughter church to GORRAN

GORRAN (Cong/FIEC) Mount Zion, Gorran Haven. Erected 1812
OR None

GORRAN (Ind) Old Chapel f late 18th century, replaced by High Lanes chapel
1813

GORRAN (Wes) High Lanes. Erected 1817
OR C 1886-1971 M 1906-73 (CRO)

GORRAN (Wes) Gorran Haven. Erected 1830 [1882 Return]

GORRAN (Wes) Church Town [1882 Return]

GORRAN (Bible Christian) Boswinger [1882 Return]

GORRAN (Prim Meth) [Kelly 1856]

GRADE St Grada and Holy Cross [Kerrier Hundred; Helston Union] [306] United
1958 with RUAN MAJOR, RUAN MINOR. Now also with LANDEWEDNACK
OR C 1700-1988 M 1707-1944 B 1707-1964 (CRO) No earlier registers noted in
  1831
BT CMB 1674-1736, 1741-72 (CRO); CMB 1597-1673, 1737-40, 1773-1812, 1816-51
  (DRO)
Cop M 1674-1812 (Ptd Phillimore: 1917); CMB 1597-1704 from BT; C 1700-1837
  B 1707-1837 (DCRS/WSL); M 1813-37 (CMI); M 1597-1673 (SG); M 1674-1812
  from OR; M 1607-73 from BT (Boyd); M 1790-1812 (Pallot); B 1813-37 (CBI)
Cop (Mf) C 1707-1954 M 1707-1944 B 1708-1959 (RIC); CMB 1597-1812 (Mf of BT
  at DRO: CRO,CSL); M 1813-1925 (Ross); Extr C 1597-1704, 1707-1885
  M 1674-1703, 1707-1875 (IGI); C 1597-1704, 1813-75 M 1674-1703
  (SLC)
MI (Ptd CFHS)

GRAMPOUND   *see* CREED

GRAMPOUND ROAD   in LADOCK q.v. and PROBUS

GREENBOTTOM   *see* KENWYN

GRIMSCOTT   *see* LAUNCELLS

GROGOTH   *see* CORNELLY

GRUGWITH   *see* ST KEVERNE

GULVAL or LANESLY St Gulval [Penwith Hundred; Penzance Union] [1467]
Now with MARAZION
OR C 1599-1886 M 1598-1882 B 1599-1925 (CRO)
BT CMB 1674-1736, 1741-72 (CRO); CMB 1608-73, 1737-40, 1773-1812, 1813,
    1815, 1825, 1827-30, 1832-36, 1838-54, 1858-61 (DRO)
Cop CMB 1598-1812 (Ptd G.Millett, W.Bolitho *The Parish Registers of
    Gulval...*: 1893); M 1687-1741 (Ptd Phillimore: 1907); CMB 1813-37
    (Ts CSL); M 1813-37 (CMI); B 1813-37 (CBI); M 1598-1812 (Boyd);
    M 1800-12 (Pallot)
Cop (Mf) C 1599-1960 MB 1598-1960 (RIC); CMB 1600-1812 (Mf of BT at DRO:
    CRO,CSL); M 1813-1925 (Ross); Extr C 1599-1842, 1871-75
    M 1588-1876, 1883-95 (IGI); C 1599-1712, 1813-37 M 1588-1812 (SLC)

GULVAL Trythall Mission Church. Erected 1885

GULVAL (Wes) Erected 1822 [1882 Return] Now Wesley Villa, private house

GULVAL (Wes) Tolverth

GULVAL (Wes) Trevarrack [Kelly 1889]

GULVAL (Wes) Gear. Erected 1814 [Kelly 1889]

GULVAL (Bible Christian) Carfury. Erected 1833   [1882 Return]

GULVAL (Teetotal Wes/Free Meth) New Mill. Erected 1844 [Kelly 1889]

GULVAL (Meth) Erected 1884

GUNNISLAKE   *see* CALSTOCK

GUNPIPER   *see* FEOCK

GUNWALLOE or WINNINGTON St Winwalloe [Kerrier Hundred; Helston Union] [284]
Chapelry in BREAGE. United 1836 with CURY. Now also with ST MAWGAN IN
MENEAGE
OR C 1717-1993 M 1716-1837 B 1716-1994 (CRO) No earlier registers noted in
    1831. *see* BREAGE
BT CMB 1676-1736, 1741-72 (CRO); CMB 1608-71, 1737-40, 1773-1814, 1816-31,
    1834 (DRO)
Cop C 1608-1848 M 1608-1837 B 1608-1845 (CSL); CMB 1716-1845 with index
    (CRO,CFHS); C 1717-99 (DCRS/WSL); C 1717-99 M 1608-73 from BT (CSL);
    M 1813-37 (CMI); M 1608-65 (SG); M 1716-1837 (Boyd); B 1813-37 (CBI)
Cop (Mf) C 1717-1958 M 1716-1959 B 1716-1960 (RIC); CMB 1608-1812 (Mf of BT
    at DRO: CRO,CSL); M 1608-65, 1813-1925 (Ross); Extr C 1676-1885
    M 1676-1714, 1716-1896 (IGI); C 1676-1875 (SLC)
MI (Ptd CFHS)

GUNWALLOE (Wes) Gunwalloe [1882 Return]

GUNWALLOE (Wes/UMFC) Beripper Union, Gunwalloe [1882 Return]
OR C 1911-80 M 1921-75 (CRO)

GWAVAS   *see* SITHNEY

GWEEK   in CONSTANTINE q.v. and WENDRON

GWENNAP St Weneppa [Kerrier Hundred; Redruth Union] [8539] United with
STITHIANS, PERRAN-AR-WORTHAL
OR C 1658-1891 M 1660-1990 B 1658-1924 (CRO)
BT CMB 1674-1736, 1741-72 (CRO); CMB 1610-70, 1737-40, 1773-1824, 1826-38
    (DRO)
Cop M 1660-1812 (Ptd Phillimore: 1917); C 1658-1825 MB 1628-1845 (CSL);
    CMB 1658-1845 (Ts with index, RIC,CRO,CFHS); M 1813-37 (Ts RIC);
    M 1841-75 (Ms RIC); M 1813-37 (CMI); B 1813-37 (CBI); M 1610-1819 (SG);
    M 1660-1812 from OR; M 1610-70 from BT (Boyd); M 1790-1812 (Pallot);
    M 1876-1900 (CFHS)
Cop (Mf) CMB 1610-1812 (Mf of BT at DRO: CRO,CSL); M 1813-75 (Ross);
        Extr C 1674-1772 from BT (IGI); C 1674-1772 from BT (SLC)

GWENNAP Holy Trinity, St Day. Chapelry of St Day in GWENNAP. Erected 1828.
Separate parish 1829. Closed. Replaced by church centre 1967. Now with
CHACEWATER, CARHARRACK
OR C 1833-1935 M 1835-1962 B 1833-1919 (CRO)
BT None
Cop C 1833-59 M 1835-37 B 1833-45 including Gwennap Nonconformist registers
    1820-45 (CSL,CFHS); C 1833-75 M 1876-1900 (CFHS); M 1836-75 (Photocopy
    of Ms, RIC); M 1813-37 (CMI); B 1813-37 (CBI)
Cop (Mf) M 1835-75 (Ross);
MI (Ptd CFHS)

GWENNAP Christ Church, Lanner. Parish created 1844 from GWENNAP. Erected
1845. United with REDRUTH, TRELEIGH
OR C 1845-1975 M 1845-1966 B 1846-1952 (CRO)

GWENNAP St Piran, Carharrack. Erected 1884. Licensed mission church, now in
parish of St Paul, Chacewater (KENWYN)

GWENNAP (Wes) Gwennap Circuit
OR C 1837-81, 1917-34 (CRO)
Cop C 1843-51 (SG)

GWENNAP (Wes) Carharrack Wesley f 1760. Erected 1768; rebuilt 1815
[1882 Return]
OR C 1820-51 (PRO); C 1940-83 (CRO)
Cop ZC 1820-42 (SG)
Cop (Mf) C 1820-51 (DCRS/WSL); Extr C 1820-51 (IGI); C 1820-51 (SLC)

GWENNAP (Wes) St Day, West End [1882 Return]
OR C 1848-94 (CRO)

GWENNAP (Wes) Gwennap Pit. Erected 1836

GWENNAP (Wes) Lanner Wesley. Erected 1828. Rebuilt 1844 [1882 Return]
OR C 1840-79 (CRO)

GWENNAP (Wes) Crofthandy. Erected 1844 [1882 Return]

GWENNAP (Wes) Frogpool. Erected 1843 [1882 Return]

GWENNAP (Wes) Busveal, near St Day [1882 Return]

GWENNAP (Wes) Sunny Corner [1882 Return]

GWENNAP (Wes) Trevarth [Kelly 1889]

GWENNAP (Bible Christian/U Meth) Carharrack Billy Bray Memorial [Kelly 1889]
Demolished 1986
OR C 1943-76 (CRO)

GWENNAP (Bible Christian) Great Deliverance, Carharrack. Erected 1840; now a
farm shed. New chapel 1883; demolished 1988.

GWENNAP (Bible Christian) Hicks Mill. Erected 1821 [1882 Return]

GWENNAP (Bible Christian) Lanner. Erected 1856 [1882 Return] Now village
hall

GWENNAP (Prim Meth) St Day Circuit
OR C 1858-1936 (CRO)

GWENNAP (Prim Meth) St Day [1882 Return]

GWENNAP (Prim Meth) Lanner Moor [1882 Return]
OR C 1935-75 (CRO)

GWENNAP Burial grounds
OR B 1855-1938 (CRO)

GWINEAR St Winnear [Penwith Hundred; Redruth Union] [2728] Now part of
GODREVY Team Mission
OR CMB 1560+ (Inc) Vol.1 CMB 1560-1737 described in 1831 as "very
    defective"
BT CMB 1679-1736, 1741-72 (CRO); CMB 1607-73, 1736-40, 1773-1824, 1826-35
    (DRO)
Cop M 1560-1812 (Ptd Phillimore: 1907); C 1737-83, 1799-1817 (Morrab);
    C 1737-1812 (CSL); M 1813-37 (CMI); M 1560-1812 (Boyd); M 1800-12
    (Pallot)
Cop (Mf) C 1560-1960 MB 1560-1959 (RIC); CMB 1608-1813 (Mf of BT at DRO:
         CRO,CSL); M 1601-36, 1813-1925 (Ross); Extr C 1560-1885 M 1736-1895
         (IGI); C 1560-1735, 1813-75 (SLC)
MI (Ptd CFHS)

GWINEAR (Wes) Deveral. Erected 1793-94. [1882 Return] Closed by 1980
OR C 1902-73 (CRO)

GWINEAR (Wes) Wall. Erected 1829 [1882 Return]
OR C 1862-1945 M 1899-1990 (CRO)

GWINEAR (Wes) Connor Downs [1882 Return]

GWINEAR (Wes) Carnhell Green [Kelly 1889]

GWITHIAN St Gwithian [Penwith Hundred; Redruth Union] [539] Chapelry in
PHILLACK. Original oratory in the sands. Present church erected 1865. Now
part of GODREVY Team Mission
OR C 1560-1894 M 1560-1837 B 1560-1916 (CRO) Noted in 1831: Vol 1 C 1718+ M
    1717+ B 1724+ "containing loose leaves of Bap Bur of the 16th and 17th
    centuries"
BT CMB 1684-1736, 1741-72 (CRO); CMB 1597-1673, 1737-40, 1773-1858 (DRO)
Cop M 1560-1812 (Ptd Phillimore: 1903); M 1560-1812 (CRO); C 1559-1837
    B 1560-1837 (Morrab); M 1813-37 (CMI); M 1560-1812 (Boyd); M 1837-1925
    (CFHS); B 1560-1837 (CSL); M 1790-1812 (Pallot); B 1813-37 (CBI)

GWITHIAN cont.

Cop (Mf) CM 1560-1959 B 156C-1960 (RIC); CMB 1597-1812 (Mf of BT at DRO: CRO,CSL); M 1813-1925 (Ross); Extr C 1560-1875 M 1838-95 (IGI); C 1560-1875 (SLC)

MI (Ptd CFHS)

GWITHIAN (Wes) Erected 1820. Church Town [1882 Return]
OR C 1966-91 (CRO)

HALAMANNING   see ST HILARY

HALBATHIC   see LISKEARD

HALSE TOWN   or HALSETOWN see ST IVES

HALTON QUAY   see ST DOMINICK

HALVOSSO   see MABE

HAMPT   see STOKE CLIMSLAND

HARLAND CROSS   see BREAGE

HARROWBARROW   see CALSTOCK

HARROWBRIDGE   see ST NEOT

HAYLE   see PHILLACK

HEAMOOR   see MADRON

HELFORD   see MANACCAN

HELLAND St Helena [Trigg Hundred; Bodmin Union] [285]
OR C 1722-1812 M 1722-1836 B 1722-1812 (CRO) No earlier registers noted in 1831
BT CMB 1677-1736, 1741-72 (CRO); CMB 1608-73, 1737-40, 1773-1833, 1835 (DRO)
Cop M 1677-1812 (Ptd Phillimore: 1903); M 1813-37 (CMI); CB 1722-1812 M 1608-1812 (SG); M 1677-1812 from OR; M 1608-73 from BT (Boyd); M 1790-1812 (Pallot)
Cop (Mf) CMB 1608-1812 (Mf of BT at DRO: CRO,CSL); M 1813-37 (Ross); Extr C 1677-1719, 1722-1811 M 1677-1812 (IGI); C 1677-1719 (SLC)
MI (Ptd CFHS)

HELLAND (Wes) [Kelly 1856]; [1882 Return]

HELLESVEOR   see ST IVES

HEL(L)IGAN   see ST MABYN

HELSTON or HELSTON-IN-KERRIER St Michael [Kerrier Hundred; Helston Union] [3293] Chapelry and borough in WENDRON. Rebuilt 1761. Separate parish 1845. United with WENDRON
OR C 1599-1641, 1646-53, 1696-1972 M 1599-1641, 1647-53, 1696-1974 B 1598-1639, 1696-1975 (CRO)
BT CMB 1675-1736, 1741-72 (CRO); CMB 1608-78, 1737-40, 1773-1842, 1844-50, 1852 (DRO)

HELSTON cont.
Cop M 1599-1812 (Ptd Phillimore: 1912); CB 1599-1837 (DCRS/WSL); M 1813-37
    (CRO); C 1698-1812 M 1696-1753 B 1698-1791 (RIC); C 1837-75 M 1876-1900
    (CFHS); M 1837-60 (Ms RIC); M 1813-37 (CMI); M 1599-1812 (Boyd);
    M 1800-12 (Pallot); B 1813-37 (CBI)
Cop (Mf) C 1599-1690 M 1599-1653 B 1598-1639 (RIC); CMB 1608-1812 (Mf of BT
    at DRO: CRO,CSL); M 1610-73, 1813-75 (Ross); Extr C 1599-1837
    M 1599-1853 (IGI); C 1599-1837 M 1599-1853 (SLC)
MI Ch,cy,cemetery (Ptd CFHS)

HELSTON All Saints, Meneage Street. Mission church erected 1882 adjacent to
new cemetery. Closed 1970s

HELSTON Chaplaincy, Royal Naval Air Station, Culdrose

HELSTON (RC) House of John Plomer 1845-51, 1857+. Wendron Street
[1882 Return] Served from Penzance 1845-51,1858-65; from Camborne 1857-58,
1865-88. Modern parish St Mary f 1968
OR No early registers: see PENZANCE, CAMBORNE

HELSTON (RC) Holy Redeemer, Royal Naval Air Station, Culdrose: served from
Helston

HELSTON (Bapt) Coinage Hall Street f 1805; rebuilt 1888-89
OR Z 1814-37 (PRO)
Cop Z 1814-37 (SG)
Cop (Mf) Z 1814-37 (DCRS/WSL); Extr Z 1814-37 (IGI); Z 1814-37 (SLC)

HELSTON (Bapt) Wendron Street. Erected 1802. Rebuilt 1837. [Bapt. Manual
1850; Handbook 1869] Later a cinema

HELSTON (Bapt) Lower Road f 1877 [Bapt.Handbook 1881]

HELSTON (Bapt) Lower Town n.d. [Bapt.Handbook 1881]

HELSTON (Presb) fl 1672-90

HELSTON (Wes) Helston Circuit
OR ZC 1804-37 (PRO); C 1837-1930 (CRO)
Cop ZC 1804-37 (SG)
Cop (Mf) ZC 1804-37 (DCRS/WSL); Extr ZC 1804-37 (IGI); ZC 1804-37 (SLC)

HELSTON (Wes) Coinagehall Street. Erected 1797. Rebuilt 1888
OR C 1936-81 (CRO)

HELSTON (Wes) Degibna [1882 Return]

HELSTON (Bible Christian) Circuit
OR C 1838-1907 (CRO)

HELSTON (Bible Christian/U Meth) Meneage Street [1882 Return]
OR C 1918, 1955-61 (CRO)

HELSTON (Wes Meth Ass/UMFC/U Meth) Church Street [1882 Return]
OR C 1863-90, 1897-1929, 1953-68 M 1899-1968 (CRO)

HELSTON (U Meth) Circuit
OR C 1913-32 (CRO)

HELSTON (Meth) Circuit
OR C 1933-52 (CRO)

HELSTON (Meth) Circuit. Constantine section
OR C 1946-51 (CRO)

HELSTON (S of F) Erected 1731. Part of FALMOUTH MM

HELSTON (Latter Day Saints) Clodgey Lane

HELSTON Poor Law Union
OR D 1914-59 (CRO)

HELSTONE   see LANTEGLOS BY CAMELFORD

HENDRA   see BREAGE

HENDRA   see ST STITHIANS

HENWOOD   see LINKINHORNE

HERODSFOOT   see DULOE

HESSENFORD   see ST GERMANS

HIGH LANES   see GORRAN

HIGH LANES   see PILLATON

HIGHER KEHELLAND   see CAMBORNE

HIGHERTOWN   see TRURO

HIGHLANES   see MANACCAN

HIGHLANES   see PHILLACK

HIGHWAY   see TYWARDREATH

HIGHWAY   see LANTEGLOS BY FOWEY

ST HILARY St Hilary [Penwith Hundred; Penzance Union] [1728] United with
PERRANUTHNOE
OR C 1687-1889 M 1679-1975 B 1677-1954 including entries for St Michael's
    Mount (CRO)
BT CMB 1676-1734, 1741-72 (CRO); CMB 1609-73, 1737-40, 1773-1853, 1855-57
    (DRO)
Cop M 1676-86, 1692-1812 (Ptd Phillimore: 1906); C 1671-1812 B 1677-1812
    (Morrab); M 1813-37 (CMI); M 1676-1812 from OR; M 1609-73 from BT
    (Boyd); M 1800-12 (Pallot); B 1753-1812 (CFHS); B 1813-37 (CBI)
Cop (Mf) C 1671-1959 M 1679-1959 B 1677-1959 (RIC); CMB 1609-1812 (Mf of BT
        at DRO: CRO,CSL); C 1671-1812 M 1609-1812 B 1677-1812 (SG);
        M 1813-1910 (Ross); Extr C 1687-1875 (IGI); C 1687-1875 (SLC)

ST HILARY All Saints, Marazion. Marazion or Market Jew an ancient market town and chapelry in St Hilary [1393]. Chapel of St Hermes rebuilt 1735. Separate parish 1823. Present church 1861. Now with GULVAL
OR C 1813-1979 B 1813-1944 (CRO) Noted in 1831: "The entries of Baptisms are made in the Registers of the Mother Church of St Hilary; no Burials or Marriages take place at this Chapel"
BT CMB 1813-16, 1830, 1832-34, 1838-57 (DRO) For the earlier period see St Hilary
Cop C 1813-57 B 1839-45 (CSL,CFHS); CMB 1813-45 with index (CRO); C 1692-1812 (Morrab); CB 1813-45 (Ts RIC); C 1754-1812 (SG); Banns 1838-99 (CFHS)
Cop (Mf) Banns 1838-99 (Ross)
MI (Ptd CFHS)

ST HILARY St Michael's Mount [West Hundred; Penzance Union] [161] Extra-parochial place in Mounts Bay. 14th century chapel of St Aubyn family (Lord St Levan)
OR *see* St Hilary
Cop B 1754-1812 (Morrab,SG); B 1813-37 (CBI)

ST HILARY (Bapt) Marazion f 1823 [*Bapt. Manual* 1850; *Handbook* 1881]

ST HILARY (Wes) Erected 1836

ST HILARY (Wes) Marazion Circuit
OR C 1841-83, 1888-1954 (CRO)
Cop C 1868-83 (CFHS)

ST HILARY (Wes) Marazion. Erected 1811 [1882 Return]

ST HILARY (Wes) Halamanning. Erected 1854 [1882 Return]

ST HILARY (Wes) Relubbus. Erected 1875 [1882 Return]; [Kelly 1889]

ST HILARY (Wes) St Michael's Mount. Erected c.1820

ST HILARY (Wes) Penberthy Cross. Erected c.1840

ST HILARY (Bible Christian) Rudgevean, or Rosudgeon. Erected c.1830 [Kelly 1889]

ST HILARY (Bible Christian) Ebenezer, High Street, Marazion. Erected 1840 [1882 Return]

ST HILARY (UMFC/U Meth) Ebenezer, Marazion [1882 Return]
OR C 1877-1922 (CRO)

ST HILARY (Meth) Marazion Circuit
OR C 1927-86 (CRO)

ST HILARY (S of F) Land's End and Marazion Monthly Meeting f 1676 from FALMOUTH MM; later named Penzance MM until 1783, when joined FALMOUTH MM
OR Z 1653-1730 B 1659-1782 in CORNWALL QM register RG 6/1578 (PRO); Z 1653-1787 M 1657-1708, 1713-77 B 1658-1780 in Cornwall West Division registers RG 6/261,951,1169,1233 (PRO)

ST HILARY cont.
Cop M 1661-1777 'with names of those who subscribed their approbation'
B 1653-1781, in 1828 copy of old register book of Cornwall QM (CRO);
Z 1674-1782 M 1694, 1706 B 1688-98 Marazion, Penzance and Lands End:
extracted from MM registers 1838 (CRO); ZMB 1711-17: 1856 copy from
Minute Book (CRO)
Cop (Mf) M 1659-1782 (Ross)

ST HILARY (S of F) Marazion Meeting f 1679. Erected 1688. Meetings ceased
1842, resumed 1918. Currently [1998] at Beacon Road
OR Marazion and Penryn Z 1672-1780 M 1678-1777 B 1659-1782 in Cornwall West
Division register RG 6/1503 (PRO); B 1867-76, 3 entries; B notes,
Marazion burial ground 1838-43 (CRO)
Cop M 1670-1777 (CFHS)

HILL, NORTH or NORTHILL St Torney [East Hundred; Launceston Union] [1155]
United with LEWANNICK
OR C 1630-1979 M 1555-1990 B 1630-1959 (CRO) No earlier CB registers noted
in 1831
BT CMB 1675-1736, 1741-72 (CRO); CMB 1608-73, 1737-40, 1773-1812, 1827,
1831-32, 1836, 1839-76, 1880 (DRO)
Cop CB 1630-1865 M 1555-1865 (DCRS/WSL); C 1638-1754 M 1730-76 B 1630-1742
(CRO); C 1621-1865 M 1555-1840 B 1630-1840 (Ts RIC,SG); M 1813-37 (CMI);
B 1813-37 (CBI); M 1608-73 from BT (Boyd)
Cop (Mf) C 1813-1960 M 1754-1960 B 1813-1959 (RIC); CMB 1608-1812 (Mf of BT
at DRO: CRO,CSL); M 1555-1925 (Ross); Extr C 1630-1772, 1813-75
M 1555-1837 (IGI); C 1630-1772, 1813-75 M 1555-1837 (SLC)
MI (DCRS/WSL); ch,cy 1971 (Ts SG)

HILL, NORTH (Wes) North Hill Circuit
OR C 1848-1975 (CRO)

HILL, NORTH (Wes) North Hill. Erected 1810 [1882 Return]
OR C 1780-1990 (CRO)

HILL, NORTH (Wes) Coads Green. Erected 1826; rebuilt 1849 [1882 Return]
OR B 1828-1968 (CRO)
MI (Ptd CFHS)

HILL, NORTH (Bible Christian) Middlewood [1882 Return]

HILL, NORTH (Meth) North Hill Circuit
OR C 1915-75 (CRO)

HILL, SOUTH or SOUTHILL St Sampson [East Hundred; Liskeard Union] [530]
Now with CALLINGTON
OR C 1543-1996 M 1566-1975 B 1550-1897 (CRO) Noted in 1831: B deficient
1579-1620
BT CMB 1676-1736, 1741-72 (CRO); CMB 1738-40, 1773-1841 (DRO);
for CMB 1597-1673 *see* CALLINGTON
Cop M 1566-1837 (Ts with index, RIC,CRO); M 1566-1812 (CFHS); M 1813-37
(CMI); B 1813-37 (CBI)
Cop (Mf) CMB 1614-1812 (Mf of BT at DRO: CRO,CSL); M 1566-1837 (Ross);
Extr C 1676-1772 (IGI); C 1676-1772 (SLC)
MI (Ptd CFHS)

HILL, SOUTH (Wes) Golberdon Bethel [1882 Return]
OR M 1910-91 (CRO)
MI (Ptd CFHS)

HOLMBUSH   *see* STOKE CLIMSLAND

HORSEDOWNS   *see* CROWAN

HUGUS   *see* KEA

ILLOGAN Parish church [Penwith Hundred; Redruth Union] [6072] Rebuilt on new
site 1846. *see also* CAMBORNE Tuckingmill, ST AGNES Mount Hawke
OR C 1539-1882 M 1600-1902 B 1540-1886 (CRO) Noted in 1831: Vol.1
    transcribed in 1801 from the original and mutilated register: C 1539-
    1731, deficient 1547-57, 1589-1614, 1618-64, 1666-84. Vol 2 B 1540-1731
    deficient 1543-59, 1646-53, 1695-99
BT CMB 1681-1736, 1741-72 (CRO); CMB 1613-73, 1737-40, 1773-1812, 1817-18,
    1821-24, 1826-28, 1830-31, 1835, 1837-49 (DRO)
Cop C 1539-1858 M 1601-1837 B 1540-1845 (CSL,CFHS); CMB 1613-73 from BT;
    CMB 1600-1837 (DCRS/WSL); CMB 1539-1845 (Ts with index, RIC,CRO);
    CMB 1540-1731 (CRO); CB 1613-36, 1663-73 M 1600-1812 (CSL); M 1613-74
    (SG); M 1613-73 from BT (Boyd); M 1813-37 (CMI); M 1856-74 (CFHS);
    B 1813-37 (CBI)
Cop (Mf) CMB 1609-1812 (Mf of BT at DRO: CRO,CSL); M 1600-1875 (Ross);
      Extr C 1613-73, 1683-1773 M 1600-1837 (IGI); C 1613-73, 1683-1773
      M 1600-1837 (SLC)

ILLOGAN St Illogan, Trevenson Moor, Pool. Chapel-of-ease to Illogan. Erected
1806-09
MI (Ptd CFHS)

ILLOGAN St Mary, Portreath. Chapel-of-ease to ILLOGAN. Erected 1841

ILLOGAN (Wes) Bridge [1882 Return]
OR C 1844-1922 (CRO)

ILLOGAN (Wes) Carn Brea
OR C 1938-81 (CRO)

ILLOGAN (Wes) Illogan Downs [1882 Return]
OR C 1839-1971 (CRO)

ILLOGAN (Wes) Illogan Highway. Erected 1809; new chapels 1839, 1908
[1882 Return]

ILLOGAN (Wes) Rosecroggan, Red River [1882 Return]; Rosecroggan [Kelly 1897]
OR C 1916-90 (CRO)

ILLOGAN (Wes) Voguebeloth. [1882 Return] Rebuilt 1886
OR C 1841-1985 (CRO)

ILLOGAN (Wes) Forest. Erected 1829; rebuilt 1882 [1882 Return] [Kelly 1897]

ILLOGAN (Wes) Carnkie [Kelly 1897]

ILLOGAN (Wes) Pool [1882 Return]; [Kelly 1897]

ILLOGAN (Wes) Porth Town [Kelly 1897]

ILLOGAN (Wes) Portreath [1882 Return]; [Kelly 1897]

ILLOGAN (Wes) A building, Tregagorran [1882 Return]

ILLOGAN (Wes) Ebenezer, Broad Lanes [1882 Return]

ILLOGAN (Prim Meth) Treskillard [Kelly 1897]
OR C 1942-79 (CRO)

ILLOGAN (Prim Meth) Broad Lane =? Prim Meth erected 1859 rebuilt 1889
[Kelly 1897] = ? Brown Lane [1882 Return]
OR C 1942-87 (CRO)

ILLOGAN (Prim Meth) Carnkie [1882 Return]; [Kelly 1897]

ILLOGAN (Prim Meth) Illogan Highway [Kelly 1897]

ILLOGAN (Bible Christian/U Meth) Brea
OR M 1962-92 (CRO)

ILLOGAN (UMFC/U Meth) Pool St Martin's
OR C 1877-1903 (CRO)

ILLOGAN (UMFC/U Meth) Rosecroggan
OR C 1880-1930 (CRO)

ILLOGAN (UMFC/U Meth) Illogan Highway, Chill Road. Erected 1850. [1882
Return] Demolished
OR C 1892-1934 M 1959-72 (CRO)

ILLOGAN (UMFC) Paynters Lane End [1882 Return]

ILLOGAN (UMFC) Tolskithy [1882 Return]

ILLOGAN (UMFC) Portreath [Kelly 1889]

ILLOGAN (S of F) Erected 1731, part of FALMOUTH MM

INDIAN QUEENS   see ST COLUMB MAJOR

ST ISSEY or EGLOSCROOK St Issey [Pydar Hundred; St Columb Major Union] [720]
Peculiar of the Bishop of Exeter. United with ST PETROC MINOR
OR C 1596-1863 M 1597-1617, 1632-1837 B 1602-1872 (CRO) Noted in 1831:
    M deficient 1618-31, 1753-55
BT CMB 1608-1842 (DRO)
Cop M 1596-1617, 1632-1812 (Ptd Phillimore: 1909); C 1596-1774 B 1602-1840
    (CSL); CMB 1596-1850 (CRO); CMB 1663-1772 from BT (DCRS/WSL); M 1813-37
    (CMI); B 1813-37 (CBI); CB 1596-1812 (SG); M 1596-1812 (Boyd)
Cop (Mf) C 1596-1957 M 1597-1958 B 1602-1959 (RIC); CMB 1608-1812 (Mf of BT
        at DRO: CRO,CSL); M 1813-1925 (Ross); Extr C 1596-1875 (IGI);
        C 1596-1875 (SLC)
MI (Ptd CFHS)

ST ISSEY (Ind/Cong) f 1819. Church Town [1882 Return] Closed 1969
OR None known

ST ISSEY (Wes) Trenance [1882 Return]

ST IVE or **ST EVE** St Ive [East Hundred; Liskeard Union] [656] United with
QUETHIOCK
OR C 1683-1937 M 1686-1972 B 1686-1927 (CRO) Noted in 1831: CMB 1651+
BT CMB 1675-1736, 1741-72 (CRO); CMB 1614-72, 1737-40, 1773-1815, 1821,
    1823-24, 1830, 1833-34, 1837-63 (DRO)
Cop M 1813-37 (CMI); M 1614, 1623-33, 1664-65, 1670-84, 1686-1837 Banns
    1754-1812 (RIC,CFHS,SG); M 1614-72 from BT (Boyd); B 1813-37 (CBI)
Cop (Mf) CMB 1614-1812 (Mf of BT at DRO: CRO,CSL); M 1682-1875 (Ross);
       Extr C 1675-1805 (IGI); C 1675-1805 (SLC)
MI (Ptd CFHS)

ST IVE Pensilva Mission Church. Licensed school room [Kelly 1885]; iron
church [Kelly 1935]

ST IVE (Wes) [Kelly 1856]; [1882 Return]
MI (Ptd CFHS)

ST IVE (Wes) Bodmin Land [1882 Return]

ST IVE (Wes) Marsh Gate [1882 Return]

ST IVE (Prim Meth) A building in the occupation of Richard Pearce, The
Church Town of St Ive [1882 Return]

ST IVE (Bible Christian) Cheriton Cross [1882 Return]

ST IVE (Bible Christian) Bodmin Lands [1882 Return]

ST IVE (Wes Reform) [Kelly 1889]

ST IVE Pensilva Cemetery
OR B 1865-1954 (CRO)

ST IVES St Ia the Virgin [Penwith Hundred; Penzance Union] [4776] Chapelry
in LELANT. Separate parish 1826
OR C 1651-1940 M 1653-1977 B 1653-1964 (CRO)
BT CMB 1679-1736, 1741-72 (CRO); CMB 1614-72, 1737-40, 1774-1812,1814-15,
    1817-18, 1820, 1823-26, 1828-29, 1831 (DRO)
Cop M 1653-1812 (Ptd Phillimore: 1909); C 1651-1812 M 1837-60 B 1653-1812
    (Ms RIC); C 1813-88 M 1837-1900 B 1653-1700 (CFHS); Extr 1607-74 (Ms
    RIC); M 1614-1837 (CRO); M 1813-37 (CMI); M 1653-1812 from OR; M 1607-74
    from BT (Boyd); M 1800-12 (Pallot); B 1813-37 (CBI)
Cop (Mf) C 1651-1812 B 1653-1812 (Mf of transcript, RIC); CMB 1608-1812
       (Mf of BT at DRO: CRO,CSL); M 1813-75 (Ross); Extr C 1651-1812
       (IGI); C 1651-1812 (SLC)
MI (Ptd CFHS); Barnoon cemetery (CFHS)

ST IVES St Nicholas Chapel, St Ives Head. Mediaeval. Rebuilt 1911

ST IVES St Nicholas Chapel, Norway Square. Mariners' mission church
[Kelly 1889, 1935]

ST IVES St John's in the Fields, Halsetown. Parish created 1846 from
ST IVES. Erected 1866
OR C 1848-1944 M 1860-1970 B 1901-76 (CRO)
Cop (Mf) C 1848-77 (CFHS); M 1860-75 (Ross)

ST IVES (RC) An 18th century mission served by Franciscan Friars. Sacred
Heart and St Ia f 1902
OR C 1818-37, 1841-1908 (CRO)

ST IVES (Lady Hunt Conn) Zion Chapel, Fore Street. f 1804. Chapel 1824
[*Cong.Yearbook* 1850] associated with a chapel at Hellesveor f 1824
[1882 Return]
OR C 1800-22 (PRO)
Cop ZC 1800-22 (SG)
Cop (Mf) C 1800-22 (DCRS/WSL); Extr C 1800-22 (IGI)

ST IVES (Wes) St Ives Circuit
OR ZC 1818-37 (PRO); C 1818-37, 1841-1908 (CRO)
Cop ZC 1818-37 (SG)
Cop (Mf) ZC 1818-37 (DCRS/WSL); Extr ZC 1818-37 (IGI); ZC 1818-37 (SLC)

ST IVES (Wes) Wesley, Street-an-Garrow. Erected 1784

ST IVES (Wes) Lower Chapel or Bank Chapel. Erected 1824

ST IVES (Wes/UMFC) Wesley; later Wesley and Bedford Road
OR C 1908-93 (CRO)

ST IVES (Wes) Hallesveor. Erected 1844. [1882 Return] New building 1937
moved from Trezelah. Madron

ST IVES (Wes) Halsetown. Erected 1833 [1882 Return]

ST IVES (Teetotal Wes) Halsetown. Erected 1845. fl *c.*1851

ST IVES (Bible Christian/U Meth) St Peter Street. Erected 1824
OR C 1912-34 (CRO)

ST IVES (Bible Christian) Ebenezer, Halsetown. Erected 1832 [1882 Return]
[Kelly 1889]

ST IVES (Bible Christian) Back Road. Erected 1858 [Kelly 1889]

ST IVES (Prim Meth) Circuit
OR ZC 1832-37 (PRO); C 1832-1932 (CRO)
Cop ZC 1832-37 (SG)
Cop (Mf) ZC 1832-37 (DCRS/WSL); Extr ZC 1832-37 (IGI); ZC 1832-37 (SLC)

ST IVES (Prim Meth) Ebenezer, Fore Street. Erected 1831

ST IVES (Prim Meth) Chyanchy. Erected 1831 [1882 Return]

ST IVES (Prim Meth) Trevalgan. Erected 1835 [1882 Return]

ST IVES (Prim Meth) Balnoon [1882 Return]

ST IVES (Meth New Conn) Circuit
OR None known

ST IVES (Meth New Conn/U Meth) Bedford Road
OR C 1860-1993 (CRO)

ST IVES (Meth New Conn) Halsetown. Erected mid-19th century

ST IVES (Meth New Conn) Fore Street [1882 Return]

ST IVES (Meth New Conn) Chapel Street [Kelly 1889]

JACOBSTOW or STOW ST JAMES St James [Stratton Hundred; Stratton Union] [638]
United with ST GENNYS, WARBSTOW, TRENEGLOS
OR   C 1653-1869 M 1656-1837 B 1653-1811 (CRO)
BT   CMB 1674-1736, 1741-72 (CRO); CMB 1612-73, 1737-40, 1773-1812, 1814,
     1819-20, 1826-29, 1836-37 (DRO)
Cop M 1656-1812 (Ptd Phillimore: 1917); CMB 1612-73 from BT; M 1612-37 with
     BOYTON (DCRS/WSL); M 1813-37 (CMI); Extr CB 1612-73; M 1612-1837 (SG);
     M 1656-1812 from OR; M 1612-73 from BT (Boyd); M 1790-1812 (Pallot);
     B 1813-37 (CBI)
Cop (Mf) C 1653-1869 M 1656-1960 B 1653-1960 (RIC); CMB 1612-1812 (Mf of BT
          at DRO: CRO,CSL); M 1813-1907 (Ross); Extr C 1612-34, 1653-1811,
          1813-69 M 1612-1895 (IGI); C 1612-34, 1813-69 M 1612-1837 (SLC)
MI   (Ptd CFHS)

JACOBSTOW (Bible Christian) Eden Chapel, Eden Cross [1882 Return]

JACOBSTOW (Prim Meth) [Kelly 1856]

ST JOHN St John the Baptist [Part Roborough Hundred (Devon), part East
Hundred (Cornwall); St Germans Union] [150] United with MILLBROOK (MAKER)
OR   C 1582-1970 M 1621-1978 B 1621-1980 (CRO)
BT   CMB 1675-1736, 1741-72 (CRO); CMB 1611-73, 1737-40, 1773-1836, 1838-40,
     1844-51, 1853-57, 1859-61 (DRO)
Cop M 1612-1812 (Ts RIC,CFHS); M 1813-37 (CMI); M 1881-97 (CFHS); M 1611-74
     (SG); M 1611-73 from BT (Boyd); B 1813-37 (CBI)
Cop (Mf) CMB 1612-1812 (Mf of BT at DRO: CRO,CSL); M 1675-1875 (Ross);
          Extr C 1675-1772 from BT (IGI); C 1675-1772 from BT (SLC)
MI   (Ptd CFHS); Ch (Ptd Jewers 12-13)

ST JOHN (Wes) [1882 Return]

ST JOHN (Prim Meth) [Kelly 1856]

ST JULIOT St Julitta [Lesnewth Hundred; Camelford Union] [271]
OR   C 1657-1979 M 1646-1958 B 1663-1983 (CRO) Noted in 1831: C deficient
     1733-38, 1782-84 M deficient 1657-63, 1669-75, 1728-34, 1752-56, 1759-73
     B deficient 1665-69, 1671-74, 1778-85
BT   CMB 1679-1736, 1741-72 (CRO); CMB 1623-73, 1737-40, 1773-1812, 1838,
     1840 (DRO)
Cop M 1656-1812 (Ptd Phillimore: 1900); M 1813-37 (CMI); M 1623-1812 (SG);
     M 1656-1812 from OR; M 1623-73 from BT (Boyd); M 1800-12 (Pallot);
     M 1876-1900 (CFHS);B 1813-37 (CBI)
Cop (Mf) CMB 1623-1812 (Mf of BT at DRO: CRO,CSL); Extr C 1682-1805
          M 1656-1812 (IGI); C 1682-1805 (SLC)
MI   (Ptd CFHS)

ST JULIOT (Bible Christian) Tresparrett [1882 Return]; Meth [Kelly 1935]

ST JUST IN PENWITH St Just [Penwith Hundred; Penzance Union] [4667]
United with SANCREED
OR C 1630-1922 M 1599-1980 B 1599-1975 (CRO)
BT CMB 1679-1736, 1741-72 (CRO); CMB 1612-67, 1737-40, 1773-1813, 1815-16,
    1820-21, 1826, 1830-31, 1834, 1836-39, 1841-42, 1844-49 (DRO)
Cop M 1599-1812 (Ptd Phillimore: 1903); C 1612-1812 B 1599-1711 (Ptd parish
    magazine: CSL, Morrab); CMB 1612-73 from BT (DCRS/WSL); M 1813-37 (CRO);
    C 1612-1812 B 1599-1711 (RIC,SG); M 1813-37 (CMI); M 1599-1812 (Boyd);
    M 1800-12 (Pallot); B 1813-37 (CBI)
Cop (Mf) C 1630-1960 MB 1599-1960 (RIC); CMB 1612-1812 (Mf of BT at DRO:
        CRO,CSL); C 1612-1812 B 1599-1711 (SG); M 1813-1925 (Ross);
        Extr C 1612-1875 M 1592-1877 (IGI); C 1612-1875 M 1754-1877 (SLC)
MI Ch,cy,cemetery (Ptd CFHS)

ST JUST IN PENWITH St John the Baptist, Pendeen. Temporary chapel 1849. New
church 1850-51. Parish created from ST JUST IN PENWITH. United with MORVAH
OR C 1849-1956 M 1854-1984 B 1854-1975 (CRO)
Cop M 1876-1900 (CFHS)
Cop (Mf) C 1849-1960 MB 1854-1959 (RIC); M 1854-76 (Ross); Extr C 1800-75 ?
        (IGI); C 1800-75 ? (SLC)
MI (Ptd CFHS)

ST JUST IN PENWITH (Wes) Circuit
OR C 1856-1913 (CRO)

ST JUST IN PENWITH (Wes) Chapel Street. Erected 1833 [1882 Return]
OR B 1849-1913 (CRO)
MI (Ptd CFHS)

ST JUST IN PENWITH (Wes) Trewellard. Erected c.1815. New chapel 1833
[1882 Return]
OR C 1894-1924 (CRO)

ST JUST IN PENWITH (Wes) Bojewyan. Erected 1841 [1882 Return]

ST JUST IN PENWITH (Wes) Nanquidno. Erected 1829 [1882 Return]

ST JUST IN PENWITH (Wes) Dowran. Erected 1838 [1882 Return]

ST JUST IN PENWITH (Wes) Botallack. Erected 1844 [1882 Return]

ST JUST IN PENWITH (Wes) Pendeen [Kelly 1889]

ST JUST IN PENWITH (Bible Christian) St Just Circuit
OR C 1861-75, 1881-1907 (CRO)

ST JUST IN PENWITH (Bible Christian) Queen Street. Erected 1842
[1882 Return] Demolished

ST JUST IN PENWITH (Bible Christian) Boscaswell. Erected 1840 [1882 Return]

ST JUST IN PENWITH (Bible Christian) Cripples Hill [1882 Return]

ST JUST IN PENWITH (Bible Christian) Pendeen [Kelly 1889]

ST JUST IN PENWITH (Wes Reform U) St Just Circuit; joined Liskeard Meth
Circuit 1959
Cop C 1851-1957 (CRO,CFHS)

ST JUST IN PENWITH (Wes Reform U) Bosorne Terrace. Erected 1860

ST JUST IN PENWITH (UMFC/U Meth) Cape Cornwall Street
OR M 1919-34 (CRO)

ST JUST IN PENWITH (Free Meth) Pendeen [Kelly 1889]

ST JUST IN PENWITH (Teetotal Wes) Trewellard Cross. Erected 1843

ST JUST IN PENWITH (U Meth) Circuit
OR C 1908-33 (CRO)

ST JUST IN PENWITH (Meth) Pendnandrea

ST JUST IN PENWITH (S of F) Part of PENZANCE MM. Meeting house 1696. Burial
ground used 1659-1789

ST JUST IN ROSELAND St Just [Powder Hundred; Truro Union] [1558] United with
PHILLEIGH
OR C 1540-1970 M 1538-1978 B 1538-1955 (CRO) Noted in 1831: M deficient
    1540-99, 1602-04
BT CMB 1678-1736, 1741-72 (CRO); CMB 1597-1673, 1737-40, 1773-1820, 1822-
    23, 1825, 1827-28, 1832-34, 1836, 1838-42 (DRO)
Cop M 1538-1837 with St Mawes (Ptd Phillimore: 1935); M 1538-1837 (Ms CSL);
    C 1540-1837 B 1538-1837 (DCRS/WSL); M 1813-37 (CMI); M 1597-1673 from BT
    (Boyd); M 1790-1837 (Pallot); B 1813-37 (CBI)
Cop (Mf) C 1540-1852 M 1538-1900 B 1538-1955 (RIC); CMB 1597-1812 (Mf of BT
        at DRO: CRO,CSL); M 1538-1900 (Ross); Extr C 1540-1853 (IGI);
        C 1540-1853 (SLC)
MI (Ptd CFHS); Ch,cy (Wall,40-47, Ms SG)

ST JUST IN ROSELAND St Mawes, St Mawes. Ancient chapelry. Erected 1812; not
used until 1837; rebuilt 1883-84
OR C 1921-95 (Inc); C after 1995 registered at St Just. No MB

ST JUST IN ROSELAND (RC) Our Lady Star of the Sea and St Anthony, St Mawes
f 1937

ST JUST IN ROSELAND (Ind/Cong) St Mawes f 1784; rebuilt 1809 [Kelly 1856,
1889] Closed
OR Z 1798-1837 (PRO)
Cop ZC 1798-1837 (SG)
Cop (Mf) Z 1798-1837 (DCRS/WSL); Extr Z 1798-1837 (IGI); Z 1798-1837 (SLC)

ST JUST IN ROSELAND (Wes) Erected 1812. St Just Lane [1882 Return]

ST JUST IN ROSELAND (Wes) St Mawes Circuit
OR C 1826-37 (PRO); C 1838-1992; membership roll 1968-91 (CRO)
Cop ZC 1826-37 (SG)
Cop (Mf) C 1826-37 (DCRS/WSL); Extr ZC 1826-37 (IGI); ZC 1826-37 (SLC)

ST JUST IN ROSELAND (Wes) St Mawes. Erected 1816 [Kelly 1856]; [1882 Return]

ST JUST IN ROSELAND (Bible Christian) Salem, Trethewell. Erected 1836.
[1882 Return] Now a house

ST JUST IN ROSELAND (Bible Christian) St Mawes [1882 Return]

ST JUST IN ROSELAND (Meth) St Mawes Circuit, later called Roseland Circuit
OR C 1948-51 (CRO)

KEA or LANDEGE All Hallows [Powder Hundred; Truro Union] [3896] Chapelry in
KENWYN. Rebuilt 1802 and 1895. Separate parish 1883
OR C 1618-1983 M 1559-1858 B 1571-1915 (CRO)
BT CMB 1678-1736, 1741-72 (CRO); CMB 1607-73, 1737-40, 1773-1842 (DRO)
Cop M 1559-1812 in section wrongly headed Kenwyn (Ptd Phillimore: 1914);
     C 1618-1837 M 1559-1837 B 1571-1837 (DCRS/WSL); CMB 1753-1812 (Ms RIC);
     M 1813-37 (CMI); M 1607-74 from BT (SG); M 1599-1812 wrongly given as
     Kenwyn (Boyd); M 1800-12 (Pallot); B 1813-37 (CBI); B 1779-1800 (CRO)
     Banns 1868-1900 (CFHS)
Cop (Mf) CMB 1607-1812 (Mf of BT at DRO: CRO,CSL); M 1813-58 (Ross);
     Extr C 1607-1837 from BT (IGI); C 1607-1837 from BT (SLC)
MI (Ptd CFHS)

KEA Old Kea. Mission church attached to tower of old church. Erected 1863

KEA St Michael and All Angels, Baldhu. Parish created 1847 from KEA, KENWYN,
CHACEWATER. Erected 1848. Redundant 1987. United with KENWYN All Saints
Highertown
OR C 1847-1975 M 1848-1978 B 1848-1973 (CRO); B 1973+ (Inc, Highertown)
     No CM 1978-87: church then not in regular use, but served by KEA parish.
Cop M 1876-1900 (CFHS)
Cop (Mf) M 1848-75 (Ross)
MI (Ptd CFHS)

KEA (Ind) Baldhu [Kelly 1856]

KEA (Wes) Hugus. Erected 1830
OR C 1927-61 (CRO)

KEA (Wes) Porth. Erected 1869; [1882 Return]

KEA (Wes) Hugus, Baldhu. Erected 1830

KEA (Wes) Baldhu. Erected 1889 [1882 Return]

KEA (Wes) Penweathers. Erected 1842. Now a house

KEA (Bible Christian) Bethel, Baldhu 1842. Closed

KEA (Bible Christian) Quenchwell Chapel, Chycowling Downs [1882 Return]

KEA (S of F) Come to Good. Part of FALMOUTH MM. Moved from FEOCK 1697;
rebuilt 1707-10 [1882 Return] Closed late 19th century. Now revived
OR M 1711-59 B 1658-1775 in CORNWALL QM register RG 6/1578 (PRO);
     Z 1679-1728 M 1664-1701 B 1656-1730 in Cornwall West Division register
     RG 6/1582 (PRO); B notes 1836-38, 1850-60, 1865-66 Truro and Kea burial
     ground (CRO)
Cop Z 1664-1713 M 1701-17 B 1659-1728 extracted from MM registers 1838
     (CRO); B notes Kea and Truro Vean burial ground 1839-49 (CRO)
MI (Ptd CFHS)

KEHELLAND   *see* CAMBORNE

KELLINGTON   *see* CALLINGTON

KELLY BRAY   *see* STOKE CLIMSLAND

KENNEGGY DOWNS *see* BREAGE

KENWYN St Keyne [Powder Hundred; Truro Union] [8492] United with ST ALLEN
OR C 1662-1971 M 1662-1988 B 1670-1977 (CRO) Noted in 1831: Vols 1 and 2
  "much injured and partially illegible": C 1613-43, 1653-98 M 1559-1611,
  1653-66, 1674-92 B 1612-43, 1653-1700. Interrupted by Vol.3 "in equally
  bad condition": C 1662-79 M 1662 B 1693
BT CMB 1678-1736, 1741-72 (CRO); CMB 1608-73, 1737-40, 1773-1812, 1819,
  1822-23, 1825-27, 1829-43 (DRO)
Cop M 1607-1812 in section wrongly headed Kea (Ptd Phillimore: 1914);
  CMB 1608-36 from BT; C 1662-1837 B 1670-1837 (DCRS/WSL); CMB 1608-36
  (CRO); M 1813-37 (CMI); B 1813-37 (CBI); M 1607-74 from BT (SG);
  M 1653-1812 from OR, M 1607-73 from BT all wrongly given as Kea (Boyd);
  M 1800-12 (Pallot)
Cop (Mf) CM 1662-1959 B 1670-1959 (RIC); CMB 1608-1812 (Mf of BT at DRO:
  CRO,CSL); M 1813-1900 (Ross); Extr C 1608-36, 1662-1859 (IGI);
  C 1608-36, 1662-1859 (SLC)
MI (Ptd CFHS)

KENWYN St Paul, Chacewater. Chapelry in KENWYN. Erected 1828. Separate
parish 1829 from KENWYN and KEA. United with ST DAY, CARHARRACK (GWENNAP)
OR C 1828-1964 M 1837-1974 B 1828-1936 (CRO)
BT None
Cop M 1837-75 (CFHS); B 1813-37 (CBI)
Cop (Mf) M 1837-75 (Ross)
MI Ch,cy, cemetery (Ptd CFHS)

KENWYN St George, Carvedras. Parish created 1846 from KENWYN. Erected 1855.
Later called Truro St George. United with Kenwyn St John
OR C 1847-1964 M 1856-1984 (CRO)
Cop (Mf) M 1856-75 (Ross); M 1856-1900 (CFHS)
MI (Ptd CFHS)

KENWYN St John, Lemon Street. Erected 1827. Parish created 1865 from KENWYN.
Later called Truro St John. United with Truro St George
OR C 1852-1957 M 1865-1966 (CRO)
Cop (Mf) M 1865-75 (Ross)
MI (Ptd CFHS)

KENWYN All Saints, Highertown. Mission church erected 1889. New church 1980.
Separate parish 1984. Now united with BALDHU
OR C 1968-86 (CRO)

KENWYN (Bapt) Chacewater fl.1764-1840. Connected with FALMOUTH and TRURO
OR Z 1789-1807 in Falmouth records (CRO)

KENWYN (Wes) Chacewater. Station Road. Erected 1832 [1882 Return]
OR C 1844-1960 (CRO)

KENWYN (Wes) Short Lanes End. Erected 1840 [1882 Return]; [Kelly 1889]

KENWYN (Bible Christian) Greenbottom [1882 Return]

KENWYN (Bible Christian) Gloweth [1882 Return]

KENWYN (Bible Christian/U Meth) Creegbrawse or Cox Hill Zion
OR C 1963, 1969 (CRO)

KENWYN (Prim Meth) Chacewater, East End. Erected 1830; [1882 Return] Closed by 1980. Now a house

KENWYN (Prim Meth) Mount Horem [1882 Return]

KENWYN (Prim Meth) Criegbraws [1882 Return]

KENWYN (Prim Meth) Wheal Busy [1882 Return]

KENWYN (UMFC) Salem School [1882 Return]

KERRIS   *see* PAUL

KESTLE MILL *see* NEWLYN, EAST

ST KEVERNE St Keverne [Kerrier Hundred; Helston Union] [2437]
OR C 1581-88, 1606-1982 M 1608-50, 1654-1972 B 1605-47, 1651-1990 (CRO)
BT CMB 1679-1736, 1741-73 (CRO); CMB 1597-1673, 1737-40, 1773-1812,
      1823-24, 1835-44 (DRO)
Cop CMB strays (Ptd *'The First register at St Keverne'*: CFHSJ 23: 1982);
      M 1600-17 (I CSL); M 1608-1812 (Ptd Phillimore: 1904); CMB 1597-1704
      from BT; C 1580-1837 B 1605-1837 (DCRS/WSL); M 1813-37 (CMI);
      M 1597-1812 (SG); M 1608-1812 from OR; M 1597-1673 from BT (Boyd);
      M 1800-12 (Pallot); M 1887-1925 (CFHS); B 1813-37 (CBI)
Cop (Mf) C 1580-1959 M 1608-1959 B 1605-1959 (RIC); CMB 1597-1812 (Mf of BT
         at DRO: CRO,CSL); M 1813-75 (Ross); Extr C 1580-1875 (IGI);
         C 1580-1875 (SLC)
MI (Ptd CFHS)

ST KEVERNE St Peter, Coverack. Mission church erected 1885
MI (Ptd CFHS)

ST KEVERNE (Ind) Coverack f 1821 [*Cong.Yearbook* 1850] Closed
OR None known

ST KEVERNE (Wes) Circuit
OR C 1874-1943 (CRO)

ST KEVERNE (Wes) [1882 Return]
OR C 1843-58 (CRO)

ST KEVERNE (Wes) Coverack; Coverack Bridges [1882 Return]

ST KEVERNE (Wes) Porthoustock [1882 Return] [Kelly 1935]

ST KEVERNE (Wes) Tregarn [1882 Return]

ST KEVERNE (Wes) Grugwith [1882 Return]

ST KEVERNE (Bible Christian) Zoar. Erected 1877 [Kelly 1935]

ST KEVERNE (Bible Christian) Ponsongath. Erected 1833. A building in the possession of Alexander Pengilly [1882 Return] [Kelly 1935]

ST KEVERNE (Bible Christian) Coverack [1882 Return]

ST KEVERNE (Bible Christian) Porthallow [1882 Return] [Kelly 1935]

ST KEVERNE (Bible Christian) Crowsa Downs [1882 Return]

ST KEVERNE (UMFC/U Meth) Rosuick [1882 Return]
OR C 1873-1964 (CRO)

ST KEVERNE (Meth) Trenithon [Kelly 1935]

ST KEVERNE (S of F) Erected 1672-73; rebuilt 1731; closed 18th century.
Part of FALMOUTH MM

ST KEW or LANOWE St James the Great [Trigg Hundred; Bodmin Union] [1316]
United with ST ENDELLION, PORT ISAAC
OR C 1564-1891 M 1564-1976 B 1564-1910 (CRO)
BT CMB 1677-1736, 1741-72 (CRO); CMB 1611-73, 1737-40, 1773-1813, 1823-29,
    1831-40 (DRO)
Cop M 1564-1812 (Ptd Phillimore: 1904); CB 1564-1680 (DCRS/WSL); M 1813-37
    (CMI); M 1563-1812 (Boyd); M 1790-1812 (Pallot); B 1813-37 (CBI)
Cop (Mf) CB 1564-1960 M 1564-1959 (RIC); CMB 1611-1812 (Mf of BT at DRO:
        CRO,CSL); M 1813-1900 (Ross); Extr C 1564-1875 M 1680-1875 (IGI);
        C 1564-1875 M 1680-1875 (SLC)
MI (Ptd CFHS); Ch cy (Ptd J.Maclean *Parochial and Family History of the
    church of Lanowe alias St Kew*: 1874)

ST KEW (Wes/Wes Meth Assn) Trelill. Erected 1812 or 1817 [Kelly 1889]
MI (CFHS)

ST KEW (Bible Christian) [Kelly 1856] = ? (Wes/Bible Christian) erected 1815
[Kelly 1889]

ST KEW (Wes Meth Assn) Chapel Amble. Erected 1828; rebuilt 1840 ? [1882
Return]; Meth [Kelly 1835]
MI (Ptd CFHS)

ST KEW (Wes Meth Assn) St Kew Highway. Erected 1840 [1882 Return]; [Kelly
1889]

ST KEW (Free Meth) Pendoggett. Erected 1830 [Kelly 1889]

ST KEW (Free Meth) Trequite [Kelly 1889]

ST KEYNE St Keyna [West Hundred; Liskeard Union] [201] United with LISKEARD,
ST PINNOCK, MORVAL, BRADOC
OR C 1721-1839 Banns 1874-1994 M 1722-1949 B 1721-1978 (CRO) No earlier
    register noted in 1831. For 1538+ *see* RIC copy, below
BT CMB 1685-1736, 1741-72 (CRO); CMB 1601-73, 1737-40, 1773-1812, 1838-43
    (DRO)
Cop CMB 1612-1720 from BT; CMB 1539-1837 (DCRS/WSL); CMB 1538-1600?
    (photocopy of OR, illegible, RIC); CMB 1601-1720 with many gaps (CRO);
    M 1722-1837 (Ts with index, RIC,CRO); M 1722-1812, 1837-75 (CFHS);
    M 1813-37 (CMI); B 1813-37 (CBI); M 1601-74, 1722-1837; Extr C 1533-1609
    B 1555-1790 (SG); M 1608-73 from BT (Boyd)
Cop (Mf) CMB 1601-1812 (Mf of BT at DRO: CRO,CSL); M 1601-1875 (Ross);
        Extr C 1539-48, 1555-1837 M 1597-1837 (IGI); C 1539-48, 1555-1837
        M 1597-1837 (SLC)
MI (Ptd CFHS)

ST KEYNE (Wes) Zion. Erected 1861. Closed 1932. Now a house

ST KEYNE (Bible Christian) High Gate Chapel, near St Keyne village
[1882 Return]

ST KEYNE (Meth Reform) [Kelly 1935]

ST KEYNE (S of F) Lametton. fl.c.1679-1702. Part of East Cornwall MM

KILKHAMPTON or WEEKHAMPTON St James the Great [Stratton Hundred; Stratton
Union] [1126] United with MORWENSTOW
OR C 1539-1823 M 1539-1966 B 1537-1961 (CRO)
BT CMB 1676-1736, 1741-72 (CRO); CMB 1608-73, 1737-40, 1773-1815, 1817-36,
    1838 (DRO)
Cop M 1539-1812 (Ptd Phillimore: 1912); CMB 1539-1839 (DCRS/WSL); M 1813-37
    (CMI); M 1539-1812 (Boyd); M 1800-12 (Pallot); B 1813-37 (CBI)
Cop (Mf) CMB 1539-1960 (RIC); CMB 1608-1812 (Mf of BT at DRO: CRO,CSL);
          M 1813-99 (Ross); Extr C 1539-1875 M 1539-1876 (IGI); C 1539-1875
          M 1539-1839 (SLC)
MI (Ptd R.Dew Kilkhampton Church: c.1933); ch c.1927 (Ts SG)

KILKHAMPTON Parochial chapelry at Stebb [Kelly 1889]

KILKHAMPTON Parochial chapelry at Thurdon [Kelly 1889]

KILKHAMPTON (Wes) Circuit
OR C 1838-61 (CRO); C 1861-1927 (DRO)
Cop (Mf) Extr C 1839-60 (IGI)

KILKHAMPTON (Wes) Erected 1884 [Kelly 1889] Burial ground
MI [Ptd CFHS]

KILKHAMPTON (Wes) Thurdon. Erected 1840. Closed c.1982. Now a house

KILKHAMPTON (Bible Christian) Circuit
OR ZC 1817-36 (PRO); C 1838-95 (CRO)
Cop ZC 1817-36 (CFHS,SG)
Cop (Mf) ZC 1817-36 (DCRS/WSL); Extr ZC 1817-85 (IGI); C 1817-36 (SLC)

KILKHAMPTON (Bible Christian) Ebenezer Jubilee Chapel [1882 Return]

KILLINGTON   see CALLINGTON

KINGSAND   see MAKER

KISTLE   see ST EWE

KUGGAR   see RUAN MINOR

LADOCK St Ladoca [Powder Hundred; Truro Union] [761] United with PROBUS,
GRAMPOUND, CREED, ST ERME
OR C 1662-1964 M 1684-1970 B 1678-1934 (CRO)
BT CMB 1684-1736, 1741-72 (CRO); CMB 1609-70, 1737-40, 1773-1819, 1821,
    1824-28, 1830-42 (DRO)
Cop M 1686-1812 (Ptd Phillimore: 1915); M 1813-37 (CMI); B 1813-37 (CBI);
    C 1669-1837 M 1609-1837 B 1675-1837 (SG); C 1669-1837 (CFHS);
    M 1686-1812 from OR; M 1609-70 from BT (Boyd); M 1800-12 (Pallot)
Cop (Mf) C 1675-1959 M 1686-1959 B 1682-1959 (RIC); CMB 1609-1812 (Mf of BT
          at DRO: CRO,CSL); M 1813-1925 (Ross); Extr C 1669-1875 M 1684-1876
          (IGI); C 1669-1875 (SLC)
MI (Ptd CFHS)

LADOCK (Ind) New Mills f 1825 [1851 Religious Census]

LADOCK (Wes) Grampound Road. Erected 1866 [1882 Return]
OR C 1867-1958 (CRO)
Cop C 1867-1958 (CRO,CFHS)

LADOCK (Wes) A building, Bissick [1882 Return]

LADOCK (Prim Meth) New Mills, The London Apprentice [1882 Return]
OR C 1938-92 (CRO)

LADOCK (Bible Christian/U Meth) Ebenezer, New Mills [1882 Return]
OR C 1952-86 (CRO)

LADOCK (Bible Christian/U Meth) Scarcewater [1882 Return]
OR C 1952-86 (CRO)

LAMETTON   see ST KEYNE

LAMORRAN St Moran [Powder Hundred; Truro Union] [96] Superseded as parish
church by Holy Trinity, Tresillian. United with MERTHER, ST MICHAEL PENKIVEL
OR C 1612-1915 M 1572-1893 B 1574-1948 (CRO); M 1935+ (Inc)
BT CMB 1692-1736, 1741-72 (CRO); CMB 1621-36, 1737-40, 1773-1812, 1819,
    1821, 1824-25, 1828, 1834, 1839-41, 1843-44, 1846 (DRO)
Cop M 1572-1754, 1762-1812 Banns 1762-1812 (Ts CRO,RIC,CFHS,CSL,SG);
    M 1813-37 (CMI); M 1876-93 (CFHS); B 1813-37 (CBI); M 1621-36 from BT
    (Boyd)
Cop (Mf) C 1612-1914 M 1572-1714 B 1574-1948 (RIC); CMB 1621-1812 (Mf of BT
    at DRO: CRO,CSL); C 1699-1805 (SG); M 1572-1875, 1905-10 (Ross);
    Extr C 1612-1804, 1813-71 M 1572-1714, 1718-72 (IGI); C 1699-1701,
    1711-72 M 1572-1714 (SLC)
MI (Ptd CFHS)

LAMORRAN Holy Trinity, Tresillian, Erected 1904. Now used as parish church
OR C 1903+ M 1975+ B 1994+; photocopy of B 1954+ (Inc)

LAND'S END   see SENNEN; for (S of F) see ST HILARY and SENNEN

LANDEGE   see KEA

LANDEWEDNACK St Winwallow [Kerrier Hundred; Helston Union] [406]
OR C 1578-1964 M 1654-1971 B 1653-1928 (CRO) No earlier MB noted in 1831
BT CMB 1674-1736, 1741-72 (CRO); CMB 1598-1673, 1737-40, 1773-1843 (DRO)
Cop M 1654-1812 (Ptd Phillimore: 1917); CMB 1598-1634; C 1578-1837
    B 1653-1837 (DCRS/WSL); C 1578-1812 MB 1653-1772 (RIC); M 1813-37 (CMI);
    M 1598-1812 (SG); M 1654-1812 from OR; M 1598-1673 from BT (Boyd);
    M 1790-1812 (Pallot); M 1876-1900 (CFHS); B 1813-37 (CBI)
Cop (Mf) CMB 1598-1812 (Mf of BT at DRO: CRO,CSL); M 1813-75 (Ross);
    Extr C 1578-1837 (IGI); C 1578-1837 (SLC)
MI (Ptd CFHS)

LANDEWEDNACK (Wes) Lizard [1882 Return]

LANDEWEDNACK (UMFC/U Meth) Lizard [1882 Return]
OR C 1865-1924 (CRO)

LANDRAKE St Michael [East Hundred; St Germans Union] [872 including
St Erney] St Erney was original mother church of Landrake, but by 16th
century was united and subordinate to it. Peculiar of the Bishop of Exeter.
United with ST ERNEY and BOTUS FLEMING
OR C 1585-1981 M 1583-1978 B 1687-1987 (CRO) Noted in 1831: C 1603-1709
M 1600-1730 B 1603-1762 'very defective'
BT CMB 1612-1835, 1839-41 (DRO)
Cop M 1583-1812 (Ptd Phillimore: 1912); C 1585-1837 M 1583-1837 B 1687-1837
(DCRS/WSL); M 1583-1812 (Ts RIC,CFHS); M 1583-1812 Banns 1754-1812
including some St Erney M 1754+ (SG); M 1813-37 (CMI); M 1583-1812
(Boyd); M 1800-12 (Pallot); Banns 1837-1900 (CFHS); B 1813-37 (CBI)
Cop (Mf) CMB 1612-1812 (Mf of BT at DRO: CRO,CSL); Extr C 1585-1812
M 1583-1756 (IGI); C 1585-1812 (SLC); *and see* ST ERNEY

LANDRAKE (Wes) [1882 Return]
OR M 1903-80 (CRO)

LANDRAKE (Bible Christian) Erected 1860; closed 1970. Now a house

LANDRAKE (Prim Meth) [1882 Return]

LANDRAKE (S of F) Brightor. fl c.1696-post-1821. Part of East Cornwall MM

LANDULPH St Leonard and St Dilpe [East Hundred; St Germans Union] [570]
United with ST DOMINICK, ST MELLION, PILLATON
OR C 1540-1979 M 1540-1977 B 1540-1978 (CRO) Noted in 1831: CMB deficient
1588-1602; M deficient 1630-49
BT CMB 1675-1736, 1741-72 (CRO); CMB 1623-72, 1737-40, 1773-1815, 1817-36
(DRO)
Cop CB 1540-1837 (DCRS/WSL); M 1540-1812 Banns 1755-1812 (Ts RIC,CFHS,SG);
CB 1540-1747 (CRO); M 1813-37 (CMI); M 1541-1812 (Boyd); M 1800-12
(Pallot); B 1813-37 (CBI)
Cop (Mf) CMB 1540-1922 (RIC); CMB 1624-1812 (Mf of BT at DRO: CRO,CSL);
M 1813-75 (Ross); Extr C 1540-1872 M 1540-1837 (IGI); C 1540-1872
M 1540-1837 (SLC); M 1549-1812, 1876-1900 (CFHS)
MI (Ptd CFHS); cy n.d. (Ms SG)

LANDULPH (Bapt) Cargreen f 1837 [Kelly 1856, 1889]

LANDULPH (Presb) fl. 1672-90

LANDULPH (Wes) Erected 1874 [1882 Return]

LANDULPH (Wes) Cargreen [Kelly 1856, 1889]

LANDULPH (Bible Christian) Cargreen [Kelly 1889]

LANEAST St Gulval and St Sidwell [East Hundred; Launceston Union] [279]
United with ALTARNON, BOLVENTOR, ST CLETHER
OR CB 1700-1812 M 1700-1902 (CRO) No earlier registers in 1831
BT CMB 1676-1736, 1741-72 (CRO); CMB 1597-1673, 1737-40, 1773-1812, 1815,
1833-36, 1838 (DRO)
Cop M 1680-1812 (Ptd Phillimore: 1902); M 1813-37 (CMI); M 1597-1812 (SG);
M 1680-1812 from OR; M 1597-1673 from BT (Boyd); M 1790-1812 (Pallot);
M 1876-1900 (CFHS); B 1813-37 (CBI)
Cop (Mf) CMB 1700-1960 (RIC); CMB 1597-1812 (Mf of BT at DRO: CRO,CSL);
M 1813-75, 1903-10 (Ross); Extr C 1676-97, 1701-1885 M 1680-97,
1701-1837 (IGI); C 1676-97, 1813-75 (SLC)
MI (Ptd CFHS)

LANEAST (Wes) [1882 Return]
OR C 1935-65 (CRO)

LANEAST (Wes) Tregeare. Erected 1844 [1882 Return]
MI (Ptd CFHS)

LANEAST (Wes) Trewethen [1882 Return]

LANESLY   see GULVAL

LANGORE   see ST STEPHENS BY LAUNCESTON

LANHARGY   see LINKINHORNE

LANHERNE   see MAWGAN IN PYDAR

LANHYDROCK Sy Hydrock [Pydar Hundred; Bodmin Union] [239] United with
BODMIN, LANIVET
OR C 1561-1919 M 1559-1837 B 1558-1812 (CRO)
BT CMB 1609-41, 1814-17, 1823, 1830, 1832-37, 1844, 1846, 1871-73 (DRO)
Cop M 1559-1812 (Ptd Phillimore: 1903); M 1813-37 (CMI); CB 1558-1812 (SG);
     M 1559-1812 (Boyd); M 1790-1812 (Pallot)
Cop (Mf) CMB 1616-35 (Mf of BT at DRO: CRO,CSL); M 1813-37 (Ross);
         Extr C 1561-1812 M 1559-1812 (IGI); C 1561-1812 (SLC)
MI (Ptd CFHS)

LANIVET St Leonard [Pydar Hundred; Bodmin Union] [922] United with BODMIN,
LANHYDROCK
OR C 1656-1945 M 1670-1965 B 1670-1968 (CRO)
BT CMB 1678-1736, 1741-72 (CRO); CMB 1608-67, 1737-40, 1773-1838, 1841-43
     (DRO)
Cop M 1608-1812 (Ptd Phillimore: 1902); CMB 1608-65 from BT; C 1656-1837
     B 1670-1837 (DCRS/WSL); CMB 1608-65 from BT (Ms CRO); M 1813-37 (CMI);
     B 1813-37 (CBI); M 1608-1812 (Boyd); M 1790-1812 (Pallot)
Cop (Mf) C 1656-1959 M 1670-1959 B 1670-1957 (RIC); CMB 1608-1812 (Mf of BT
         at DRO: CRO,CSL); C 1608-1727 (SG); M 1813-1900 (Ross);
         Extr C 1656-1875 M 1670-1875 B 1670-1726 (IGI); C 1608-1754,
         1813-75 (SLC)
MI (Ptd CFHS)

LANIVET St Stephen, Nanstallon. Licensed mission room

LANIVET (Wes) Erected 1842 [1882 Return] Later a shop

LANIVET (Wes) Nanstallon [1882 Return]

LANIVET (Wes) St Lawrence [Kelly 1889]

LANIVET (Bible Christian) [Kelly 1889]

LANIVET (Bible Christian) Tretoil [Kelly 1889]

LANIVET (Bible Christian) Bethany, Nanstallon [1882 Return]

LANLIVERY St Brevita [Powder Hundred; Bodmin Union] [1687] United with
LUXULYAN
OR C c1600-1945 M c1600-1951 B c1600-1850 (CRO) see copies below
BT CMB 1678-1736, 1741-72 (CRO); CMB 1608-73, 1737-40, 1773-1838 (DRO)
Cop M 1600-1812 (Ptd Phillimore: 1906); CB 1583-1837 (DCRS/WSL); M 1813-37
    (CMI); B 1813-37 (CBI); C 1583-1812 B 1600-1812 (SG); M 1600-1812
    (Boyd); M 1800-12 (Pallot)
Cop (Mf) C 1583-1944 M 1583-1951 B 1583-1961 (RIC); CMB 1608-1812 (Mf of BT
    at DRO: CRO,CSL); M 1813-97 (Ross); Extr C 1583-1875 M 1600-1876
    (IGI); C 1583-1875 M 1600-1754 (SLC)
MI (Ptd CFHS)

LANLIVERY (Wes) [Kelly 1856]; Ebenezer Chapel, near Sweet's House
[1882 Return] [Kelly 1889]

LANLIVERY (UMFC) [1882 Return] = ? (Free Meth) Sweets House [Kelly 1889]

LANLIVERY (UMFC) Redmoor [1882 Return]

LANLIVERY (Wes) Pennant [Kelly 1889]

LANLIVERY (S of F) Milton Meeting f 1692. Rejoined Tregangeeves (ST AUSTELL)
1694
Cop Z 1590-1783 Tregangeeves and Milton meetings, extracted from MM
    registers 1838 (CRO)

LANNER   or LANNARTH see GWENNAP

LANNER MOOR   see GWENNAP

LAWNOWE   or LANHO see ST KEW

LANREATH St Marnarck [West Hundred; Liskeard Union] [651] Now with PELYNT
OR CB 1555-1992 M 1555-1993 (CRO)
BT CMB 1676-1736, 1741-72 (CRO); CMB 1597-1673, 1737-40, 1773-1812,
    1814-17, 1820, 1822-24, 1826, 1833, 1836-42 (DRO)
Cop CMB 1555-1850 (DCRS/WSL); CMB 1555-1795 (CRO); C 1741-1837 M 1730-1837
    B 1720-1837 (Ms RIC); M 1813-37 (CMI); CB 1813-37 M 1597-1668 (SG);
    M 1597-1673 from BT (Boyd); B 1813-37 (CBI)
Cop (Mf) C 1555-1910 M 1555-1837 B 1555-1890 (RIC); CMB 1597-1812 (Mf of BT
    at DRO: CRO,CSL); C 1555-1674 (SG); M 1555-1850 (Ross);
    Extr C 1555-1875 M 1837-50 (IGI); C 1555-1812 M 1837-50 (SLC)
MI (Ptd CFHS)

LANREATH (Ind) Ebenezer f 1816. Closed
OR ZC 1816-24 (PRO)
Cop ZC 1816-24 (SG)
Cop (Mf) ZC 1816-24 (DCRS/WSL); Extr ZC 1816-24 (IGI)

LANREATH (Wes) [1882 Return]
OR M 1946-90 (CRO)

LANREATH (Prim Meth) [Kelly 1856]

LANSALLOS St Ildierna [West Hundred; Liskeard Union] [884] Now with TALLAND
OR C 1600-1993 M 1600-1946 B 1600-1989 (CRO)
BT CMB 1682-1736, 1741-72 (CRO); CMB 1607-72, 1737-40, 1773-1838, 1841-44
(DRO)
Cop M 1600-1837 (CRO,RIC,SG); M 1600-1812, 1837-75 (CFHS); M 1813-37 (CMI);
B 1813-37 (CBI); M 1607-72 from BT (Boyd)
Cop (Mf) CMB 1608-1812 (Mf of BT at DRO: CRO,CSL); M 1600-1875 (Ross);
Extr C 1682-1736, 1741-1805 (IGI); C 1682-1736, 1741-1805 (SLC)
MI (Ptd CFHS)

LANSALLOS (Wes) [Kelly 1889]
MI = ? Lansallos Ebenezer and General Burial Ground (Ptd CFHS)

LANSALLOS (Bible Christian) Crumplehorn [1882 Return]

LANSALLOS (Bible Christian) A building, Trenewan [1882 Return]

LANSALLOS (Free Meth) [Kelly 1889]

LANTEGLOS BY CAMELFORD St Julitta [Lesnewth Hundred; Camelford Union] [1359]
United with ADVENT
OR C 1558-1993 M 1558-1975 B 1558-1973 (CRO)
BT CMB 1684-1736, 1741-72 (CRO); CMB 1607-65, 1737-40, 1773-1842 (DRO)
Cop M 1558-1812 (Ptd Phillimore: 1900); C 1558-1808 M 1558-1797 B 1558-1812
(CRO); M 1813-37 (CMI); M 1558-1812 (Boyd); M 1790-1812 (Pallot);
B 1813-37 (CBI)
Cop (Mf) CMB 1607-1812 (Mf of BT at DRO: CRO,CSL); Extr C 1684-1736,
1741-1805 M 1558-1812 (IGI); C 1684-1736, 1741-1805 (SLC)
MI (Ptd CFHS)

LANTEGLOS BY CAMELFORD St Thomas of Canterbury, Camelford. Borough of
Camelford in LANTEGLOS. Chapel-of-ease erected 1938

LANTEGLOS BY CAMELFORD (Wes) Camelford Circuit
OR C 1801-1932 (CRO) *see also* WADEBRIDGE

LANTEGLOS BY CAMELFORD (Wes) Chapel Street, Camelford. Erected 1810
[1882 Return] Now closed
OR B 1805-1975 (CRO)

LANTEGLOS BY CAMELFORD (Wes) Camelford and St Austell
OR ZC 1800-37 (PRO)
Cop ZC 1800-37 (SG)
Cop (Mf) ZC 1800-37 (DCRS/WSL, SG)

LANTEGLOS BY CAMELFORD (Wes, later Bible Christian) Helstone. Erected 1826

LANTEGLOS BY CAMELFORD (Wes) Trewalder. Erected 1803 = ? (UMFC) Building,
the property of William Sloggatt [1882 Return]

LANTEGLOS BY CAMELFORD (Bible Christian) Camelford Circuit *see* MICHAELSTOW

LANTEGLOS BY CAMELFORD (Bible Christian) Victoria Road. Erected 1841. Bethel
Chapel, Victoria Buildings [1882 Return]

LANTEGLOS BY CAMELFORD (UMFC) Camelford Circuit
OR C 1863-1911 (CRO)

LANTEGLOS BY CAMELFORD (UMFC/U Meth) Fore Street, Camelford. Erected 1837 =
? (UMFC) Building used as a chapel, the property of Richard Harris Burt, at
or near the Market-place, Camelford [1882 Return]
OR C 1911-34 (CRO)

LANTEGLOS BY CAMELFORD (U Meth) Camelford and Wadebridge Circuit
OR C 1925-32 (CRO)

LANTEGLOS BY CAMELFORD (Meth) Camelford and Wadebridge Circuit, Camelford
section
OR C 1934-72 (CRO)
MI Methodist (Ptd CFHS)

LANTEGLOS BY FOWEY St Wyllow [West Hundred; Liskeard Union] [1208]
OR C 1661-1944 M 1678-1967 B 1678-1936 (CRO)
BT CMB 1674-1736, 1741-72 (CRO); CMB 1607-73, 1737-40, 1773-1821, 1824-28,
    1830-47 (DRO)
Cop CB 1678-1836 M 1610-1836 (Ts with index, RIC,CFHS); M 1678-1837 (CRO);
    M 1813-37 (CMI); B 1813-37 (CBI); M 1610-74 (SG); M 1607-73 from BT
    (Boyd); M 1876-1900 (CFHS)
Cop (Mf) CMB 1610-1812 (Mf of BT at DRO: CRO,CSL); M 1678-1875 (Ross);
         Extr C 1674-1719, 1721-73 (IGI); C 1674-1719, 1721-73 (SLC)

LANTEGLOS BY FOWEY St Saviour, Polruan. Chapel-of-ease erected 1890-91
replacing ancient chapelry

LANTEGLOS BY FOWEY St John the Baptist, Bodinnick. f 1948 in converted
stable; dedicated 1949
OR for C see LANTEGLOS St Wyllow. No MB

LANTEGLOS BY FOWEY (Ind) Polruan f 1837. Closed
OR None known

LANTEGLOS BY FOWEY (Wes) West Street, Polruan [1882 Return] = ? (Wes) 1880
[Kelly 1889]
OR C 1908-64 (CRO)

LANTEGLOS BY FOWEY (Wes) Highway [1882 Return]

LANTEGLOS BY FOWEY (UMFC/U Meth) Fore Street, Polruan [1882 Return]
= ? (Free Meth) f 1879 [Kelly 1889]
OR C 1883-1957 (CRO)

LAUNCELLS St Andrew and St Swithen [Stratton Hundred; Stratton Union] [848]
United with STRATTON
OR C 1708-1989 M 1642-1977 B 1708-1988 (CRO) Noted in 1831: C 1700+
    MB 1708+ with M 1642-1700 on eight loose sheets of vellum
BT CMB 1674-1736, 1741-72 (CRO); CMB 1618-73, 1737-40, 1773-1812, 1817,
    1819-20, 1824-26, 1831-33, 1835 (DRO)
Cop M 1642-1812 (Ptd Phillimore: 1915); CMB 1618-1707 from BT; CMB 1708-39
    (DCRS/WSL); M 1813-37 (CMI); CB 1618-1708 (SG); M 1642-1812 from OR;
    M 1618-73 from BT (Boyd); M 1800-12 (Pallot); B 1813-37 (CBI)
Cop (Mf) CMB 1618-1812 (Mf of BT at DRO: CRO,CSL); M 1813-1960 (Ross);
         Extr C 1618-1836 M 1618-1720, 1723-1804, 1813-36 (IGI); C 1618-1836
         M 1618-1720, 1813-36 (SLC)
MI (Ptd CFHS); ch, cy c.1927 (Ts SG)

LAUNCELLS (Wes) Grimscott. Erected 1836 [1882 Return]
MI (Ptd CFHS)

LAUNCELLS (Bible Christian) Grimscott [1882 Return]; rebuilt 1885
[Kelly 1889]
MI (Ptd CFHS)

LAUNCESTON or DUNHEVED St Mary Magdalene [East Hundred; Launceston Union]
[2231] United with ST THOMAS BY LAUNCESTON, ST STEPHENS BY LAUNCESTON
OR C 1559-1949 M 1559-1952 B 1559-1960 (CRO)
BT CMB 1681-1736, 1741-72 (CRO); CMB 1608-73, 1737-40, 1773-1847 (DRO)
Cop M 1559-1812 (Ptd Phillimore: 1915); M 1813-37 (CMI); B 1813-37 (CBI);
    M 1559-1812 (Boyd); M 1800-12 (Pallot)
Cop (Mf) CMB 1608-1812 (Mf of BT at DRO: CRO,CSL); M 1813-37 (Ross);
         Extr C 1559-1808 M 1563-1753 (IGI); C 1681-1749, 1752-72 (SLC)
MI (Ptd CFHS)

LAUNCESTON (RC) St John Fisher and St Thomas More f 1886; later renamed St
Cuthbert Mayne

LAUNCESTON (Bapt) Madford Lane. Madford House, erected late 18th century,
purchased 1928 and converted to chapel

LAUNCESTON (Bapt) f 1876 [Bapt.Handbook 1881]; Oddfellows Hall, Western Road
[Kelly 1889]

LAUNCESTON (Presb) f Werrington [Devon] 1672. Moved to Castle Street by
1715; closed by 1772

LAUNCESTON (Ind/Cong) Castle Street f 1788; chapel (erected 1712) purchased
from Presb. [Cong.Yearbook 1850] [Kelly 1889]
OR ZC 1777-1837 (PRO); C 1874-80, 1904-36 M 1904-08 B 1874, 1904-09 (CRO)
Cop ZC 1777-1837 (SG)
Cop (Mf) ZC 1777-1837 (DCRS/WSL); Extr ZC 1777-1837 (IGI); ZC 1777-1837
         (SLC)

LAUNCESTON (Wes) Circuit
OR ZC 1794-1837 B 1823-37 (PRO); C 1837-1932 B 1819-1905 (CRO)
Cop ZC 1794-1837 B 1823-37 (SG)
Cop (Mf) ZC 1794-1837 B 1823-37 (DCRS/WSL); Extr ZC 1794-1837 (IGI);
         ZC 1794-1837 (SLC)

LAUNCESTON (Wes) f 1764 Back Lane, now Tower Street (demolished 1865)
Castle Street 1810, rebuilt 1862, 1869-70

LAUNCESTON (Bible Christian) Circuit
OR C 1841-1910 (CRO)

LAUNCESTON (Bible Christian/U Meth) Tower Street. Chapels erected 1851
(now a house) and 1897 (closed 1975, demolished) [1882 Return]
OR M 1950-72 (CRO)

LAUNCESTON (UMFC/U Meth) St Thomas Road. Erected 1840 [Kelly 1889]
OR C 1868-1909 (CRO)

LAUNCESTON (UMFC) New North Road [1882 Return]

LAUNCESTON (U Meth) Circuit
OR C 1909-26 (CRO)

LAUNCESTON (Meth) Circuit, formerly Wes
OR C 1932-51 (CRO)

LAUNCESTON (Meth) Circuit, formerly U Meth
OR C 1930-44 (CRO)

LAUNCESTON (Salvation Army) Tower Street

LAUNCESTON (S of F) f pre 1661. Part of East Cornwall MM. Meetings after
c.1703 often held at CALLINGTON
OR Z 1661-89 in CORNWALL QM register RG 6/1578; Z 1661-99 M 1660-94:
     RG 6/1249 (PRO)

LAUNCESTON Poor Law Union
OR D 1899-1950 (CRO)

LAVABE   see MABE

LAWHITTON St Michael [East Hundred; Launceston Union] [485] Peculiar of the
Bishop of Exeter. United with LEZANT. SOUTH PETHERWIN, TREWIN
OR C 1640-1947 M 1640-1982 B 1640-1952 (CRO)
BT CMB 1608-1812, 1815-16, 1818-23, 1831, 1838-39, 1841 (DRO)
Cop M 1608-14, 1623-29, 1638, 1640-1812 Banns 1754-1812 (CRO,RIC,CFHS,SG);
     M 1813-37 (CMI); M 1876-1900 (CFHS); B 1813-37 (CBI); M 1608-75 from BT
     (Boyd)
Cop (Mf) CMB 1608-1812 (Mf of BT at DRO: CRO,CSL)
MI (Ptd CFHS)

LAWHITTON (Wes) Carzantic
OR C 1935-63 (CRO)

LAWHITTON (Wes) Tregada [1882 Return]
MI (Ptd CFHS)

ST LAWRENCE   see LANIVET

LEA   see ST NEOT

LEEDSTOWN   see CROWAN

LEEK SEED CHAPEL   see ST BLAZEY

LELANT or UNY LELANT St Uny [Penwith Hundred; Penzance Union] [1602]
United with CARBIS BAY. see also ST IVES, TOWEDNACK
OR C 1669-1901 M 1716-1988 B 1716-1928; clerk's copies CMB 1827-66 (CRO)
     Noted in 1831: Vol.1 C 1684-1724. No earlier registers
BT CMB 1679-1736, 1741-72 (CRO); CMB 1607-74, 1737-40, 1773-1861 (DRO)
Cop M 1679-1812 (Ptd Phillimore: 1906); C 1684-1810 M 1679-1812 B 1716-1810
     (Ms RIC); M 1813-37 (CMI); B 1813-37 (CBI); M 1611-1812 (SG);
     M 1679-1812 from OR; M 1611-74 from BT (Boyd); M 1800-12 (Pallot)
Cop (Mf) C 1684-1958 M 1716-1958 B 1716-1960 (RIC); CMB 1611-1812 (Mf of BT
         at DRO: CRO,CSL); M 1813-1900 (Ross); Extr C 1669-1810, 1813-75
         M 1716-82 (IGI); C 1669-1810, 1813-75 M 1716-82 (SLC)
MI (Ptd CFHS)

LELANT St Anta and All Saints, Carbis Bay. Erected 1927-29. Parish created
1948 from LELANT. United with LELANT
OR CM 1929+ (Inc) No burial ground
MI (CFHS)

LELANT (Bapt) [Kelly 1856]

LELANT (Wes) Erected 1834. [1882 Return] Closed
OR C 1906-77 (CRO)

LELANT (Wes) Carbis Water. Erected 1840 [1882 Return]

LELANT (Wes) Lelant Downs. Erected 1844 [1882 Return]

LELANT (Wes) Polpeor. Erected 1831 [1882 Return]

LELANT (Wes) Ninnes [Kelly 1889]

LELANT (Prim Meth) Erected 1859; [1882 Return] Closed 1909. Village hall
OR C 1906-77 (CRO)

LELANT (Prim Meth) Balnoon [1882 Return]

LELANT (Prim Meth) Ninnes Bridge. Erected 1873 [1882 Return] [Kelly 1935]

LELANT (Meth New Conn/U Meth) Chyangwheal. Erected 1849 ?
OR C 1886-1900 (CRO)

LELANT (Meth New Conn) Carbis Bay [Kelly 1889]

LELANT (Meth New Conn) Lelant Down [Kelly 1889]

LERRYN   village in ST VEEP and ST WINNOW

LESNEWTH St Michael and All Angels [Lesnewth Hundred; Camelford Union] [127]
OR C 1577-1979 M 1569-1932 B c.1563-1980 (CRO)
BT CMB 1676-1735, 1741-72 (CRO); CMB 1609-73, 1737-40, 1773-1829, 1831-33,
    1835 (DRO)
Cop M 1569-1812 (Ptd Phillimore: 1909); C 157[7]-1848 M 1569-1837
    B 156[4]-1844 (Ts RIC,CFHS); M 1813-37 (CMI); B 1813-37 (CBI);
    M 1569-1812 (Boyd); M 1876-1900 (CFHS)
Cop (Mf) CMB 1608-1812 (Mf of BT at DRO: CRO,CSL); M 1813-75 (Ross);
        Extr C 1682-1805 M 1569-1811 (IGI); C 1682-1805 (SLC)
MI (Ptd CFHS)

LESNEWTH (Bible Christian) Freworwall f 1838 [Kelly 1897]

ST LEVAN St Levan [Penwith Hundred; Penzance Union] [515] Formerly in
ST BURYAN parish: Royal Peculiar. Separate parish 1850. Now with ST BURYAN,
SENNEN
OR C 1700-1870 M 1700-1981 B 1700-1973 (CRO) No earlier registers noted in
    1831. see ST BURYAN
BT CMB 1694-1847 (CRO) None at Exeter
Cop M 1694-1812 (Ptd Phillimore: 1903); CMB 1694-99 from BT; CB 1700-1812
    (DCRS/WSL, CSL, Morrab); C 1699-1812 B 1700-1812 (Ms RIC); M 1813-37
    (CMI); C 1694-1812 B 1700-1812 (SG); M 1694-1812 (Boyd); M 1790-1812
    (Pallot); M 1832-1910 (CFHS); B 1813-37 (CBI)
Cop (Mf) CMB 1694-1959 (RIC); M 1813-1900 (Ross); Extr C 1694-1875
        M 1694-1812 (IGI); C 1694-1875 (SLC)
MI (Ptd CFHS)

ST LEVAN (Bapt) f post-1800

ST LEVAN (Wes) Sowah. Erected pre-1800. fl c.1851

ST LEVAN (Wes)
OR C 1875-1969 (CRO)

ST LEVAN (Wes) Treen. Erected 1834 [1882 Return]

ST LEVAN (Wes) Trethewey. Erected 1868

ST LEVAN (Wes) Chygnidden [1882 Return]

ST LEVAN (Wes) Bottoms. Erected 1831. fl c.1851

ST LEVAN (Prim Meth) [Kelly 1856]

LEWANNICK St Martin [East Hundred; Launceston Union] [643] United with NORTH
HILL
OR C 1660-1977 M 1755-1992 B 1738-1895 (CRO) Noted in 1831: C deficient
    1662-71. No earlier MB registers
BT CMB 1675-1736, 1741-72 (CRO); CMB 1597-1673, 1737-40, 1773-1812, 1814,
    1816-17, 1821-30, 1832-33, 1835, 1837-39 (DRO)
Cop M 1675-1812 (Ptd Phillimore: 1909); M 1813-37 (CMI); B 1813-37 (CBI);
    C 1600-1812 M 1597-1812 B 1738-1812 (SG); M 1675-1812 from OR;
    M 1597-1673 from BT (Boyd); M 1800-12 (Pallot); M 1877-1900 (CFHS)
Cop (Mf) CMB 1597-1812 (Mf of BT at DRO: CRO,CSL); Extr C 1660-1812 (IGI);
    C 1660-1812 (SLC)
MI (Ptd CFHS)

LEWANNICK (Bapt) Trebartha f post-1800

LEWANNICK (Ind) Polyphant f 1817. Closed by 1850
OR None known

LEWANNICK (Wes) Polyphant
OR B 1890-1986 (CRO)
MI (Ptd CFHS)

LEWANNICK (Wes) Trevadlock Cross. Erected 1810. Rebuilt 1849 [1882 Return]
OR C 1845-1992 (CRO)

LEWANNICK (Bible Christian) [Kelly 1856]

LEZANT St Briochus [East Hundred; Launceston Union] [841] Peculiar of the
Bishop of Exeter. United with LAWHITTON, SOUTH PETHERWIN, TREWEN
OR CMB 1539-1981 (CRO)
BT CMB 1608-1845, 1847-51 (DRO)
Cop M 1539-1812 (Ptd Phillimore: 1907); M 1813-37 (CMI); B 1813-37 (CBI);
    CB 1539-1812 (SG); M 1539-1812 (Boyd); M 1790-1812 (Pallot); M 1876-1900
    (CFHS)
Cop (Mf) CMB 1609-1812 (Mf of BT at DRO: CRO,CSL); M 1539-1812 (SG);
    Extr C 1539-1812 (IGI); C 1539-1812 (SLC)
MI (Ptd CFHS)

LEZANT Trecarrel. Medieval chapel of manor house of Trecarrel family

LEZANT (Bapt) [Kelly 1889]

LEZANT (Wes) [Kelly 1889]

LEZANT (Wes) Trebullett f 1819 [Kelly 1889, 1935]
OR C 1945-77 (CRO)
MI (Ptd CFHS)

LEZANT (Reform Wes) [Kelly 1889]

LEZANT (UMFC/U Meth) Treburley [1882 Return] [Kelly 1935]
OR C 1903-81 (CRO)
MI (Ptd CFHS)

LEZANT (UMFC) Rezare [1882 Return]

LEZANT (Meth) Tregada [Kelly 1889, 1935]

LINKINHORNE St Mellor [East Hundred; Liskeard Union] [1159]
OR C 1576-1910 M 1576-1966 B 1576-1894 (CRO) Noted in 1831: CMB 1616+
BT CMB 1675-1735, 1741-72 (CRO); CMB 1611-72, 1737-40, 1773-1813, 1817-19,
   1823-29, 1831-37 (DRO)
Cop M 1576-1812 (Ptd Phillimore: 1910); M 1813-37 (CMI); B 1813-37 (CBI);
   C 1576-1812 B 1641-1812 (SG); M 1576-1812 (Boyd); M 1790-1812 (Pallot)
Cop (Mf) C 1576-1908 M 1576-1902 B 1576-1894 (RIC); CMB 1611-1812 (Mf of BT
      at DRO: CRO,CSL); M 1813-1925 (Ross); Extr C 1576-1876 M 1570-1876
      (IGI); C 1576-1876 M 1570-1876 (SLC)
MI (Ptd CFHS)

LINKINHORNE St Paul, Upton Cross. Chapel-of-ease erected 1887
MI (Ptd CFHS)

LINKINHORNE (Bapt} Plusha Bridge [Kelly 1889]

LINKINHORNE (Wes) Lanhargy [1882 Return]
OR C 1871-1956 B 1912-85 (CRO)
MI (Ptd CFHS)

LINKINHORNE (Wes) Rilla Mill. Erected 1846 [1882 Return]
OR C 1841-80 (CRO)
MI (Ptd CFHS)

LINKINHORNE (Wes) Upton Cross [1882 Return]
OR C 1933-58 (CRO)

LINKINHORNE (Prim Meth, then Wes) Cheeswring
OR C 1969-78 (CRO)

LINKINHORNE (Prim Meth) Henwood [1882 Return]

LINKINHORNE (UMFC/U Meth) Darley
OR C 1837-1907 (CRO)

LINKINHORNE (Free Meth) Railway [Kelly 1889]

LINKINHORNE (Free Meth) Cradon [Kelly 1889]

LISKEARD St Martin [West Hundred; Liskeard Union] [1189] United with
ST KEYNE, ST PINNOCK, MORVAL, BRADOC
OR C 1539-1911 M 1539-1958 B 1539-1940 (CRO)
BT CMB 1691-1736, 1741-72 (CRO); CMB 1597-1665, 1737-40, 1773-1812,
    1814-17, 1819-29, 1831, 1833-35 (DRO)
Cop C 1669-1830 M 1539-1837 B 1669-1900 (Ts with index, CRO,RIC,CFHS);
    C 1830-83 Banns 1946-69 M 1837-63 B 1838-83 (CRO); M 1813-37 (CMI);
    M 1813-30 (Ts WSL); M 1597-1638 (SG); M 1597-1665 from BT (Boyd);
    B 1813-37 (CBI)
Cop (Mf) CMB 1599-1813 (Mf of BT at DRO: CRO,CSL); M 1538-1876 (Ross);
    Extr C 1691-1773 (IGI); C 1691-1773 (SLC)
MI Cemetery (CFHS)

LISKEARD St Peter, Dobwalls. Chapel-of-ease erected 1839

LISKEARD (RC) Our Lady and St Neot, West Street f 1840. Served 1840-56 from
Trelawne or Sclerder (see PELYNT, TALLAND)
OR CDB 1856+ M 1875+ Confirmations 1858+ (Inc)

LISKEARD (Bapt) f 1876 [Bapt.Handbook 1881] Barn Street [Kelly 1889]

LISKEARD (Presb/Ind/Cong) f.1701 [Cong.Yearbook 1850] = ? Congregational
Chapel (Ind) Dean Street erected 1865 [1882 Return]
OR C 1809-43 (CRO)

LISKEARD (Wes) Circuit
OR ZC 1806-37 (PRO); C 1834-1936 (CRO)
Cop ZC 1806-37 (SG)
Cop (Mf) ZC 1806-37 (DCRS/WSL); Extr ZC 1806-37 (IGI); ZC 1806-37 (SLC)

LISKEARD (Wes) Dobwalls. Erected 1859; [1882 Return]
Cop B 1859-1997 (CFHS)

LISKEARD (Wes) Barn Street. Erected 1841. Burnt down. Rebuilt 1846
[1882 Return]

LISKEARD (Wes) Trevelmond [1882 Return]; Meth [Kelly 1935]

LISKEARD (Wes) Bye Lane End [Kelly 1889]

LISKEARD (Prim Meth) Circuit. Ceased 1924, chapels joining North Hill
Wesleyan Circuit
OR C 1856-1924 (CRO); see also CALLINGTON

LISKEARD (Prim Meth) Castle Hill [Kelly 1889]

LISKEARD (Bible Christian) Circuit. Known as St Neot Circuit until 1846.
Continued as U Meth, below
OR C 1837-1905 (CRO)

LISKEARD (Bible Christian) Trewidland. Erected 1835 [1882 Return]

LISKEARD (Bible Christian) Barn Street. Erected 1858 [1882 Return];
[Kelly 1889]

LISKEARD (Bible Christian) Dobwalls [1882 Return]

LISKEARD (Wes Reform U) Circuit
OR C 1934-58 (CRO)

LISKEARD (Wes Meth Assn) Greenbank Road. Erected 1838; United Free Church [1882 Return]

LISKEARD (UMFC) Circuit
OR C 1902-05 (CRO)

LISKEARD (UMFC/U Meth) Greenbank
OR C 1872-1909 (CRO)

LISKEARD (UMFC) Moorswater [Kelly 1889]

LISKEARD (U Meth, formerly Bible Christian) Circuit
OR C 1905-32 (CRO)

LISKEARD (Meth) Circuit, formerly Wes
OR C 1932-48 (CRO)

LISKEARD (Meth) Circuit, formerly U Meth
OR C 1932-70 (CRO)

LISKEARD (Meth) Circuit, Dobwalls section
OR C 1933-43 (CRO)

LISKEARD (Meth) Circuit
OR C 1974-80 (CRO)

LISKEARD (Prot Diss) Union Chapel [1882 Return]

LISKEARD (Free Church) Trewidland [Kelly 1889]

LISKEARD (Salvation Army) Church Street

LISKEARD (S of F) Monthly Meeting f 1668
OR Z 1723-73 M 1659-1771 B 1659-90 in Cornwall QM register RG 6/1578;
   Z 1647-1794 M 1659-1792 B 1659-1796 in Cornwall East Division register
   RG 6/1339; Z 1659-98 B 1659-89: RG6/1498 (PRO)
Cop Z 1659-1771 B 1659-90 in 1828 copy of old register book of Cornwall QM;
   Z 1660-1792 M 1660-1792 B 1676-1796 extracted from MM registers 1838
   (CRO)

LISKEARD (S of F) Liskeard Meeting f c.1659. Part of St Austell/East
Cornwall MM [1882 Return] Meeting houses in Liskeard: Pound Street erected
1796 [Kelly 1889] and at Halbathic. Currently [1998] meeting at Public
Rooms, West Street
OR Z M 1798-1835 B 1686-1760 in EAST CORNWALL MM register RG 6/185,1314
   (PRO); Z 1659-1746 M 1659-1734 B 1659-1738: RG 6/1249 (PRO); Halbathic
   B 1865-66; B notes 1838-48; B notes with D certs 1848-1904 (CRO)
Cop (Mf) M 1659-1837 (Ross)
MI (Ptd CFHS)

LISKEARD Nonconformist cemetery, Barn Street [Kelly 1897]

LITTLE **BOSULLOW**   *see* MADRON

LITTLE **COLAN**   *see* COLAN

LITTLE **PETHERICK**   *see* PETHERICK, LITTLE

LIZARD   *see* LANDEWEDNACK

LIZARDTOWN   see LANDEWEDNACK

LONDON APPRENTICE   see ST AUSTELL

LONGCOE   see ST MARTIN BY LOOE

LONGROCK   see LUDGVAN

LONGSTONE   see ST MABYN

LOOE St Mary, East Looe [West Hundred; Liskeard Union] [865] Chapelry in
ST MARTIN. United 1845 with West Looe
OR C 1709-1894 M 1850-1982 (CRO); see also ST MARTIN
BT see ST MARTIN
Cop C 1709-1807 (Ts CRO,RIC,CSL,CFHS,SG); M 1879-1900 (CFHS)
Cop (Mf) CMB 1670-73 (Mf of BT at DRO: CRO,CSL); M 1670-73, 1850-69 (Ross)

LOOE St Nicholas, West Looe, sometimes called Portbyan or Portbighan
[West Hundred; Liskeard Union] [Borough 593] Part of TALLAND. United 1845
with East Looe. United with ST MARTIN
BT CMB 1820 (DRO)

LOOE (RC) Our Lady and St Nicholas, West Looe f 1923

LOOE (Cong) Riverside United, Quay Street, West Looe f 1777 [1882 Return]
OR ZC 1787-1836 B 1819-36 (PRO); C 1893-1966 M 1893-1984 B 1819-1919,
    1928-66 (CRO)
Cop ZC 1787-1836 B 1819-36 (SG); B 1819-54; names from headstones 1801-86
    (CFHS)
Cop (Mf) ZC 1787-1836 B 1819-36 (DCRS/WSL); Extr ZC 1787-1836 (IGI);
         ZC 1787-1836 (SLC)

LOOE (Wes) Circuit
OR C 1871-93, 1899-1940 (CRO)

LOOE (Wes) East Looe f 1814 [1882 Return]
OR ZC 1815-36 (PRO); M 1941-65 (CRO)
Cop ZC 1815-36 (SG)
Cop (Mf) ZC 1815-26 (DCRS/WSL); Extr ZC 1815-36 (IGI); ZC 1815-36 (SLC)

LOOE (Bible Christian) Circuit
OR C 1848-1935 (CRO)

LOOE (Bible Christian/U Meth) West Looe. Erected 1846; = ? (UMFC) Tower
Hill, West Looe [1882 Return]
OR M 1946-64 (CRO)

LOOE (Free Meth) East Looe [Kelly 1889]

LOOE (Meth) Circuit
OR C 1941-70 (CRO)

LOOE (S of F) East Looe f 1690 from DULOE. Existed 1836. Part of EAST
CORNWALL MM
OR Z 1727-73 M 1659-1771 in CORNWALL QM register RG 6/1578; M 1798-1835 in
    Cornwall East Division register RG 6/185 (PRO); B notes 1839-40, 1849
    (CRO)

LOSTWITHIEL St Bartholomew [Powder Hundred; Bodmin Union] [1548] United with
ST WINNOW, ST NECTAN'S CHAPEL, ST VEEP, BOCONNOC
OR C 1609-1947 M 1609-1980 B 1609-1949 (CRO)
BT CMB 1678-1736, 1741-71 (CRO); CMB 1616-36, 1737-40, 1773-1815, 1820-22,
   1824, 1828-30, 1832-36, 1851-71 (DRO)
Cop M 1609-1812 (Ptd Phillimore: 1905); CMB 1609-1837 (DCRS/WSL); M 1813-37
   (CMI); M 1609-1812 (Boyd); M 1790-1812 (Pallot); M 1876-1900 (CFHS);
   B 1813-37 (CBI)
Cop (Mf) CMB 1616-1812 (Mf of BT at DRO: CRO,CSL); M 1813-75 (Ross);
         Extr CM 1609-1837 (IGI); CM 1609-1837 (SLC)
MI Ch, cy, Castle Hill Cemetery, Restormel Road Cemetery (Ptd CFHS)

LOSTWITHIEL (Presb) fl 1672-90

LOSTWITHIEL (Ind/Cong) Restormel Road. f 1810. Closed 1899
OR ZC 1812-37 (PRO)
Cop ZC 1812-37 (SG)
Cop (Mf) ZC 1812-37 (DCRS/WSL); Extr ZC 1812-37 (IGI); ZC 1912-37 (SLC)

LOSTWITHIEL (Wes) Bodmin Circuit: Lostwithiel section
OR C 1881-1932 (CRO)

LOSTWITHIEL (Wes) Restormel Rood. Erected 1880 [Kelly 1889]
OR M 1900-59 (CRO)

LOSTWITHIEL (Prim Meth) Knight's Long Room [1882 Return]

LOSTWITHIEL (UMFC) Lostwithiel and Bodmin Circuit
OR C 1866-1907 (CRO)

LOSTWITHIEL (U Meth) Lostwithiel and Bodmin Circuit
OR C 1907-33 (CRO)

LOSTWITHIEL (UMFC/U Meth) Lostwithiel Bank [1882 Return]
OR M 1901-86 (CRO)

LOSTWITHIEL (Wes Meth Ass) [1882 Return]

LOSTWITHIEL (UMFC) Albert Terrace. Erected 1835 [Kelly 1889]

LOSTWITHIEL (Meth) Circuit
OR *see* BODMIN

LOWER BOLENOWE   *see* CAMBORNE

LOWER LANKE   *see* ST BREWARD

LUCKETT   *see* STOKE CLIMSLAND

LUDGVAN St Ludgvan and St Paul [Penwith Hundred; Penzance Union] [2322]
OR C 1564-1974 M 1563-1980 B 1563-1959 (CRO)
BT CMB 1674-1736, 1741-72 (CRO); CMB 1608-73, 1737-40, 1773-1846, 1849-53
   (DRO)
Cop M 1563-1812 (Ptd Phillimore: 1903); C 1712-97, 1813-40 MB 1813-37
   (Ms RIC); M 1813-37 (CMI); CB 1813-37 (CRO,SG); M 1563-1812 (Boyd);
   B 1813-37 (CBI)

LUDGVAN cont.
Cop (Mf) C 1564-1959 M 1563-1959 B 1563-1960 (RIC); CMB 1608-1812 (Mf of BT
          at DRO: CRO,CSL); M 1813-1925 (Ross); Extr C 1564-1875 M 1563-1875
          (IGI); C 1564-1711, 1805-75 (SLC)
MI   (Ptd CFHS)

LUDGVAN (Wes) Canons Town. f 1843 [1882 Return]
OR   C 1855-91 (CRO)

LUDGVAN (Wes) Crowlas f 1834 [1882 Return]
MI   [Ptd CFHS]

LUDGVAN (Wes) White Cross. Erected 1810 [Kelly 1889]

LUDGVAN (Wes) Longrock [Kelly 1889]

LUDGVAN (Wes) Trenowin. Erected 1847 [Kelly 1889]

LUDGVAN (Bible Christian) Tregurthen. Erected 1842 [Kelly 1889]

LUDGVAN (Wes) Newtown. Erected 1837 fl c.1851

LUDGVAN (Wes) Truthwell. Erected 1841 fl c.1851

LUDGVAN (Prim Meth) Cockwells [1882 Return] [Kelly 1889]

LUDGVAN (Prim Meth) Castel an Dinas [Kelly 1889]

LUXULYAN St Cyrus and St Julitta [Powder Hundred; Bodmin Union] [1288]
United with LANLIVERY
OR   C 1594-1881 M 1594-1902 B 1594-1898 (CRO)
BT   CMB 1682-1736, 1741-72 (CRO); CMB 1610-73, 1737-40, 1773-1812, 1814,
          1817-18, 1823, 1825-29, 1838-51 (DRO)
Cop M 1594-1812 (Ptd Phillimore: 1905); CB 1594-1837 (DCRS/WSL); B 1594-1812
          (CRO); B 1910-60 (Ms RIC); M 1813-37 (CMI); B 1813-37 (CBI);
          CB 1594-1812 (SG); M 1594-1812 (Boyd); M 1790-1812 (Pallot); M 1876-1900
          (CFHS)
Cop (Mf) C 1594-1881 M 1594-1837 B 1594-1895 (RIC); CMB 1610-1812 (Mf of BT
          at DRO: CRO,CSL); C 1594-1711 (SG); M 1813-75 (Ross);
          Extr C 1594-1875 (IGI); C 1594-1875 (SLC)
MI   (Ptd CFHS)

LUXULYAN (Wes) [Kelly 1856]; a building, Rosemellen [1882 Return]

LUXULYAN (Wes) Gunwen, Lower Town [1882 Return]
MI   (Ptd CFHS)

LUXULYAN (Prim Meth) Mrs Roach's schoolroom, Churchtown [1882 Return]

LUXULYAN (Bible Christian) Circuit *see* BODMIN

LUXULYAN (Bible Christian) f 1820. Rebuilt 1846. Bodmin Common [1882 Return]
OR   ZC 1820-37 (PRO)
Cop ZC 1820-37 (SG)
Cop (Mf) ZC 1820-37 (DCRS/WSL); Extr ZC 1820-37 (IGI); ZC 1820-37 (SLC)

MABE or LAVABE St Laudus [Kerrier Hundred; Falmouth Union] [512] Chapelry in
MYLOR. Peculiar of the Bishop of Exeter. Separate parish 1868
OR C 1654-1904 M 1654-1975 B 1654-1960 (CRO)
BT CMB 1610-1813, 1816, 1818-22, 1835-36, 1838-39, 1841-44, 1846-66 (DRO)
Cop CMB 1654-1837 (DCRS/WSL); M 1650-1812 (Ms RIC); M 1657-1812
      Banns 1762-96 (Morrab); M 1813-37 (CMI); B 1813-37 (CBI); M 1611-1812
      (SG); M 1610-75 from BT (Boyd)
Cop (Mf) C 1564-1959 M 1657-1959 B 1653-1959 (RIC); CMB 1610-1812 (Mf of BT
      at DRO: CRO,CSL); M 1657-1925 (Ross); Extr C 1653-1742, 1757-1875
      (IGI); C 1653-1742, 1813-75 (SLC)
MI (Ptd CFHS)

MABE St Michael and All Angels, Ponsanooth, *see* ST GLUVIAS

MABE (Wes) Halvosso [1882 Return]
OR C 1937-82 (CRO)

MABE (Wes) Burnt House [1882 Return]

MABE (Wes) Trenoweth [Kelly 1889]

MABE (Meth) Edgecumbe
MI (Ptd CFHS)

MABE (S of F) f 1696, part of FALMOUTH MM

ST MABYN St Mabena [Trigg Hundred; Bodmin Union] [793] United with ST TUDY,
MICHAELSTOW
OR C 1562-1846 M 1562-1983 B 1562-1890 (CRO)
BT CMB 1683-1736, 1741-72 (CRO); CMB 1608-71, 1737-40, 1773-1842 (DRO)
Cop M 1562-1812 (Ptd Phillimore: 1902); C 1562-1846 M 1562-1837 B 1562-1890
      (RIC,CRO); M 1813-37 (CMI); CB 1652-1812 (SG); M 1562-1812 (Boyd);
      M 1790-1812 (Pallot); M 1837-1900 (CFHS); B 1813-37 (CBI)
Cop (Mf) C 1562-1846 M 1562-1837 B 1562-1890 (Mf of transcript, RIC);
      CMB 1608-1812 (Mf of BT at DRO: CRO,CSL); M 1813-75 (Ross);
      Extr CM 1562-1812 (IGI); C 1562-1812 (SLC)
MI (Ptd CFHS)

ST MABYN (Presb) Heligan fl 1662-90

ST MABYN (Wes) Longstone f 1875 [1882 Return] [Kelly 1889]

ST MABYN (Wes/Free Meth) f 1820 [Kelly 1897]

ST MABYN (Wes Meth Assn/UMFC/U Meth) f 1851 ?; UMFC [1882 return]
OR C 1905-71 (CRO)

MADRON St Maddern [Penwith Hundred; Penzance Union] [2058]
see also PENZANCE, MORVAH, NEWLYN
OR C 1592-1888 M 1577-1870 B 1577-1877 (CRO)
BT CMB 1674-1736, 1741-72 (CRO); CMB 1597-1673, 1738-39, 1772-1821, 1823-
      26, 1830, 1832-33, 1836-37, 1839-46 (DRO)
Cop C 1592-1725 M 1577-1678 B 1577-1681 (Ptd G.Millett *The first book of the
      parish registers of Madron*: 1877); M 1674-1812 (Ptd Phillimore: 1907);
      C 1737-88 B 1737-97 (Ms RIC); M 1813-37 (CMI); C 1592-1687, 1700-1810
      M 1577-1837 B 1577-1681, 1700-1810 (SG); M 1577-1812 (Boyd); M 1790-1812
      (Pallot); M 1577-1884 (CFHS); B 1813-37 (CBI)

MADRON cont.
Cop (Mf) C 1591-1959 MB 1577-1959 (RIC); CMB 1597-1799 (Mf of BT at DRO:
          CRO,CSL); M 1577-1678, 1700-1876 (SG); M 1814-1909 (Ross);
          Extr C 1577-1875 M 1577-1695, 1700-1876 (IGI); C 1577-1787
          M 1577-1678 (SLC)
MI (Ptd Millett, above); (Ptd CFHS); cemetery (CFHS)

MADRON St Thomas, Heamoor. Mission church erected 1892

MADRON (Wes) Tregavara. Erected 1822
OR C 1892-1950 (CRO)

MADRON (Wes) Wesley Rock ? Heamoor. Erected 1844 ?
MI (Ptd CFHS)

MADRON (Wes) Trezelah. Erected 1842[1882 Return]

MADRON (Wes) Little Bosullow. Erected 1845 [1882 Return]

MADRON (Wes) Boswarthen. Erected 1842 [1882 Return]

MADRON (Wes) Church Village. Erected 1800

MADRON (Prim Meth) Church Town. fl.c.1851 [1882 Return]

MADRON (Bible Christian) Heamoor [Kelly 1889]

MADRON (Bible Christian) Polminnick. f.c.1819. fl c.1851

MADRON (UMFC) New Mill [1882 Return]

MADRON (Meth) Carnkie. Erected 1900

MAKER St Mary and St Julian [Part East Hundred (Cornwall), part Roborough
Hundred (Devon) until 1844; St Germans Union] [1545 in Cornwall portion]
United with RAME
OR C 1630-1843 M 1630-1837 B 1630-1849 (CRO)
BT CMB 1676-1735, 1741-72 (CRO); CMB 1607-73, 1737-40, 1773-1816, 1818-21,
    1823-24, 1836-30, 1833-74 (DRO)
Cop CMB 1653-1849 (DCRS/WSL); CM 1630-1724 B 1630-65, 1715-25
    (Ts RIC,CFHS); M 1813-37 (CMI); B 1813-37 (CBI); CMB 1630-1837 (I, CRO);
    C 1630-1843 M 1607-1837 B 1630-1849 (SG); M 1607-73 from BT (Boyd)
Cop (Mf) CMB 1607-1812 (Mf of BT at DRO: CRO,CSL); M 1630-1837 (Ross);
        Extr C 1630-1812 M 1630-1837 (IGI); C 1630-1812 M 1630-1750 (SLC)
MI Ch (Ptd Jewers 183-202)

MAKER All Saints, Millbrook. Chapelry in MAKER. Separate parish 1869.
Erected 1895. United with ST JOHN
OR C 1867-1958 M 1869-1975 B 1870-1968 (CRO)
Cop M 1876-1900 (CFHS)
MI (Ptd CFHS)

MAKER (Bapt) West Street, Milbrook f 1821 [*Bapt. Manual* 1850] Demolished
1960s

MAKER (Ind Bapt) Bethany, Millbrook [1882 Return]

MAKER (Wes) Kingsand [Kelly 1856]; [1882 Return]
OR C 1842-1967 (Plymouth Record Office, Devon)

MAKER (Wes) New Street, Millbrook. Erected 1874 [1882 Return]
OR C 1855-1907 M 1907-84 (Plymouth Record Office, Devon)

MAKER (S of F) Millbrook f by 1668. Part of CORNWALL Eastern division.
transferred to Western Division of DEVON MM; joined to Plymouth meeting
OR Z 1776-93 in Devon QM register RG 6/492 (PRO)

MALPAS   see ST CLEMENT

MANACCAN or MINSTER St Manaccus and St Dunstan [Kerrier Hundred; Helston
Union] [654] United with ST ANTHONY IN MENEAGE, ST MARTIN IN MENEAGE
OR C 1624-1981 M 1633-1995 B 1638-1981 (CRO)
BT CMB 1679-1736, 1741-72 (CRO); CMB 1597-1673, 1737-40, 1773-1833, 1835-
    36, 1838 (DRO)
Cop M 1633-1812 (Ptd Phillimore: 1904); CMB 1597-1679 from BT; C 1624-1837
    B 1638-1837 (DCRS/WSL); CMB 1597-1763 from BT (CRO); M 1633-1753
    incomplete; M 1614-73 from BT (CFHS); M 1813-37 (CMI); B 1813-37 (CBI);
    M 1597-1812 (SG); M 1633-1812 from OR; M 1597-1673 from BT (Boyd);
    M 1800-12 (Pallot): M 1837-1900 (CFHS)
Cop (Mf) CB 1638-1959 M 1633-1956 (RIC); CMB 1597-1812 (Mf of BT at DRO:
    CRO,CSL); M 1813-1900 (Ross); Extr C 1597-1875 M 1633-1895 (IGI);
    C 1597-1812 M 1633-1875 (SLC)
MI (CFHS)

MANACCAN (Wes) Highlanes [1882 Return]
OR C 1842-74 (CRO)

MANHAY   see WENDRON

MARAZION   see ST HILARY

MARHAMCHURCH St Marwenne [Stratton Hundred; Stratton Union] [659] Now with
BUDE HAVEN
OR C 1558-1866 M 1558-1977 B 1558-1890 (CRO)
BT CMB 1681-1736, 1741-72 (CRO); CMB 1612-73, 1737-40, 1773-1842 (DRO)
Cop M 1558-1812 (Ptd Phillimore: 1915); CB 1558-1837 (DCRS/WSL); M 1813-37
    (CMI); M 1558-1812 (Boyd); M 1800-12 (Pallot); B 1813-37 (CBI)
Cop (Mf) CMB 1612-1812 (Mf of BT at DRO: CRO,CSL); M 1813-37 (Ross);
        Extr C 1559-1837 M 1813-37 from BT (IGI); C 1559-1837 M 1813-37
        from BT (SLC)
MI (Ptd CFHS); ch, cy 1923 (Ts SG)

MARHAMCHURCH (Wes) [Kelly 1856] [1882 Return] [Kelly 1889]

MARHAMCHURCH (Wes) Tetson [Kelly 1889]

MARHAMCHURCH (Wes Meth Assn) [Kelly 1856]

MARHAMCHURCH (Bible Christian) [Kelly 1856]; [1882 Return]

MARHAMCHURCH (UMFC) [1882 Return]

MARKET JEW   see MARAZION (ST HILARY)

NARSH GATE   see ST IVE

ST MARTIN   see SCILLY ISLES

ST MARTIN BY LOOE St Martin [West Hundred; Liskeard Union] [455] United with
EAST LOOE, WEST LOOE
<u>OR</u> C 1653-1968 M 1653-1974 B 1653-1957 (CRO) Noted in 1831: Vol.4 "Bap.at
     East Looe Chapel 1710-1807"
<u>BT</u> CMB 1676-1736, 1741-72 (CRO); CMB 1597-1673, 1737-40, 1773-1812, 1814-
     20, 1822-32 (DRO)
<u>Cop</u> CMB 1597-1836 from BT; CMB 1653-1837 (DCRS/WSL); M 1813-37 (CRO);
     M 1813-37 (CMI); M 1597-1836 (CSL); M 1597-1673 (SG); M 1597-1673 from
     BT (Boyd); B 1813-37 (CBI)
<u>Cop (Mf)</u> CMB 1597-1812 (Mf of BT at DRO: CRO,CSL); M 1597-1875 (Ross);
          Extr C 1597-1633, 1653-1837 M 1597-1836 (IGI); C 1597-1633,
          1697-1772 M 1597-1836 (SLC)
<u>MI</u> (Ptd CFHS); (DCRS/WSL)

ST MARTIN BY LOOE (S of F) Longcoe. fl.1702-26. Part of East Cornwall MM

ST MARTIN IN MENEAGE St Martin [Kerrier Hundred; Helston Union] [508]
Chapelry of MAWGAN IN MENEAGE. United with MANACCAN, ST ANTHONY IN MENEAGE
<u>OR</u> C 1571-1909 M 1571-1963 B 1571-1958 (CRO)
<u>BT</u> CMB 1676-1736, 1741-72 (CRO); CMB 1608-71, 1738-40, 1773-1836 (DRO)
<u>Cop</u> M 1571-1812 (Ptd Phillimore: 1909); CMB 1571-1837 (DCRS/WSL); M 1813-37
     (CMI); M 1571-1812 (Boyd); M 1800-12 (Pallot); M 1837-1920 (CFHS);
     B 1813-37 (CBI)
<u>Cop (Mf)</u> C 1697-1957 M 1695-1957 B 1695-1958 (RIC); CMB 1608-1811 (Mf of BT
          at DRO: CRO,CSL); C 1694-1730 (SG); M 1813-1925 (Ross);
          Extr C 1571-1875 (IGI); C 1571-1730, 1813-75 (SLC)
<u>MI</u> (Ptd CFHS)

ST MARTIN IN MENEAGE (Bible Christian) Tregidden. A building in the
occupation of John Kemeys [1882 Return]

ST MARTIN IN MENEAGE (Wes) St Martin's Green [1882 Return]

ST MARTIN IN MENEAGE (Meth) Association Chapel, owned by W.Johns, near
St Martin's Green [1882 Return]; St Martin's Green [Kelly 1897,1935]

ST MARY   see SCILLY ISLES

MARYFIELD   see ANTONY

ST MAWES   see ST JUST IN ROSELAND

MAWGAN CROSS   see MAWGAN IN PYDAR

ST MAWGAN IN MENEAGE or MAWGAN IN KERRIER St Mawgan Kerrier Hundred; Helston
Union] [1094] United with CURY, GUNWALLOE. see also ST MARTIN IN MENEAGE
<u>OR</u> C 1559-1914 M 1563-1971 B 1559-1918 (CRO) Noted in 1831: CMB 1678+
<u>BT</u> CMB 1676-1736, 1741-72 (CRO); CMB 1610-73, 1737-40, 1773-1812; post 1812
     unfit for production (DRO)
<u>Cop</u> M 1563-1812 (Ptd Phillimore: 1909); CB 1559-1837 (DCRS/WSL, CSL);
     M 1813-37 (CMI); M 1563-1812 (Boyd); M 1800-12 (Pallot); B 1813-37 (CBI)
<u>Cop (Mf)</u> C 1599-1959 M 1563-1959 B 1559-1958 (RIC); CMB 1610-1811 (Mf of BT
          at DRO: CRO,CSL); M 1813-1925 (Ross); Extr C 1559-1652, 1662-1875
          (IGI); C 1559-1652, 1662-1837 (SLC)

ST MAWGAN IN MENEAGE (Bapt) Rosevear f 1813; [Kelly 1856]

ST MAWGAN IN MENEAGE (Wes) Garras. Erected early 19th century [1882 Return]
+ UMFC, below ?

ST MAWGAN IN MENEAGE (Wes Meth Assn) 2 chapels [Kelly 1856]

ST MAWGAN IN MENEAGE (UMFC/U Meth) Garras [1882 Return]
OR   C 1864-1948 M 1926-47 (CRO)

ST MAWGAN IN MENEAGE (UMFC) Bowgyhere. Association Chapel owned by John
Basset, Esquire [1882 Return]

MAWGAN IN PYDAR St Mawgan [Pydar Hundred; St Columb Major Union] [745]
United with ST ERVAN, ST EVAL
OR   C 1674-1983 M 1686-1971 B 1686-1887 (CRO)
BT   CMB 1676-1736, 1741-72 (CRO); CMB 1608-73, 1737-40, 1773-1843 (DRO)
Cop M 1608-1812 (Ptd Phillimore: 1909); CMB 1608-73 from BT (DCRS/WSL);
     M 1608-84 (Ms from BT, RIC); CM 1608-74 from BT (I CSL); M 1813-37
     (CMI); Extr CB 1608-73 (SG); M 1608-1812 (Boyd); M 1800-12 (Pallot);
     B 1813-37 (CBI)
Cop (Mf) C 1675-1959 M 1686-1958 B 1686-1959 (RIC); CMB 1608-1812 (Mf of BT
         at DRO: CRO,CSL); M 1813-76 (Ross); Extr C 1674-1875 M 1608-73,
         1676-1875 (IGI); C 1674-1875 M 1608-73, 1676-1875 (SLC)
MI   (Ptd CFHS)

MAWGAN IN PYDAR Chaplaincy, R.A.F. St Mawgan
OR   C 1952-58, 1967-68, 1972-82 (AFCC)

MAWGAN IN PYDAR (RC) Lanherne. St Joseph and St Anne. Domestic chapel of
Arundell family. Convent of Carmelite nuns, refugees from Antwerp, from
1794.
OR   CM 1710+ B 1797+ (Reverend Mother); Confirmations 1857, 1868, 1876,
     1883+ (Plymouth Diocesan Archives)
Cop M 1710-1834 (Ptd Phillimore: 1909); C 1710-1819 M 1710-1834
     Confirmations 1769-1836, 1857-1909 B 1797-1808 (Catholic FHS);
     M 1710-1834 (SG); M 1710-1834 (Boyd)
Cop (Mf) M 1850-1925 (Ross); Extr C 1710-1819 M 1710-1834 (IGI); C 1710-1819
         (SLC)
MI   (Ptd CFHS)

MAWGAN IN PYDAR (RC) Chaplaincy, R.A.F. St Mawgan

MAWGAN IN PYDAR (Wes) [Kelly 1897, 1935]; Church Town [1882 Return]

MAWGAN IN PYDAR (Wes) Mawgan Cross [1882 Return]

MAWGAN IN PYDAR (Wes) Trenance [1882 Return]

MAWGAN IN PYDAR (Bible Christian) Mawgan Cross [1882 Return];
Meth [Kelly 1935]

MAWNAN St Mawnan [Kerrier Hundred; Falmouth Union] [578]
OR   C 1582-1931 M 1553-1966 B 1553-1889 (CRO)
BT   CMB 1674-1736, 1741-72 (CRO); CMB 1597-1672, 1737-40, 1773-1838, 1840
     (DRO)
Cop M 1553-1812 (Ptd Phillimore: 1904); C 1582-1837 B 1553-1837 (DCRS/WSL);
     C 1581-1809 M 1553-1654 B 1553-1812 (Ts and Ms, RIC); M 1813-37 (CMI);
     M 1553-1812 (Boyd); M 1800-12 (Pallot); M 1851-1920 (CFHS); B 1813-37
     (CBI)
Cop (Mf) C 1581-1959 M 1553-1959 B 1553-1959 (RIC); CMB 1597-1813 (Mf of BT
         at DRO: CRO,CSL); M 1813-1925 (Ross); Extr C 1581-1875 M 1813-37
         (IGI); C 1581-1875 (SLC)

MAWNAN St Michael's Chapel. Erected 1876
Cop **(Mf)** M 1879-1959 (RIC)

MAWNAN (RC) St Edward, Mawnan Smith f 1966

MAWNAN (Bapt) f 1828

MAWNAN (Wes) Carwinion Road, Mawnan Smith. Erected 1848 [1882 Return]

MAWNAN (Wes) Durgan [1882 Return]

MAWNAN (Bible Christian/U Meth) Carlidnack
OR C 1931-64 (CRO)

MEADS   see POUNDSTOCK

MEDROSE   see ST TEATH

ST MELLION St Melanus [East Hundred; St Germans Union] [330] United with
ST DOMINICK, LANDULPH, PILLATON
OR C 1558-1880 M 1558-1979 B 1558-1932 (CRO)
BT CMB 1675-1736, 1741-72 (CRO); CMB 1609-88, 1737-40, 1773-1812, 1814-16,
    1818-47 (DRO)
Cop M 1558-1812 (Ptd Phillimore: 1910); M 1813-37 (CMI); CB 1558-1812 (SG);
    M 1558-1812 (Boyd); M 1790-1812 (Pallot); B 1813-37 (CBI)
Cop **(Mf)** CMB 1610-1812 (Mf of BT at DRO: CRO,CSL); Extr CM 1558-1812 (IGI);
          C 1558-1812 M 1558-1625 (SLC)
MI (Ptd CFHS)

ST MELLION (Wes) Bealburgh [1882 Return]; Bealbury [Kelly 1897]; Meth [Kelly
1935]

MENHENIOT St Lalluwy [East Hundred; Liskeard Union] [1253]
OR C 1554-1944 M 1554-56, 1566-1986 B 1554-1924 (CRO) Noted in 1831:
    C 1660-63 "have been wilfully cut out"
BT CMB 1677-1736, 1741-72 (CRO); CMB 1608-73, 1737-40, 1773-1846, 1848-55
    (DRO)
Cop M 1554-1812 (Ptd Phillimore: 1906); CB 1554-1837 (DCRS/WSL); M 1813-37
    (CMI); M 1554-1812 (Boyd); M 1800-12 (Pallot); M 1837-1900 (CFHS);
    B 1813-37 (CBI)
Cop **(Mf)** CMB 1608-1812 (Mf of BT at DRO: CRO,CSL); Extr C 1554-1837 (IGI);
          C 1554-1837 (SLC)
MI (CFHS)

MENHENIOT St Mary, Merrymeet. Mission church erected 1905

MENHENIOT (Ind) f 1821. closed by 1850
OR None known

MENHENIOT (Wes) Merrymeet
OR B 1911-96 (Index CRO)

MENHENIOT (Wes) Church Town [1882 Return]

MENHENIOT (Wes) Trengrove [1882 Return]

MENHENIOT (Bible Christian/U Meth) f 1854 ?; Pengover Green [1882 Return]

MENHENIOT (S of F) Bodway fl.c.1702-26. Part of East Cornwall MM

MERRYMEET *see* MENHENIOT

ST MERRYN St Merryn [Pydar Hundred; St Columb Major Union] [576] Peculiar of the Bishop of Exeter
OR C 1688-1929 M 1688-1952 B 1688-1892 (CRO) Noted in 1831: C deficient 1781-90
BT CMB 1616-1812, 1814, 1832, 1834, 1838-43 (DRO)
Cop M 1689-1812 (Ptd Phillimore: 1903); CMB 1616-99 from BT (DCRS/WSL); M 1813-37 (CMI); CB 1688-1812 M 1616-1812 (SG); M 1689-1812 from OR; M 1616-89 from BT (Boyd); M 1790-1812 (Pallot); B 1813-37 (CBI)
Cop (Mf) C 1688-1959 M 1688-1953 B 1688-1960 (RIC); CMB 1616-1812 (Mf of BT at DRO: CRO,CSL); C 1813-77 (CFHS,SG); M 1813-1925 (Ross); Extr C 1688-1877 M 1616-1875 (IGI); C 1688-1877 M 1616-1754 (SLC)
MI (Ptd CFHS)

ST MERRYN St George's Chapel, R.N. Air Station (H.M.S. Curlew)
OR C 1949-55 (MoD)

ST MERRYN (Presb) Trevethan fl 1662-90

ST MERRYN (Wes) [Kelly 1856]

ST MERRYN (Wes) Towan [1882 Return]

ST MERRYN (Bible Christian) [Kelly 1856]

MERTHER St Cohan [Powder Hundred; Truro Union] [411] Chapelry in PROBUS. Separate parish 1787. Closed 1943 and replaced as parish church by Holy Trinity, Tresilian. United with LAMORRAN, ST MICHAEL PENKIVEL
OR C 1675-1903 M 1690-1975 B 1680-1992 (CRO)
BT CMB 1685-1736, 1741-72 (CRO); CMB 1608-65, 1737-40, 1773-1837 (DRO)
Cop M 1608-34, 1665, 1685, 1690-1812 Banns 1754-1812 (Ts CRO,RIC,CFHS,SG); M 1813-37 (CMI); M 1851-1900 (CFHS); B 1813-37 (CBI); CMB 1613-66 (SG); M 1608-65 from BT (Boyd)
Cop (Mf) C 1658-1903 M 1690-1903 B 1682-1903 (RIC); CMB 1608-1812 (Mf of BT at DRO: CRO,CSL); M 1685-1905 (Ross); Extr C 1658-1799, 1813-75 M 1677-1767, 1838-95 (IGI); C 1813-75 (SLC)
MI (Ptd CFHS); cy 1979 (Ms SG)

MERTHER Holy Trinity, Tresillian. Erected 1904. Chapel-of-ease to Merther, now used as parish church
OR C 1903+ M 1975+ B 1994+, copy reg 1954+ (Inc)
Cop (Mf) M 1905-56 B 1904-59 (RIC)

MERTHER (Wes) [Kelly 1856]; Merther lane [Kelly 1880]

METHEREL *see* CALSTOCK

MEVAGISSEY St Peter [Powder Hundred; St Austell Union] [2169] United with ST EWE
OR C 1590-1961 M 1598-1961 B 1598-1967 (CRO)
BT CMB 1684-1736, 1741-72 (CRO); CMB 1598-1665, 1737-40, 1773-1812, 1814, 1816-17, 1824-25, 1827-30, 1833, 1835, 1837-38 (DRO)
Cop C 1590-1841 MB 1598-1838 (RIC,SG); M 1813-37 (CMI); B 1813-37 (CBI); M 1598-1673 from BT (Boyd)
Cop (Mf) C 1590-1959 MB 1598-1959 (RIC); CMB 1598-1812 (Mf of BT at DRO: CRO,CSL); M 1598-1900 (Ross); Extr C 1590-1875 M 1598-1876 (IGI); C 1590-1875 M 1598-1838 (SLC)
MI (Ptd CFHS)

MEVAGISSEY (Ind/Cong/URC) St Andrew's f 1776 [1882 Return] Rebuilt 1882
OR ZC 1786-1837 (PRO); ZC 1843-1990 M 1887-1904 (CRO)
Cop (Mf) ZC 1786-1837 (DCRS/WSL); Extr C 1786-1837 (IGI); C 1786-1837 (SLC)

MEVAGISSEY (Wes) Circuit
OR C 1838-71, 1875-1927 (CRO)

MEVAGISSEY (Wes) Fore Street. Erected 1842 [1882 Return] [Kelly 1889]
OR M 1916-66 (CRO)

MEVAGISSEY (Bible Christian) Circuit
OR C 1838-1907 (CRO)

MEVAGISSEY (UMFC) Tregony Hill [1882 Return]

MEVAGISSEY (Bible Christian) Erected 1826 [Kelly 1889]

MEVAGISSEY (Bible Christian/U Meth) River Street; = ? Mevagissey Town [1882
Return]
OR C 1946-75 M 1967-94 (CRO)

MEVAGISSEY (U Meth) Circuit
OR C 1907-36 (CRO)

MEVAGISSEY (Meth) Circuit, formerly Wes
OR C 1932-49 (CRO)

MEVAGISSEY (Free Meth) Erected 1857 [Kelly 1889]

MEVAGISSEY (S of F) f 1710. Part of ST AUSTELL MM. fl c.1737

ST MEWAN St Mewan [Powder Hundred; St Austell Union] [1306]
OR C 1693-1978 M 1693-1970 B 1693-1962 (CRO)
BT CMB 1678-1736, 1741-72 (CRO); CMB 1607-73, 1737-40, 1773-1813, 1820,
    1826, 1838-41 (DRO)
Cop CMB 1607-92 from BT; CMB 1693-1837 (DCRS/WSL); M 1813-37 (CMI);
    B 1813-37 (CBI); M 1607-74 (SG); M 1607-73 from BT (Boyd)
Cop (Mf) CMB 1607-1959 (transcript pre-1692, RIC); CMB 1607-1812 (Mf of BT
        at DRO: CRO,CSL); M 1607-1900 (Ross); Extr C 1607-1875 M 1607-1837
        (IGI); C 1607-1742 M 1607-1837 (SLC)
MI (Ptd CFHS)

ST MEWAN St Mark, Sticker. Mission chapel of St Mark, Polgooth, erected 1877
OR M 1991+ (Inc) for CB see St Mewan

ST MEWAN (Wes) Trewoon [1882 Return]; [Kelly 1902]

ST MEWAN (Wes) Polgooth [Kelly 1902]

ST MEWAN (Wes) Sticker. Erected 1876 ? [1882 Return]; [Kelly 1902]

ST MEWAN (UMFC/U Meth) Trelowth. Erected 1872 [Kelly 1889]
OR C 1882-1960 (CRO)

ST MICHAEL CAERHAYS or CARHAYS St Michael [Powder Hundred; St Austell Union]
[197] Chapelry of ST STEPHEN IN BRANNEL until 1832. United with GORRAN
OR C 1590-1900 M 1594-1900 B 1588-1900 (CRO)
BT CMB 1677-1736, 1741-72 (CRO); CMB 1608-73, 1737-40, 1773-1814, 1816-34,
  1836, 1839, 1841 (DRO)
Cop C 1590-1812 M 1594-1915 B 1588-1812 (Ts CRO,RIC); M 1813-37 (CMI);
  B 1813-37 (CBI); M 1608-73 (SG); M 1608-73 from BT (Boyd)
Cop (Mf) CMB 1608-1812 (Mf of BT at DRO: CRO,CSL); M 1594-1915 (Ross);
  Extr C 1677-1772 (IGI); C 1677-1772 (SLC)
MI (Ptd CFHS)

ST MICHAEL PENKIVEL St Michael [Powder Hundred; Truro Union] [179]
Estate church of Boscawen family (Lord Falmouth) of Tregothnan. United with
LAMORRAN, MERTHER
OR C 1546-1812 M 1577-1939 B 1576-1812 (CRO) CB 1812+ (Inc, Tresilian,
  Merther)
BT CMB 1692-1736, 1741-72 (CRO); CMB 1597-1623, 1737-40, 1773-1838, 1840-46
  (DRO)
Cop M 1577-1837 (Ptd Phillimore: 1935); C 1546-1837 B 1576-1837 (DCRS/WSL);
  M 1577-1812 Banns 1755-1812 (Ts CRO,RIC,CFHS,SG); M 1577-1836 (CSL);
  M 1813-37 (CMI); M 1597-1623 from BT (Boyd); M 1790-1812 (Pallot);
  M 1876-1900 (CFHS); B 1813-37 (CBI)
Cop (Mf) C 1546-1956 M 1577-1952 B 1576-1959 (RIC); CMB 1597-1812 (Mf of BT
  at DRO: CRO,CSL); M 1577-1875 (Ross); Extr C 1546-1875 (IGI);
  C 1546-1875 (SLC)
MI (Ptd CFHS)

ST MICHAEL PENKIVEL (Wes) Motherlane. Erected 1842

ST MICHAEL ROCK   *see* ST MINVER

ST MICHAEL'S MOUNT   *see* ST HILARY

MICHAELSTOW St Michael [Lesnewth Hundred; Camelford Union] [215] United with
ST TUDY, ST MABYN
OR C 1680-1993 M 1548-1978 B 1544-1993 (CRO) No earlier C register noted in
  1831
BT CMB 1676-1736, 1741-49 (CRO); CMB 1615-73, 1737-40, 1773-1842 (DRO)
Cop M 1548-1812 (Ptd Phillimore: 1900); B 1814-1974 (Ts CRO,RIC); M 1813-37
  (CMI); C 1680-1812 B 1544-1812 (SG); M 1548-1812 (Boyd); M 1790-1812
  (Pallot); Banns 1845-1900 (CFHS); B 1813-37 (CBI)
Cop (Mf) CMB 1617-1812 (Mf of BT at DRO: CRO,CSL); M 1813-45 (Ross);
  Extr C 1680-92, 1719-1812 M 1548-1812 (IGI); C 1680-92, 1719-1812
  (SLC)
MI (Ptd CFHS)

MICHAELSTOW (Wes) [Kelly 1856]

MICHAELSTOW (Bible Christian) Circuit, later known as Camelford Circuit
OR ZC 1822-37 (PRO); C 1837-1915 (CRO)
Cop ZC 1822-37 (SG)
Cop (Mf) ZC 1822-37 (DCRS/WSL,SG); Extr C 1822-37 (IGI); C 1822-37 (SLC)

MICHAELSTOW (Bible Christian) Treveighan. Erected 1828

MICHAELSTOW (Wes Meth Assn) [Kelly 1856]

MICHAELSTOW (Free Meth) Erected 1842 [Kelly 1889]

MIDDLEWOOD   see HILL, NORTH

MILLBROOK   see MAKER

MILLPOOL   see CARDINHAM

MILTON   see LANLIVERY

MINARD CROSS   see ST GERMANS

MINGOOSE   see ST AGNES

MINSTER   see MANACCAN

MINSTER or TALKARNE St Merteriana [Lesnewth Hundred; Camelford Union] [497]
United with FORRABURY 1958. see also BOSCASTLE
OR C 1679-1978 M 1682-1958 B 1678-1979 (CRO)
BT CMB 1676-1736, 1741-72 (CRO); CMB 1616-70, 1737-40, 1773-1847 (DRO)
Cop M 1676-1812 (Ptd Phillimore: 1900); C 1677-1846 M 1679-1837 B 1678-1845
    (Ts RIC,CFHS); M 1813-37 (CMI); M 1611-1812 (SG); M 1676-1812 from OR;
    M 1616-32 from BT (Boyd); M 1790-1812 (Pallot); B 1813-37 (CBI)
Cop (Mf) CMB 1616-1812 (Mf of BT at DRO: CRO,CSL); M 1813-75 (Ross);
         Extr C 1697-1804 M 1676-1812 (IGI); C 1697-1804 (SLC)
MI (Ptd CFHS); ch 1927 (Ts SG)

MINSTER (Meth) Rebuilt 1825 [Kelly 1935]

ST MINVER St Menefreda [Trigg Hundred; Bodmin Union] [1110] United with
ST ENODOC, ST MICHAEL ROCK
OR CB 1559-1978 Banns 1823-1961 M 1559-1812 Confirmations 1892-1996 (CRO)
BT CMB 1677-1736, 1741-72 (CRO); CMB 1608-73, 1737-40, 1773-1867, 1869
    (DRO)
Cop M 1559-1812 (Ptd Phillimore: 1903); M 1813-37 (CMI); CB 1558-1812 (SG);
    M 1559-1812 (Boyd); M 1790-1812 (Pallot); M 1837-1910 (CFHS); B 1813-37
    (CBI)
Cop (Mf) CB 1559-1961 M 1559-1960 (RIC); CMB 1608-1812 (Mf of BT at DRO:
         CRO,CSL); C 1813-77 (CFHS,SG); M 1813-1910 (Ross); Extr C 1558-1877
         M 1559-1812 (IGI); C 1558-1877 M 1559-1812 (SLC)
MI (Ptd CFHS)

ST MINVER St Enodoc, Trebetherick. Norman church: northern chapelry of
ST MINVER, buried in sand, restored 1863. United with ST MINVER, ST MICHAEL
ROCK
OR M 1995+ (Inc) and see St Menefreda
MI (Ptd CFHS)

ST MINVER St Michael, Rock, or Porthilly, Southern chapelry of ST MINVER.
12th cent. Restored 1865. United with ST MINVER, ST ENODOC
OR see St Menefreda
MI (Ptd CFHS)

ST MINVER (Wes) [Kelly 1856] = ? (Wes/Free Meth) Erected 1815; rebuilt 1874
[Kelly 1889]

ST MINVER (Wes) Rock. Erected 1842 [1882 Return] [Kelly 1889]

ST MINVER (Bible Christian) Trevanger. Erected 1872 [Kelly 1889]

ST MINVER (Wes Meth Assn) [Kelly 1856]

ST MINVER (UMFC/U Meth) Tredrizzick
OR C 1946-90 (CRO)

ST MINVER (S of F) Minver Monthly Meeting f c.1701 from ST AUSTELL MM, which it rejoined 1770.
OR Z 1609-1758 B 1669-1754 in CORNWALL QM register RG 6/1578 (PRO)
Cop Z 1701-63, 1783-99 M 1712-63, 1782-87 B 1721-68, 1784-96 'Minver or Port Isaac Monthly Meeting', extracted from MM registers 1838 (CRO)

ST MINVER (S of F) St Minver Meeting f pre-1668; moved to PORT ISAAC by 1761. Existed 1821 but little used. Meeting house Treglines [Kelly 1889]
OR Z 1609-1763 M 1708-63 B 1669-1796 in EAST CORNWALL MM registers RG 6/1314, 1020 (PRO)
Cop St Minver and Boscastle Z 1609-1758 M 1669-1754 in 1828 copy of old register book of Cornwall QM; 19th century list of those buried (CRO)

MITCHELL   former borough in ST ENODER q.v. and NEWLYN, EAST

MITHIAN   *see* ST AGNES

MOLLIONIS   *see* ST AUSTELL

MOORSWATER   *see* LISKEARD

MORVAH St Morwetha [Penwith Hundred; Penzance Union] [377] Chapelry in MADRON. United with PENDEEN
OR C 1650-1874 M 1617-1993 B 1655-1991 (CRO) for M 1772-1812 *see* MADRON
BT CMB 1683-1736, 1741-72 (CRO); CMB 1614-73, 1737-40, 1773-1814, 1816-17, 1819-20, 1822, 1824, 1826-27, 1830-32, 1834, 1842-43, 1845-48 (DRO)
Cop M 1617-1722 (Ptd Phillimore: 1907); C 1650-1837 B 1655-1837 (DCRS/WSL,SG,Morrab); C 1650-94 B 1655-98 (CRO); C 1650-1837 M 1812-37 B 1655-1837 (Ms RIC); M 1813-37 (CMI); B 1813-37 (CBI); M 1617-72 from OR; M 1614-73 from BT (Boyd); M 1851-1925 (CFHS)
Cop (Mf) C 1653-1959 M 1617-1954 B 1655-1959 (RIC); CMB 1614-1812 (Mf of BT at DRO: CRO,CSL); M 1813-1925 (Ross); Extr C 1650-1885 M 1813-95 (IGI); C 1650-1875 M 1813-37 (SLC)
MI (Ptd CFHS)

MORVAH (Wes) Erected 1744; rebuilt 1866. Church Town [1882 Return] Closed

MORVAH (Bible Christian) Erected early 19th century. Later a school; Church Town [1882 Return]

MORVAL St Wenna [West Hundred; Liskeard Union] [644] United with LISKEARD, ST KEYNE, ST PINNOCK, BRADOC
OR C 1542-1902 M 1539-1946 B 1538-1880 (CRO)
BT CMB 1682-1736, 1741-72 (CRO); CMB 1597-1670, 1737-40, 1773-1815, 1817-42 (DRO)
Cop C 1542-1837 M 1539-1837 B 1538-1837 (DCRS/WSL); M 1813-37 (Ts CRO,RIC); M 1813-37 (CMI); M 1610-71 (SG); M 1597-1670 from BT (Boyd); B 1813-37 (CBI)
Cop (Mf) CMB 1597-1812 (Mf of BT at DRO: CRO,CSL); M 1538-1875 (Ross); Extr C 1543-1837 M 1538-1837 (IGI); C 1543-1837 M 1538-1837 (SLC)
MI (Ptd CFHS)

MORVAL (Presb) fl 1672-90

MORVAL (Wes) Sandplace. Erected 1864 [1882 Return] [Kelly 1889]

MORVAL (UMFC/U Meth) Widegates [1882 Return]
OR C 1874-1932 (CRO)

MORWENSTOW St John the Baptist [Stratton Hundred; Stratton Union] [1102]
United with KILKHAMPTON
OR C 1558-1900 M 1558-1903 B 1558-1863 (CRO)
BT CMB 1676-1736, 1741-72 (CRO); CMB 1597-1673, 1737-40, 1773-1814, 1818-
   20, 1822-30, 1832, 1834 (DRO)
Cop M 1558-1812 (Ptd Phillimore: 1910); M 1813-37 (Ts CRO,WSL); M 1813-37
   (CMI); CB 1558-1837 (SG); M 1558-1812 (Boyd); M 1790-1812 (Pallot);
   M 1835-1903 (CFHS); B 1813-37 (CBI)
Cop (Mf) C 1558-1956 M 1558-1958 B 1558-1960 (RIC); CMB 1611-1812 (Mf of BT
      at DRO: CRO,CSL); C 1813-77 (SG); M 1813-1903 (Ross);
      Extr C 1558-1885 M 1558-1895 (IGI); C 1558-1875 (SLC)
MI (Ptd CFHS)

MORWENSTOW (Wes) Shop
OR M 1927-29, 1935-48 (CRO)
MI (Ptd CFHS); cy 1982 (Ts SG)

MORWENSTOW (Wes) Woodford [1882 Return]
MI (Ptd CFHS); 1982 (Ts SG)

MORWENSTOW (Wes) Woolley. Erected c.1822; [1882 Return] Closed 1971.
Now a house

MORWENSTOW (Bible Christian) Woodford. Erected 1883 [1882 Return]
[Kelly 1889] Closed. Now a cottage
MI (Ptd CFHS); 1982 (Ts SG)

MORWENSTOW (Bible Christian) Eastcott [1882 Return]

MORWENSTOW (Bible Christian) Bethel, Goosham Mill [1882 Return]

MOTHERLANE   see ST MICHAEL PENKIVEL

MOUNT CHARLES   see ST AUSTELL

MOUNT HAWKE   see ST AGNES

MOUNT HOREM   see KENWYN

MOUNTJOY   see ST COLAN

MOUSEHOLE   see PAUL

MULLION St Mellanus [Kerrier Hundred; Camelford Union] [733]
OR C 1598-1981 M 1621-1954 B 1598-1981 (CRO)
BT CMB 1674-1736, 1741-72 (CRO); CMB 1610-73, 1737-40, 1773-1820, 1822-52
   (DRO)
Cop CB 1598-1812 M 1621-1812 (DCRS/WSL, CSL); C 1750-1837 M 1813-37
   B 1747-1837 (Ms RIC); M 1813-37 (CMI); B 1813-37 (CBI); M 1610-73
   CMB 1813-37 (SG); M 1610-73 from BT (Boyd)
Cop (Mf) CB 1598-1959 M 1621-1959 (RIC); CMB 1610-1812 (Mf of BT at DRO:
      CRO, CSL); M 1610-1925 (Ross); Extr C 1598-1875 M 1622-1754 (IGI);
      C 1598-1875 (SLC)
MI ch,cy,cemetery (Ptd CFHS)

MULLION (RC) St Michael the Archangel 1925

117

MULLION (Wes) [Kelly 1856]; Church Town [1882 Return]

MULLION (Wes Meth Assn) [Kelly 1856]

MULLION (UMFC/U Meth) Church Town [1882 Return]
OR C 1864-1931 (CRO)

MULLION (UMFC/U Meth) Pradnack [1882 Return]

MYLOR St Mylor [Kerrier Hundred; Falmouth Union] [2647] Peculiar of the
Bishop of Exeter. United with FLUSHING. see also MABE
OR C 1673-1904 M 1673-1955 B 1673-1943 (CRO) Noted in 1831: C deficient
    1730-34, 1736-38, 1743-60 B deficient 1730-34, 1742-61
BT CMB 1607-1866 (DRO)
Cop M 1673-1812 (Ptd Phillimore: 1904); CMB 1601-71 from BT; CB 1673-1837
    (DCRS/WSL); M 1813-37 (CMI); M 1607-1812 (SG); M 1673-1812 from OR;
    M 1607-63 from BT (Boyd); M 1800-12 (Pallot); B 1813-37 (CBI)
Cop (Mf) CMB 1673-1959 (RIC); CMB 1607-1812 (Mf of BT at DRO: CRO,CSL);
         M 1813-1901 (Ross); Extr C 1601-33, 1663-1875 (IGI); C 1601-33,
         1663-1875 (SLC)
MI (Ptd CFHS); Ch (Wall,20-26, Ms SG)

MYLOR St Peter, Flushing. Erected 1842. Parish created 1844 from MYLOR.
United with MYLOR
OR no information
MI (Ptd CFHS)

MYLOR All Saints, Mylor Bridge. Mission church erected 1840

MYLOR (Presb) fl 1672-90

MYLOR (Unit) Flushing f 1812 from FALMOUTH. Rebuilt 1830

MYLOR (Wes) Mylor Bridge f 1820 [1882 Return]
OR ZC 1823-37 (PRO)
Cop ZC 1823-37 (SG)
Cop (Mf) ZC 1823-37 (DCRS/WSL); Extr C 1823-37 (IGI); C 1823-37 (SLC)

MYLOR (Wes) Flushing. Erected 1816 [Kelly 1889]
OR ZC 1814-37 (PRO)
Cop ZC 1817-37 (SG)
Cop (Mf) ZC 1814-37 (DCRS/WSL, SG); Extr C 1814-37 (IGI); C 1814-37 (SLC)

MYLOR (Bible Christian) Mylor Bridge [1882 Return]

MYLOR (Bible Christian) Flushing [Kelly 1889]

MYLOR (Prim Meth) Flushing. Erected 1866 [1882 Return] [Kelly 1889]

MYLOR (Prim Meth) Mylor Bridge [1882 Return]

MYLOR (S of F) f 1696, part of FALMOUTH MM.

NANCEGOLLAN   see CROWAN

NANCLEDRA   see TOWEDNACK

NANPEAN   see ST STEPHEN IN BRANNEL

NANPEAN   *see* ST STEPHEN IN BRANNEL

NANQUIDNO   *see* ST JUST IN PENWITH

NANSANT   *see* ST ISSEY

NANSANT   *see* ST BREOKE

NANSTALLON   in LANIVET q.v. and BODMIN

NASSINGTON   *see* ST PETROC MINOR

NAVARINA   *see* PETHERWIN, NORTH

ST NECTAN   *see* ST WINNOW

ST NEOT St Neot [West Hundred; Liskeard Union] [1424] United with WARLEGGAN.
see also ALTARNON Holy Trinity Bolventor
OR C 1549-1950 M 1550-1989 B 1549-1898 (CRO)
BT CMB 1676-1736, 1741-72 (CRO); CMB 1610-73, 1737-40, 1773-1834 (DRO)
Cop CB 1549-1812 M 1550-1756 (Ts CRO,RIC); CMB 1610-73, 1737-40, 1773-1834 (DRO)
    M 1550-1837 (CSL); M 1610-75 (SG); M 1610-73 from BT (Boyd)
Cop (Mf) C 1549-1855 M 1550-1947 B 1549-1898 (RIC); CMB 1610-1812 (Mf of BT
    at DRO: CRO,CSL); M 1550-1900 (Ross); Extr C 1549-1855 M 1550-1837
    (IGI); C 1549-1812, 1820-37 M 1550-1837 (SLC)

ST NEOT (Wes) [Kelly 1856]; Church Town [1882 Return]

ST NEOT (Bible Christian) Circuit *see* LISKEARD

ST NEOT (Bible Christian)
OR ZC 1821-37 (PRO)
Cop ZC 1821-37 (SG)
Cop (Mf) ZC 1821-37 (DCRS/WSL); Extr ZC 1821-37 (IGI); ZC 1821-37 (SLC)

ST NEOT (Bible Christian/U Meth) Trenant [1882 Return]
OR B 1843-1963; burial certificates and cemetery papers 1942-86 (CRO)
MI (Ptd CFHS)

ST NEOT (Bible Christian) St Luke [1882 Return]

ST NEOT (Bible Christian) Lea [1882 Return]

ST NEOT (Bible Christian) Tredinnick [Kelly 1889]

ST NEOT (Bible Christian) Harrowbridge [Kelly 1889]

NEW MILL   *see* MADRON

NEW MILLS   *see* LADOCK

NEWBRIDGE   *see* SANCREED

NEWLYN   near PENZANCE, *see* PAUL

NEWLYN, EAST or NEWLYN IN PYDAR St Newlina [Pydar Hundred; St Columb Major
Union] [1218]
OR CMB 1559+ (Inc)
BT CMB 1675-1736, 1741-72 (CRO); CMB 1609-73, 1737-40, 1773-1817, 1825-34,
    1838-41 (DRO)
Cop M 1559-1812 (Ptd Phillimore: 1909); CMB 1559-1715 (CRO); CMB 1559-1837
    (DCRS/WSL); M 1813-37 (CMI); M 1559-1812 (Boyd); M 1800-12 (Pallot)
Cop (Mf) CMB 1559-1900 (CRO); CM 1559-1959 B 1559-1958 (RIC); CMB 1609-1812
         (Mf of BT at DRO: CRO,CSL); C 1560-1720 (SG); M 1813-1900 (Ross);
         Extr C 1560-1885 M 1559-1895 (IGI); C 1560-1875 M 1559-1876 (SLC)
MI (Ptd CFHS)

NEWLYN, EAST (Wes) Newlyn East Circuit
OR C 1838-99 (CRO)
Cop C 1899-1931 (CRO,CFHS)

NEWLYN, EAST (Wes) Erected 1832
OR M 1939-55, 1957-82 (CRO)

NEWLYN, EAST (Wes) Kestle Mill [1882 Return]
OR C 1939-55 (CRO)

NEWLYN, EAST (Wes) Rejerrah, Newlyn [1882 Return]
OR C 1857-1978 (CRO)

NEWLYN, EAST (Bible Christian) Church Town [1882 Return]

NEWPORT   *see* ST STEPHEN BY LAUNCESTON or CALLINGTON

NEWQUAY   *see* ST COLUMB MINOR

NINNES   NINNES BRIDGE, *see* LELANT

NORTH COUNTRY   *see* REDRUTH

NORTH HILL   *see* HILL, NORTH

NORTH PETHERWIN   *see* PETHERWIN, NORTH

NORTH TAMERTON   *see* TAMERTON, NORTH

OTTERHAM St Denis [Lesnewth Hundred; Camelford Union] [227]
see also BOSCASTLE
OR C 1687-1979 MB 1687-1978 (CRO)
BT CMB 1674-1736, 1741-72 (CRO); CMB 1612-73, 1737-40, 1773-1835 (DRO)
Cop M 1687-1812 (Ptd Phillimore: 1900); M 1813-37 (CMI); M 1614-1812 (SG);
    M 1687-1811 from OR; M 1612-73 from BT (Boyd); M 1790-1812 (Pallot);
    M 1876-1900 (CFHS); B 1813-37 (CBI)
Cop (Mf) CMB 1612-1812 (Mf of BT at DRO: CRO,CSL); ZC 1681-1772, 1804 (SG);
         M 1813-75 (Ross); Extr C 1681-1772 M 1681-1772, 1804-05 (IGI);
         C 1681-1772 (SLC)
MI (Ptd CFHS)

PADSTOW St Petrock [Pydar Hundred; St Columb Major Union] [1822] Peculiar of the Bishop of Exeter, except for town and parish church
OR C 1599-1933 M 1599-1951 B 1599-1934 (CRO)
BT CMB 1684-1736, 1741-72 (CRO); CMB 1608-83, 1737-40, 1773-1835 (DRO)
Cop M 1599-1812 (Ptd Phillimore: 1904); C 1599-1812 M 1599-1795 B 1606-1810
    (CSL); M 1813-37 (CMI); CB 1611-1812 (SG); M 1599-1812 (Boyd);
    M 1790-1812 (Pallot); M 1837-1900 (CFHS); B 1813-37 (CBI)
Cop (Mf) CMB 1608-1812 (Mf of BT at DRO: CRO,CSL); M 1813-75 (Ross);
       Extr C 1600-1812 (IGI); C 1600-1812 (SLC)
MI (Ptd CFHS); (Ptd *Gent.Mag.* 1827 II 17-20)

PADSTOW St Saviour, Trevone. Mission church erected c.1935

PADSTOW (RC) St Saviour and St Petroc f 1909

PADSTOW (Bapt) f 1834 [*Bapt. Manual* 1850]
OR Z 1836 (PRO)
Cop Z 1836 (SG)
Cop (Mf) Z 1836 (DCRS/WSL); Extr Z 1836 (IGI)

PADSTOW (Wes) Church Lane. Erected 1827 [1882 Return] Demolished
OR ZC 1820-37 (PRO); C 1853-80 (CRO)
Cop ZC 1820-37 (SG)
Cop (Mf) ZC 1820-37 (DCRS/WSL); Extr ZC 1820-37 (IGI); ZC 1820-37 (SLC)

PADSTOW (Bible Christian) Circuit (formerly St Ervan Circuit)
OR C 1839-1933 (CRO)
Cop C 1820-37 (CRO)

PADSTOW (Bible Christian/U Meth) Ruthy's Lane. Erected 1840 [Kelly 1889]
OR M 1928-54 (CRO)

PADSTOW (U Meth) Circuit
OR C 1895-1933 (CRO)

PAR *see* ST BLAZEY

PAUL St Pol-de-Lion [Penwith Hundred; Penzance Union] [4191]
OR C 1595-1870 M 1595-1981 B 1595-1934 (CRO) Noted in 1831: "Registers anterior to 1595 burnt by the Spaniards when they set fire to the Church."
BT CMB 1677-1736, 1741-72 (CRO); CMB 1608-73, 1737-40, 1772-1812, 1836, 1838-60 (DRO)
Cop M 1595-1812 (Ptd Phillimore: 1906); CMB 1608-74 from BT (DCRS/WSL); C 1595-1844 M 1813-53 B 1747-94 (Ms RIC); C 1694-1808 M 1699-1851 (CFHS); C 1595-1802 B 1595-1800 (Morrab); C 1595-1741 (CSL); M 1813-37 (CMI); CB 1595-1812 (SG); M 1595-1812 (Boyd); M 1800-12 (Pallot); B 1813-37 (CBI)
Cop (Mf) CB 1595-1959 M 1595-1952 (RIC); CMB 1608-1812 (Mf of BT at DRO: CRO,CSL); M 1813-1925 (Ross); Extr C 1595-1885 M 1595-1753 (IGI); C 1595-1875 (SLC)
MI (Ptd CFHS); Sheffield Road Cemetery; Cholera (Ptd CFHS)

PAUL St Peter, Newlyn. Parish created 1848 from PAUL, MADRON. Erected 1865
OR C 1851-1967 M 1866-1992 (CRO)
Cop M 1876-1900 (CFHS)
Cop (Mf) C 1851-1960 M 1866-1959 (RIC); M 1866-1925 (Ross); Extr C 1851-76 (IGI); C 1851-76 (SLC)
MI (Ptd CFHS)

PAUL St Andrew, Newlyn. Chapel-of-ease, erected 1904

PAUL (Ind) Newlyn f 1812. Closed 1860
OR None known

PAUL (Wes) Erected 1823. fl c.1851

PAUL (Wes) Trinity, Newlyn. f 1830; erected 1834 [Kelly 1889]
OR C 1859-97 (CRO)
Cop C 1859-79 (CFHS); Newlyn, Truro and St Agnes Methodist baptisms 1837-75
(CFHS)

PAUL (Wes) Chapel Street, Mousehole. Erected 1783-84; rebuilt 1833
[1882 Return]

PAUL (Wes) Kerris [1882 Return]

PAUL (Wes) Jack Lane, Newlyn. Erected 1834. fl c.1851

PAUL (Prim Meth) Ebenezer, Newlyn f 1835 [1882 Return] [Kelly 1889]

PAUL (UMFC) Mount Zion, Mousehole. Erected 1844 [1882 Return]

PAUL (Teetotal Wes) Mousehole. Erected 1848

PAUL (Meth) Centenary. Erected 1927

PAWTON   see ST BREOKE

PAYNTERS LANE END   see ILLOGAN

PELYNT St Nun [West Hundred; Liskeard Union] [804] Now with LANREATH
OR C 1678-1993 M 1693-1971 B 1720-1992 (CRO)
BT CMB 1677-1736, 1741-72 (CRO); CMB 1610-73, 1737-40, 1773-1833 (DRO)
Cop CMB 1614-93 from BT; C 1678-1837 M 1693-1837 B 1720-1837 (DCRS/WSL);
    M 1693-1837 (Ts with index, CRO,RIC,SG); M 1693-1812, 1837-75 (CFHS);
    M 1813-37 (CMI); M 1610-73 from BT (Boyd); B 1813-37 (CBI)
Cop (Mf) CMB 1610-1811 (Mf of BT at DRO: CRO,CSL); M 1610-1875 (Ross);
        Extr C 1614-1837 M 1610-1837 from BT (IGI); C 1614-1837 M 1610-1837
        from BT (SLC)
MI (Ptd CFHS)

PELYNT (RC) Trelawne. Chapel of Trelawny family. Mass centre served by
French émigré priests to 1802. Chapel closed 1860
OR C 1833+ M 1856+ (Inc, Sclerder, Talland)

PELYNT (Wes) [Kelly 1856]; [1882 Return] Rebuilt 1889
OR C 1969-91 M 1974-90 (CRO)

PELYNT (Wes Meth Assn) [Kelly 1856] [Kelly 1889]

PELYNT (UMFC) Churchtown [1882 Return]

PELYNT (Wes) Trelawne [Kelly 1889]

PENCOYS   see WENDRON

PENDEEN   see ST JUST IN PENWITH

PENDOGGETT   *see* ST KEW

PENGEGON   *see* CAMBORNE

PENGELLY   *see* ST TEATH

PENGOVER GREEN   *see* MENHENIOT

PENHALLOW   *see* PERRANZABULOE

PENHALVEAN   *see* ST STITHIANS

PENHENDAR   *see* RAME

PENKIVEL   *see* ST MICHAEL PENKIVEL

PENMENNOR   *see* ST STITHIANS

PENNANT   *see* LANLIVERY

PENPOLL   *see* FEOCK

PENPONDS   *see* CAMBORNE

PENROSE   *see* ST ERVAN

PENRYN   borough in parish of ST GLUVIAS

PENTEWAN   *see* ST AUSTELL

PENTRASOE COMMON   *see* ST EWE

PENWEATHERS   *see* KEA

PENWERRIS   *see* BUDOCK

PENZANCE or BURITON St Mary [Lesnewth Hundred; Penzance Union] [6563]
Chapelry in MADRON. Erected 1680. Rebuilt 1836. Parish 1871
OR C 1789-1983 M 1837-1967 B 1789-1936 (CRO) Noted in 1831: return from
    MADRON: "Penzance registers: No.X CMB 1700-01 No.XI 1716-28 vide
    Penzance". Under PENZANCE: "Register of Bap Bur 1789-1812 vide Madron"
BT CMB Included with MADRON q.v., some headed Bur(r)iton (CRO/DRO); CMB
    1813-21, 1823-27, 1829, 1831-32 (DRO)
Cop C 1789-1900 (CRO); M 1837-75 (CFHS); B 1813-37 (CBI)
Cop (Mf) M 1837-75 (Ross); Extr C 1700-1812 (IGI); C 1700-1812 (SLC)
MI (Ptd CFHS)

PENZANCE St Paul. Erected 1843. Parish created 1867 from Penzance St Mary,
with which united 1973
OR C 1866-82 Banns 1878-1976 M 1867-1963 (CRO)
MI (Ptd CFHS)

PENZANCE St John the Baptist, Erected 1881. Parish created 1882 from
Penzance St Mary
OR C 1881+ M 1882+ (Inc)
Cop (Mf) C 1881-1900 M 1882-1900 (CRO)
MI (Ptd CFHS)

PENZANCE (RC) The Immaculate Conception f 1837
OR C 1852+ M 1854+ D 1856+ (Inc); Confirmations 1863-1935 (Plymouth
    Diocesan Archives) Pre-1852 register(s) lost

PENZANCE (Bapt) f 1802. First Chapel. Clarence Street Erected 1836 [*Bapt.
Manual* 1850; *Handbook* 1881] [Kelly 1889]

PENZANCE (Bapt) Jordan Chapel. Erected 1834 [*Bapt. Manual* 1850]

PENZANCE (Cong) Alverton
OR C 1957-66 (CRO)

PENZANCE (Presb/Cong) Market Jew Street. Erected 1707. Rebuilt 1807-08
OR CM 1898-1967 B 1897-1954 (CRO)

PENZANCE (Presb/Ind) East Street f 1662 Lower Meeting and Octagon Chapel
f 1700. Closed 1968
OR ZC 1791-1837 B 1806-37 (PRO)
Cop ZC 1791-1837 B 1806-37 (SG)
Cop (Mf) ZC 1791-1837 B 1806-37 (DCRS/WSL); Extr C 1791-1837 (IGI);
    C 1791-1837 (SLC)

PENZANCE (Unit) Clarence Street f 1832

PENZANCE (Wes, Ind, and Bapt) Bethel Seamen's Chapel fl c.1851

PENZANCE (Wes) Circuit
Cop C 1837-76 (CFHS)

PENZANCE (Wes) f 1780. Chapel Street erected 1814 [1882 Return]
OR ZC 1805-37 (PRO)
Cop ZC 1805-37 (SG)
Cop (Mf) ZC 1805-37 (DCRS/WSL); Extr C 1805-37 (IGI); C 1805-37 (SLC)

PENZANCE (Wes) St Clare Street. Erected 1834. fl c.1851

PENZANCE (Wes Meth Assn) Queen Street. pre-1800, rebuilt c.1851

PENZANCE (Prim Meth) Circuit
OR C 1844-1936 (CRO)

PENZANCE (Prim Meth) Mount Street. Erected 1839 [1882 Return] [Kelly 1889]
OR C 1910-68 (CRO)

PENZANCE (Bible Christian) Circuit
OR ZC 1821-37 (PRO); C 1839-1901 (CRO)
Cop ZC 1821-37 (SG)
Cop (Mf) ZC 1821-37 (DCRS/WSL,SG); Extr C 1821-37 (IGI); C 1821-37 (SLC)

PENZANCE (Bible Christian) Jehovah Jireh, Tredavoe. Erected 1842

PENZANCE (Bible Christian) Chapel Row, St Clare Street [1882 Return]

PENZANCE (Bible Christian) High Street. Erected 1879 [1882 Return]
[Kelly 1889]

PENZANCE (Bible Christian) Alverton Street. Erected 1851

PENZANCE (Meth New Conn) Circuit
OR None known

PENZANCE (Meth New Conn) Abbey Street [Kelly 1889]

PENZANCE (Meth New Conn/U Meth) Alexandra Road
OR M 1967-94 (CRO)

PENZANCE (UMFC/U Meth) Parade Street [1882 Return] Rebuilt 1889
OR C 1866-1967 (CRO)
Cop C 1866-1926 (CFHS)

PENZANCE (Teetotal Meth/Meth New Conn/Wes) Sheffield. Erected 1845

PENZANCE (Salvation Army) Queen Street

PENZANCE (S of F) Monthly Meeting see Marazion (ST HILARY)

PENZANCE (S of F) f c.1730 part of Land's End and Marazion, called later
Penzance MM. North Street [1882 Return] Currently [1998] at St Paul's Old
School, Taroveor Road
OR Z 1735-81 M 1733-77 B 1765-75 in CORNWALL QM register RG 6/1578;
    Z 1775-82 in West Division register RG 6/951 (PRO); M 1839-94 Falmouth,
    Truro, Redruth and Penzance (CRO)
Cop Z 1674-1782 M 1694, 1706 B 1688-98 Marazion, Penzance and Lands End:
    extracted from MM registers 1838 (CRO)

PENZANCE (Jews) Synagogue 1807-1906. New Street [1882 Return]
Cop M 1837-92 (CRO,CFHS)
MI (Ptd CFHS)

PENZANCE Heamoor Cemetery
OR B 1847-1907 (CRO)

PERRANARWORTHAL or PERRAN-AR-WORTHAL St Piran [Kerrier Hundred; Falmouth
Union] [1504] Chapelry in STITHIANS. Now with STITHIANS, GWENNAP
OR C 1739-1975 M 1739-1984 B 1739-1961 (CRO)
BT CMB 1684-1736, 1741-72 (CRO); CMB 1597-1673, 1737-40, 1773-1838, 1848
    (DRO)
Cop M 1684-1812 (Ptd Phillimore: 1904); CMB 1598-1736 from BT; CB 1739-1837
    (DCRS/WSL); M 1813-37 (CMI); M 1601-1812 (SG); M 1684-1812 from OR;
    M 1601-73 from BT (Boyd); M 1800-12 (Pallot); B 1813-37 (CBI)
Cop (Mf) CMB 1739-1959 (RIC); CMB 1597-1812 (Mf of BT at DRO: CRO,CSL);
        M 1813-37; banns 1837-1900 (Ross); Extr C 1597-1673, 1684-1736,
        1739-1875 M 1684-1739 (IGI); C 1597-1673, 1684-1736, 1739-1875
        (SLC)
MI (Ptd CFHS)

PERRANARWORTHAL (Wes) Perranwell [1882 Return]
OR C 1847-75 (CRO)

PERRANARWORTHAL (Wes) Perranwell. Erected 1867. Closed 1987
OR C 1841-1986 (CRO)

PERRANARWORTHAL (Bible Christian) Perranwell [1882 Return]

PERRANPORTH   see PERRANZABULOE

PERRANUTHNOE St Michael and St Piran [Penwith Hundred; Penzance Union]
[1033] United with ST HILARY
OR C 1562-1883 M 1589-1971 B 1562-1906 (CRO) Noted in 1831: B deficient
     1617-52, M defective 1621-98
BT CMB 1676-1736, 1741-72 (CRO); CMB 1614-70, 1737-40, 1773-1836 (DRO)
Cop C 1562-1866 M 1589-1837 B 1562-1845 (CRO,CSL,CFHS); M 1589-1812
     (Ptd Phillimore: 1909); M 1813-37 (CMI); CB 1562-1812, C 1823;
     Extr CMB 1573-1731 (Morrab); CB 1562-1812 (SG); M 1589-1812 (Boyd);
     M 1800-12 (Pallot); B 1813-37 (CBI)
Cop (Mf) CB 1562-1959 M 1589-1960 (RIC); CMB 1627-1812 (Mf of BT at DRO:
          CRO,CSL); M 1813-1910 (Ross); Extr C 1562-1885 M 1589-1875 (IGI);
          C 1562-1875 (SLC)
MI (Ptd CFHS)

PERRANUTHNOE (Wes) Goldsithney. Erected 1841. [1882 Return] Rebuilt 1984

PERRANUTHNOE (Wes Meth Assn) [Kelly 1856]

PERRANUTHNOE (Wes) Church Town [Kelly 1889]

PERRANUTHNOE (Wes) Trevean. f.1767 ? [Kelly 1889]

PERRANUTHNOE (Bible Cgristian) Rosudgeon Common. Erected 1858. Rebuilt 1904

PERRANWELL *see* PERRANARWORTHAL

PERRANZABULOE St Piran [Pydar Hundred; Truro Union] [2793] St Piran's
Oratory, and later 12th century church, both in the sands, replaced 1804 by
present church. Peculiar of the Dean and Chapter of Exeter
OR C 1558-1963 M 1663-1957 B 1653-1926 (CRO) Noted in 1831: imperfect
     fragments C 1614-36, 1643-1702 M 1603-34. No mention of C 1558+
BT CMB 1619-1837 (DRO)
Cop M 1619-35, 1663-1834 (Ptd Phillimore: 1903); C 1558-1702 B 1653-64,
     1682-1800 (CRO); CMB 1619-35 from BT; C 1558-1837 B 1653-1837
     (DCRS/WSL); M 1619-1812, B 1682-1800 with index (Ms and Ts, (RIC);
     M 1813-37 (CMI); M 1619-1812 (SG); M 1619-1812 (Boyd); M 1800-12
     (Pallot); M 1876-1900 (CFHS); B 1682-1812 index (CFHS); B 1813-37 (CBI)
Cop (Mf) CMB 1619-1811 (Mf of BT at DRO: CRO,CSL); M 1813-75 (Ross);
          Extr C 1558-76, 1614-78, 1681-1721 M 1619-1837 (IGI); C 1558-86,
          1614-78, 1681-1721 M 1619-35, 1813-37 (SLC)
MI (Ptd CFHS)

PERRANZABULOE St Michael, Perranporth. Mission church

PERRANZABULOE (RC) Christ the King, Perranporth f 1931

PERRANZABULOE (Wes) Bolingey [1882 Return]
OR C 1841-90 M 1901-78 (CRO)

PERRANZABULOE (Wes) Callestock [1882 Return]
MI (Ptd CFHS)

PERRANZABULOE (Wes) Rose. Erected 1839. Rebuilt 1865 [1882 Return]
OR C 1848-88 (CRO)
Cop C 1888-1903 (CRO)

PERRANZABULOE (Wes) Wheal Frances [1882 Return]

PERRANZABULOE (Wes) A building belonging to Mr Ezekiel Hall, Perranporth
[1882 Return]

PERRANZABULOE or **Perranarworthal** ? (Wes) Perranwell Circuit
OR C 1841-47 (CRO); for earlier and later entries see GWENNAP

PERRANZABULOE (Bible Christian) Penhallow [1882 Return]

PERRANZABULOE (Bible Christian) Goonhavern [1882 Return]

PETERVILLE   see ST AGNES

PETHERICK, LITTLE   see ST PETROC MINOR

PETHERWIN, NORTH St Paternus [East Hundred; Launceston Union] In Devon
1844-1966. United with EGLOSKERRY, TREMAINE, TRESMERE
OR C 1653-1899 M 1653-1837 B 1653-1862 (CRO)
BT CMB 1676-1736, 1741-72 (CRO); CMB 1611-73, 1737-40, 1773-1848 (DRO)
Cop M 1813-37 (CMI); M 1611-73 from BT (Boyd, Devon; SG); B 1813-37 (CBI)
Cop (Mf) CMB 1611-1812 (Mf of BT at DRO: CRO,CSL); M 1611-38, 1653-1837
          (Ross); Extr C 1676-1805 (IGI, Devon); C 1676-1805 (SLC)
MI (Ptd CFHS)

PETHERWIN, NORTH (Wes) Helscott [1882 Return]; Elscott Chapel, Petherwin
Gate [1882 Return]
MI (Ptd CFHS)

PETHERWIN, NORTH (Wes) Brazacott [1882 Return]

PETHERWIN, NORTH (Bible Christian) Salem, Maxworthy [1882 Return]

PETHERWIN, NORTH (Bible Christian) Trecrogo Lane End [1882 Return]

PETHERWIN, NORTH (Bible Christian) Navarina [Kelly 1889]

PETHERWIN, NORTH (UMFC) Copthorne [1882 Return]
MI (Ptd CFHS)

PETHERWIN, SOUTH St Paternus [East Hundred; Launceston Union] [988] Peculiar
of the Bishop of Exeter. United with LEZANT. LAWHITTON, TREWEN
OR C 1656-1979 MB 1656-1978 (CRO)
BT CMB 1608-1812; CMB 1824-37 unfit for production; 1838-40 (DRO)
Cop M 1656-1812 (Ptd Phillimore: 1910); M 1813-37 (CMI); M 1608-1812 (SG);
    M 1656-1812 from OR; M 1608-75 from BT (Boyd); M 1790-1812 (Pallot);
    B 1813-37 (CBI)
Cop (Mf) CMB 1608-1812 (Mf of BT at DRO: CRO,CSL); Extr M 1656-1812 (IGI)
MI (Ptd CFHS)

PETHERWIN, SOUTH (Bapt) Erected 1849 [Bapt.Handbook 1869]

PETHERWIN, SOUTH (Presb) fl 1662-90

PETHERWIN, SOUTH (Wes) [1882 Return]
MI (Ptd CFHS)

PETHERWIN, SOUTH (Bible Christian) Treecross [1882 Return]

PETHERWIN, SOUTH (Bible Christian) Kenner's House [1882 Return]

PETHERWIN, SOUTH (Meth) Erected 1872

ST PETROC MINOR or LITTLE PETHERICK or NASSINGTON St Petroc [Pydar Hundred; St Columb Major Union] [224] Peculiar of the Bishop of Exeter. United with ST ISSEY
OR C 1706-1984 M 1708-1837 B 1708-1993 (CRO) No earlier registers noted in 1831
BT CMB 1608-1822, 1824-44 (DRO)
Cop M 1620?, 1636, 1662, 1685-1812 (Ptd Phillimore: 1909); M 1754-1812 (Ms RIC); M 1813-37 (CMI); CB 1708-1812 (SG); M 1636-1812 from OR; M 1608-62 from BT (Boyd); M 1800-12 (Pallot); B 1813-37 (CBI)
Cop (Mf) CMB 1608-1812 (Mf of BT at DRO: CRO,CSL); M 1813-37 (Ross);
          Extr C 1705-1812 M 1636-1812 (IGI); C 1706-1812 (SLC)
MI (Ptd CFHS)

ST PETROC MINOR (Wes) [Kelly 1897]; Meth [Kelly 1935]

PHILLACK St Felicitas [Penwith Hundred; Redruth Union] [3053] Now part of GODREVY team mission, *see also* GWITHIAN
OR C 1560-1966 M 1572-1983 B 1560-1985 (CRO)
BT CMB 1684-1736, 1741-72 (CRO); CMB 1614-66, 1737-40, 1773-1858 (DRO)
Cop M 1572-1812 (Ptd Phillimore: 1902); C 1686-1837 B 1560-1837 (CRO); CMB 1614-1717 from BT; M 1837-1904 (DCRS/WSL); C 1560-1812, 1822-60 M 1837-1901 B 1560-1829 (CSL); M 1813-37 (CMI); M 1572-1812 (Boyd); M 1790-1812 (Pallot); M 1837-1900 (CFHS); B 1813-37 (CBI)
Cop (Mf) C 1560-1959 M 1572-1959 B 1560-1960 (RIC); CMB 1614-1812 (Mf of BT at DRO: CRO,CSL); C 1614-1717 (SG); M 1813-1925 (Ross);
          Extr C 1561-1875 M 1572-1875 (IGI); C 1561-1852 M 1572-1760 (SLC)
MI (Ptd CFHS)

PHILLACK St Elwyn, Hayle. Hayle a district in PHILLACK. Separate parish 1870. Erected 1886-88. Now part of GODREVY team mission
OR C 1888-1956 M 1888-1979 (CRO)
Cop (Mf) C 1889-1959 M 1888-1959 (RIC)
MI (CFHS)

PHILLACK (RC) St Joseph, Hayle f 1958

PHILLACK (Bapt) Hayle [Kelly 1856] [*Bapt.Handbook* 1881] Baptist Temperance Chapel [1882 Return]

PHILLACK (Wes) Hayle Circuit
OR C 1862-1945 (CRO)

PHILLACK (Wes) Foundry, Hayle. Erected 1845. [1882 Return] Closed
OR C 1891-1967 (CRO)

PHILLACK (Wes) Wheal Alfred [1882 Return]

PHILLACK (Wes) Angarrack [1882 Return]

PHILLACK (Wes) Chapel Lane, Copperhouse, Hayle f 1784. Rebuilt 1815-16. [1882 Return] Demolished 1973
OR ZC 1818-37 (PRO); C 1935-69 M 1903-60 (CRO)
Cop ZC 1818-37 (SG)
Cop (Mf) ZC 1818-37 (DCRS/WSL); Extr ZC 1818-37 (IGI); ZC 1818-37 (SLC)

PHILLACK (U Meth/Bible Christian) Highlanes [1882 Return]
OR C 1945-67 (CRO)

PHILLACK (UMFC) Hayle Chapel [1882 Return]

PHILLACK (Salvation Army) Salvation Warehouse, Foundry, Hayle [1882 Return]
Later in Cross Street

PHILLACK (UMFC) Ventonleague [1882 Return]

PHILLEIGH or FILLEIGH or EGLOS ROSE St Philleigh [Powder Hundred; Truro
Union] [432] United with ST JUST IN ROSELAND
OR C 1733-1954 M 1753-1979 B 1733-1955 (CRO)
    Noted in 1831: CM 1548+ B 1544+
BT CMB 1678-1736, 1741-72 (CRO); CMB 1597-1673, 1737-40, 1773-1816, 1818-
    26, 1828-29, 1831, 1833-34 (DRO)
Cop M 1613-73, 1681-1730, 1734-1837 (Ptd Phillimore: 1935); CMB 1597-1733
    from BT; CB 1733-1825 (DCRS/WSL); C 1613-1812 M 1613-1837 B 1613-1825
    (CSL); C 1837-75 M 1837-1910 (CFHS); M 1813-37 (CMI); M 1597-1673 from
    BT (Boyd); M 1790-1812 (Pallot); B 1813-37 (CBI)
Cop (Mf) C 1813-1903 M 1755-1958 B 1813-1957 (RIC); CMB 1597-1812 (Mf of BT
        at DRO: CRO,CSL); M 1813-1925 (Ross); Extr C 1612-1875 M 1613-73,
        1755-1875 (IGI); C 1612-1875 M 1613-73 (SLC)
MI (Ptd CFHS); Ch (Wall,79, Ms SG)

PHILLEIGH (Wes) 2 chapels [Kelly 1856]; Lemon Chapel, Church Town
[1882 Return]

PILLATON St Odulph [East Hundred; St Germans Union] [413] United with
ST DOMINICK, LANDULPH, ST MELLION
OR C 1557-1910 M 1557-1978 B 1557-1992 (CRO)
BT CMB 1675-1736, 1741-72 (CRO); CMB 1611-73, 1737-40, 1773-1843, 1846-47,
    1849 (DRO)
Cop M 1557-1812 (Ptd Phillimore: 1910; M 1813-37 (CMI); C 1557-1812 B 1721-
    1812 (SG); M 1557-1812 (Boyd); M 1790-1812 (Pallot); M 1838-75 (CFHS);
    B 1813-37 (CBI)
Cop (Mf) CMB 1612-1812 (Mf of BT at DRO: CRO,CSL); M 1813-75 (Ross);
        Extr CM 1557-1812 (IGI); CM 1557-1812 (SLC)
MI (Ptd CFHS)

PILLATON (Wes) [1882 Return]
OR M 1908-45 (CRO)

PILLATON (Bible Christian) Zion, Polborder. Erected 1861
MI (Ptd CFHS)

PILLATON (Bible Christian) High Lanes [Kelly 1889]

ST PINNOCK St Pinnock [West Hundred; Liskeard Union] [425] United with
LISKEARD, ST KEYNE, MORVAL, BRADOC
OR C 1566-1978 M 1539-1948 B 1546-1896 (CRO)
BT CMB 1682-1736, 1741-72 (CRO); CMB 1597-1673, 1737-40, 1773-1848, 1871
    (DRO)
Cop M 1539-1837 (Ts CRO,RIC,CSL); M 1813-37 (CMI); B 1813-37 (CBI);
    M 1597-1673 from BT (Boyd)
Cop (Mf) CMB 1597-1812 (Mf of BT at DRO: CRO,CSL); M 1539-1875 (Ross);
        Extr C 1682-1772 (IGI); C 1682-1772 (SLC)
MI (Ptd CFHS)

ST PINNOCK (Bible Christian) Bethel. Erected 1843

ST PINNOCK (Wes Reform Union/Meth) Connon. Erected 1865. Free Wes
[1882 Return]
MI (Ptd CFHS)

PIPER'S POOL	*see* TREWEN
PLAIN AN GWARRY	*see* REDRUTH
PLANTATION	*see* CAMBORNE
PLUSHA BRIDGE	*see* LINKINHORNE
POLBORDER	*see* PILLATON
POLBROCK	*see* EGLOSHAYLE
POLGOOTH	*see* ST MEWAN
POLKERRIS	*see* TYWARDREATH
POLMASSICK	*see* ST EWE
POLPEOR	*see* LELANT
POLPERRO	*see* TALLAND
POLRUAN	*see* LANTEGLOS BY FOWEY
POLYPHANT	*see* LEWANNICK
PONJARAVAH	*see* CONSTANTINE
PONSANOOTH	partly in ST GLUVIAS q.v., partly in PERRANARWORTHAL
PONSONGATH	*see* ST KEVERNE
POOL	*see* ILLOGAN
POOL, POLPERRO	*see* TALLAND
PORKELLIS	*see* WENDRON
PORT HOLLAND	or PORTHOLLAND, *see* VERYAN
PORT ISAAC	see ST ENDELLION
PORTBYAN	or PORTBIGHAN, *see* LOOE
PORTH	*see* KEA
PORTH TOWN	*see* ILLOGAN
PORTHALLOW	*see* ST KEVERNE
PORTHILLY	*see* ST MINVER
PORTHLEVEN	*see* SITHNEY
PORTHMEOR	*see* ST AUSTELL

PORTHMEOR   *see* ZENNOR

PORTHOUSTOCK   *see* ST KEVERNE

PORTHTOWAN   *see* ST AGNES

PORTLOE   *see* VERYAN

PORTREATH   *see* ILLOGAN

PORTSCATHO   *see* ST GERRANS

POUGHILL St Olaf King and Martyr [Stratton Hundred; Stratton Union] [360]
OR C 1537-1967 M 1537-1950 B 1538-1955 (CRO)
BT CMB 1676-1735, 1741-72 (CRO); CMB 1619-73, 1737-40, 1773-1813, 1815-23, 1825-35 (DRO)
Cop M 1537-1812 (Ptd Phillimore: 1912); CMB 1537-1812 (DCRS/WSL); M 1813-37 (CMI); M 1537-1812 (Boyd); M 1800-12 (Pallot); B 1813-37 (CBI)
Cop (Mf) CM 1537-1960 B 1538-1960 (RIC); CMB 1619-1812 (Mf of BT at DRO: CRO,CSL); M 1813-1925 (Ross); Extr C 1537-1875 (IGI); C 1537-1875 (SLC)
MI (Ptd CFHS); ch,cy 1927 (Ts SG)

POUGHILL (Wes) [Kelly 1897]; Meth [Kelly 1935]

POUGHILL (Bible Christian) Bush f 1869 [Kelly 1889]

POUNDSTOCK St Neot, later St Winwaloe [Lesnewth Hundred; Stratton Union] [727] United with WEEK ST MARY, WHITSTONE
OR C 1614-1974 MB 1614-1975 (CRO)
BT CMB 1676-1736, 1741-72 (CRO); CMB 1597-1673, 1737-40, 1773-1838 (DRO)
Cop CMB 1587-1673 from BT; M 1614-1837 with BOYTON (DCRS/WSL); M 1813-37 (CMI); Extr CB 1597-1673 M 1597-1837 (SG); M 1615-1812 from OR; M 1597-1673 from BT (Boyd); M 1790-1814 (Pallot); B 1813-37 (CBI)
Cop (Mf) C 1614-1854 M 1614-1959 B 1614-1887 (RIC); CMB 1618-1812 (Mf of BT at DRO: CRO,CSL); M 1838-75 (SG); M 1813-1925 (Ross); Extr C 1597-1602, 1614-1852 M 1597-1875 (IGI); C 1597-1602, 1813-52 M 1597-1875 (SLC)
MI (Ptd CFHS); ch c.1927 (Ts SG)

POUNDSTOCK Our Lady and St Anne, Widemouth Bay. Mission church

POUNDSTOCK (Wes Meth Assn/UMFC) Bangors. Erected 1840. UMFC [1882 Return] Now a house

POUNDSTOCK (Bible Christian) Ebenezer Chapel, Meads. Erected 1879 [1882 Return] [Kelly 1889]

POUNDSTOCK (Meth) Dimma [Kelly 1935]

PRADNACK   *see* MULLION

PRAZE   PRAZE AN BEEBLE *see* CROWAN

PRAZE   *see* ST ERTH

PROBUS St Probus and St Grace [Powder Hundred; Truro Union] [1350]
United with LADOCK, GRAMPOUND, CREED, ST ERME
OR C 1642-1979 M 1641-1981 B 1641-1939 (CRO) Noted in 1831: C deficient
    1646-52
BT CMB 1677-1735, 1741-72 (CRO); CMB 1597-1670, 1737-40, 1773-1836 (DRO)
Cop M 1641-1812 (Ptd Phillimore: 1915); CMB 1597-1631; C 1642-1837
    B 1641-1837 (DCRS/WSL); M 1813-37 (CMI); M 1597-1812 (SG); M 1641-1812
    from OR; M 1597-1670 from BT (Boyd); M 1800-12 (Pallot); B 1813-37 (CBI)
Cop (Mf) C 1642-1959 MB 1641-1959 (RIC); CMB 1597-1812 (Mf of BT at DRO:
    CRO,CSL); M 1813-1925 (Ross); Extr C 1597-1875 (IGI); C 1597-1875
    (SLC)
MI (Ptd CFHS); Ch (Wall, 84-85, Ms SG)

PROBUS (Presb) fl 1672-90

PROBUS (Wes) Erected 1788; rebuilt 1825; = ? Church Town [1882 Return]
OR ZC 1815-37 (PRO); C 1837-1980 (CRO)
Cop ZC 1815-37 (SG)
Cop (Mf) ZC 1815-37 (DCRS/WSL,SG); Extr ZC 1815-37 (IGI); ZC 1815-37 (SLC)

PROBUS (Wes) Tresillian. Erected 1831. A building in the occupation of
Matthew Truscott [1882 Return]

PROBUS (Bible Christian) Back Lane, later High Street. Erected 1822
[1882 Return]

PROBUS (Bible Christian) Tresillian [Kelly 1889]

PROSPIDNICK   *see* SITHNEY

QUENCHWELL   *see* KEA

QUETHIOCK or QUETHICK St Hugh [East Hundred; St Germans Union] [692]
OR C 1574-1984 M 1574-1978 B 1574-1884 (CRO) Noted in 1831: CMB deficient
    1738-59 "but imperfectly supplied by loose pages preserved by the Clerk"
BT CMB 1675-1736, 1741-72 (CRO); CMB 1597-1673, 1737-40, 1773-1848, 1850,
    1852-54 (DRO)
Cop CMB 1574-1837 (DCRS/WSL); M 1813-37 (CMI); M 1611-73 (SG); M 1597-1673
    from BT (Boyd); M 1876-1900 (CFHS); B 1813-37 (CBI)
Cop (Mf) C 1574-1852 M 1574-1836 B 1574-1889 (RIC); CMB 1597-1812 (Mf of BT
    at DRO: CRO,CSL); C 1574-1766 (SG); M 1574-1875 (Ross);
    Extr C 1573-1744, 1759-1852 M 1581-1623 (IGI); C 1573-1744,
    1759-65, 1767-1852 M 1581-1623 (SLC)
MI (Ptd CFHS)

QUETHIOCK (Wes) Erected 1839; [1882 Return]

QUETHIOCK (Bible Christian/Wes) Blunts Salem. Erected 1843.
Became Wes c.1888

QUETHIOCK (S of F) f c.1656. Moved to ST GERMANS 1697. Part of East Cornwall
MM.
OR Z 1647-88 B 1659-90 in CORNWALL QM register RG 6/1578 (PRO);
    B 1669-1712 in EAST CORNWALL MM register RG 6/1314 (PRO); Z 1647-1730
    M 1664-1731: RG 6/1249 (PRO)
Cop Z 1647-96 B 1659-90 in 1828 copy of old register book of Cornwall QM
    (CRO)

QUINTRELL DOWNS   *see* ST COLUMB MINOR

RAILWAY   *see* LINKINHORNE

RAME   hamlet in WENDRON

RAME or PENHENDAR St Germanus [East Hundred; St Germans Union] [896]
United 1943 with MAKER
OR CB 1653-1812 M 1653-1837 (CRO)
BT CMB 1813-27, 1830-31 (DRO)
Cop M 1653-1837 (Ts with index, CRO,RIC,CFHS); M 1813-37 (CMI); CB 1813-40
    M 1619-1837 (SG); M 1619-73 from BT (Boyd)
Cop (Mf) CMB 1619-1812 (Mf of BT at DRO: CRO,CSL); M 1653-1837 (Ross);
        Extr C 1653-1812 (IGI); C 1653-1812 (SLC)
MI Ch (Ptd Jewers 3-10)

RAME St Andrew, Cawsand. Chapel-of-ease to RAME. Erected 1878

RAME St Michael, Rame Head. 14th century chapel

RAME (Ind. now Cong Fed) Garrett Street, Cawsand f 1793
OR ZC 1810-37 (PRO); ZMD 1810+ (Ch Sec)
Cop ZC 1810-37 (SG)
Cop (Mf) ZC 1810-37 (DCRS/WSL); Extr ZC 1810-37 (IGI); ZC 1810-37 (SLC)

REDMOOR   *see* LANLIVERY

REDRUTH St Euny [Penwith Hundred; Redruth Union] [8191] Rebuilt 1768.
United with LANNER, TRELEIGH
OR C 1560-1984 M 1615-1972 B 1562-1969 (CRO) Noted in 1831: M 1652-89
    defective
BT CMB 1681-1736, 1741-72 (CRO); CMB 1614-73, 1737-40, 1772-1812, 1815-20,
    1822-26, 1828, 1831-32, 1835 (DRO)
Cop C 1560-1717 M 1613-89 B 1562-1716 (Ptd T.Peter *The Parish Registers of*
    Redruth in Cornwall: 1894}; M 1717-1812 (Ptd Phillimore: 1911);
    C 1717-1866 M 1717-1837 B 1717-1845 (CSL); CMB 1717-1845 (CFHS);
    CMB 1560-1845 (CRO); CMB 1560-1716, 1775-1812 (CFHS); CMB 1717-1837
    (DCRS/WSL); CMB 1775-1845 (Ts RIC); M 1813-37 (CMI); M 1560-1837 (Boyd);
    M 1800-13 (Pallot); B 1813-37 (CBI)
Cop (Mf) CMB 1560-1716 (RIC); CMB 1614-1812 (Mf of BT at DRO: CRO,CSL);
        M 1837-75 (Ross); Extr C 1560-1837 M 1614-1837 (IGI); C 1560-1830
        M 1614-1812 (SLC)

REDRUTH Chapel Street. Chapel-of-ease erected 1828. Disused
OR None

REDRUTH St Stephen, Treleigh. Parish created 1846 from REDRUTH. Services
held in blacksmith's shop at Treleigh Mine. Church erected 1865-66. United
with REDRUTH, LANNER
OR C 1862-1978 M 1866-1988 B 1866-1940 registers of grave plots 1866-1980,
    plan of graves c.1980 (CRO) No earlier registers known
Cop C 1862-80 M 1876-1909 (CFHS)

REDRUTH St Andrew. Erected 1884. Daughter church to REDRUTH St Euny
OR C 1884-1945 M 1885-1965 (CRO)

REDRUTH (RC) The Assumption f 1936

REDRUTH (Bapt) f 1802 [*Bapt. Manual* 1850; *Handbook* 1881]

REDRUTH (Presb) fl 1672-90

REDRUTH (Wes) Redruth Circuit (part only)
OR C 1839-1901 (CRO)

REDRUTH (Wes) Wesley, Fore Street. Erected 1826 [Kelly 1889]
OR M 1909-42 (CRO)

REDRUTH (Wes) South Downs
OR C 1891-1975 (CRO)

REDRUTH (Wes) = ? one of above ?
OR ZC 1805-37 (PRO)
Cop ZC 1805-37 (SG)
Cop (Mf) ZC 1805-37 (DCRS/WSL); Extr C 1805-37 (IGI); C 1805-37 (SLC)

REDRUTH (Wes) Wheal Buller
OR C 1925-78 (CRO)

REDRUTH (Prim Meth) Circuit
OR ZC 1832-37 (PRO); C 1843-1934 (CRO)
Cop ZC 1832-37 (SG)
Cop (Mf) ZC 1832-37 (DCRS/WSL); Extr ZC 1832-37 (IGI); ZC 1832-37 (SLC)

REDRUTH (Prim Meth) Plain-an-Gwarry. Erected 1882 [1882 Return]
Closed c.1975
OR M 1916-25 (CRO)

REDRUTH (Prim Meth) Redruth Highway [1882 Return]

REDRUTH (Prim Meth) Carnmarth [1882 Return]

REDRUTH (Prim Meth) North Country [1882 Return]

REDRUTH (Bible Christian) Redruth and Camborne Circuit
OR C 1876-1920 (CRO)

REDRUTH (Bible Christian) [1882 Return]

REDRUTH (Bible Christian/U Meth) Treruffe Hill. Erected 1864 [Kelly 1889]
OR C 1925-73 M 1969-75 (CRO)

REDRUTH (UMFC/U Meth) Fore Street. Erected 1838. Rebuilt 1865. [1882 Return]
Demolished 1973
OR C 1865-1969 M 1915-64 (CRO)

REDRUTH (UMFC) North Country [1882 Return]

REDRUTH (UMFC) South Downes [1882 Return]

REDRUTH (S of F) Erected 1731. Part of FALMOUTH MM. Meeting house in Church
Lane erected 1833 [1882 Return] Later used by Apostolic Church
OR Z notes 1838-43, 1847-86; B notes 1838-72, 1874-94, 1898-1945; list of
    B 1810-36; M 1839-94 Falmouth, Truro, Redruth and Penzance (CRO)
MI (Ptd CFHS)

REDRUTH (Apostolic Church) Church Lane

REDRUTH (Salvation Army) Middletons Row

REDRUTH Poor Law Union
<u>OR</u> D 1837-67, 1901-39 (CRO)

RELEATH   *see* CROWAN

RELUBBUS   *see* ST HILARY

RESCORLA   *see* ST AUSTELL

RESTORMEL   *see* LOSTWITHIEL

RETEW   *see* ST ENODER

RETIRE   *see* WITHIEL

REZARE   *see* LEZANT

RILLA MILL   *see* LINKINHORNE

RINSEY   *see* BREAGE

ROCHE St Gomonda of the Rock [Powder Hundred; St Austell Union] [1630]
United with WITHIEL
<u>OR</u> C 1571-1885 M 1579-86, 1599-1966 B 1612-39, 1710-1933 (CRO)
<u>BT</u> CMB 1681-1736, 1741-72 (CRO); CMB 1609-73, 1737-40, 1773-1814, 1817-20,
     1827-31, 1833-41 (DRO)
<u>Cop</u> M 1578-1812 (Ptd Phillimore: 1910); CMB 1571-1640, 1681-1708 (CRO);
     M 1813-37 (CMI); M 1578-1812 (Boyd); M 1790-1812 (Pallot); B 1813-37
     (CBI)
<u>Cop (Mf)</u> C 1571-1959 M 1579-1959 B 1612-1933 (RIC); CMB 1609-1812 (Mf of BT
          at DRO: CRO,CSL); M 1813-1925 (Ross); Extr C 1571-1622, 1681-1708,
          1710-73, 1800-75 M 1578-1754 (IGI); C 1571-1622, 1681-1708,
          1710-73, 1800-75 (SLC)
<u>MI</u> (Ptd CFHS)

ROCHE (Wes) Chapel Road. Erected 1835 [1882 Return]
<u>Cop</u> B 1839-1924 (CRO)
<u>MI</u> (Ptd CFHS)

ROCHE (Bible Christian/U Meth) Tresaise [1882 Return] Rebuilt 1883
<u>OR</u> C 1950-85 (CRO)

ROCHE (Bible Christian) Tregoss [1882 Return]

ROCHE (Bible Christian) Mount Pleasant, Colbiggan [1882 Return]

ROCHE (Bible Christian) Belowda [Kelly 1889]

ROCHE (Bible Christian) Tremodrett [Kelly 1889]

ROCHE (Salvation Army) Edgecumbe Road

ROCK   *see* ST MINVER

ROSCARRACK HILL *see* ST ENDELLION

ROSE   *see* PERRANZABULOE

ROSECROGGAN   *see* ILLOGAN

ROSEMELLEN   *see* LUXULYAN

ROSENANNON   *see* ST WENN

ROSENDIAN COMMON   *see* ST HILARY

ROSEVEAR   *see* ST MAWGAN IN MENEAGE

ROSEWORTHY   hamlet in CAMBORNE q.v. and GWINEAR

ROSUDGEON COMMON   *see* PERRANUTHNOE

ROSWICK   *see* ST KEVERNE

ROWLE   *see* ST GERMANS

RUAN LANIHORNE St Rumon [Powder Hundred; Truro Union] [424] United with
VERYAN
OR C 1685-1919 M 1685-1990 B 1685-1992 (CRO)
BT CMB 1682-1736, 1741-72 (CRO); CMB 1608-70, 1737-40, 1773-1847 (DRO)
Cop M 1608-1812 (Ptd Phillimore: 1935); CMB 1608-84 from BT; CB 1685-1837
   (DCRS/WSL); CMB 1608-70 from BT (CRO); M 1608-1836 (CSL); B 1829-31
   (Ts RIC); M 1813-37 (CMI); M 1608-70 from BT (Boyd); M 1790-1837
   (Pallot); C 1837-75 (CFHS); B 1813-37 (CBI)
Cop (Mf) CB 1685-1959 M 1686-1836 (RIC); CMB 1608-1812 (Mf of BT at DRO:
      CRO,CSL); M 1608-1837 (Ross); Extr C 1608-40, 1670-1875 M 1608-1836
      (IGI); C 1608-40, 1670-1875 M 1608-1836 (SLC)
MI (Ptd CFHS); Ch (Wall,30-32, Ms SG)

RUAN LANIHORNE (Wes) Tregiswin [1882 Return]; Meth [Kelly 1935]

RUAN LANIHORNE (Bible Christian) Pisgah, Treworgy [1882 Return]

RUAN MAJOR St Rumon [Kerrier Hundred; Helston Union] [162] United with
GRADE, RUAN MINOR. LANDEWEDNACK
OR C 1682-1944 M 1683-1903 B 1683-1986 (CRO)
BT CMB 1681-1736, 1741-72 (CRO); CMB 1610-73, 1737-40, 1773-1837, 1819-22,
   1824-35, 1837-43 (DRO)
Cop M 1683-1812 (Ptd Phillimore: 1917); CMB 1610-81 from BT; C 1682-1837
   B 1683-1837 (DCRS/WSL); C 1682-1812 B 1683-1722 (RIC); M 1813-37 (CMI);
   M 1611-1812 (SG); M 1681-1812 from OR; M 1610-73 from BT (Boyd);
   M 1790-1812 (Pallot); C 1837-79 (CFHS)
Cop (Mf) CMB 1610-1812 (Mf of BT at DRO: CRO,CSL); M 1813-1903 (Ross);
      Extr C 1610-1837 from BT (IGI); C 1610-1837 from BT (SLC)
MI (Ptd CFHS)

RUAN MINOR St Ruan [Kerrier Hundred; Helston Union] [269] United with GRADE,
RUAN MAJOR, LANDEWEDNACK
OR C 1654-1882 M 1667-1984 B 1653-1980 (CRO)
BT CMB 1674-1736, 1741-72 (CRO); CMB 1608-73, 1737-40, 1773-1812, 1818-20,
   1822-24, 1827-31, 1834, 1836-49, 1851, 1853 (DRO)
Cop M 1667-1812 (Ptd Phillimore: 1917); CMB 1608-1825 from BT; CB 1624-1837
   (DCRS/WSL); M 1813-37 (CMI); M 1625-1812 (SG); M 1667-1812 from OR;
   M 1608-73 from BT (Boyd); M 1790-1812 (Pallot); M 1876-1925 (CFHS);
   B 1813-37 (CBI)

RUAN MINOR cont.
Cop (Mf) C 1654-1959 M 1668-1959 B 1653-1959 (RIC); CMB 1608-1812 (Mf of BT
     at DRO: CRO,CSL); M 1813-76 (Ross); Extr C 1608-1885 M 1838-95
     (IGI); C 1608-1875 (SLC)
MI   (Ptd CFHS)

RUAN MINOR St Mary, Cadgwith. Mission Church

RUAN MINOR (Wes) [1882 Return]; 2 Meth chapels [Kelly 1935]

RUAN MINOR (Bible Christian) Ebenezer, near Mount Pleasant [1882 Return]

RUAN MINOR (UMFC) Church Town [1882 Return]; [Kelly 1897]

RUAN MINOR (UMFC) Kuggar. Building owned by John Randle [1882 Return]

RUDGEVEAN   see ST HILARY

RUMFORD   see ST ERVAN

SALTASH St Nicholas and St Faith [East Hundred; St Germans Union] [1637]
Borough and chapelry in ST STEPHENS BY SALTASH. Separate parish 1881. United
with ST STEPHENS BY SALTASH
OR   C 1687-1957 M 1881-1975 B 1753-1864 (CRO) Noted in 1831: "Marr 1740-50.
     It is supposed that these Marriages took place at St Stephens, it being
     doubtful whether any ever were solemnized in this Chapel."
BT   None. see ST STEPHENS
Cop C 1697-1728 (CRO); M 1599, 1608, 1617 (SG); B 1813-37 (CBI)
MI   Ch (Ptd Jewers 33-6)

SALTASH (RC) Our Lady of the Angels f 1884; renamed Our Lady of Perpetual
Succour

SALTASH (Bapt) Meetings in hut Silver Street/Tamar Street 1782. f 1790.
Chapel erected Culver Road 1794. United with Liberty Street (Pembroke
Street) Devonport [Devon]; separate church 1819. New building 1866
OR   M 1946-65 (CRO); see also ? Z 1779-1810 Liberty Street/Pembroke Street,
     Devonport (PRO) Other records lost in fire in 1980s. No current
     registers
MI   (Ptd CFHS)

SALTASH (Presb) fl 1662-90

SALTASH (Wes) f 1807 = ? a building, Fore Street [1882 Return] ; Mission
Room, Tamar Street [1882 Return]
OR   C 1820-37 (PRO)
Cop C 1820-37 (SG)
Cop (Mf) C 1820-37 (DCRS/WSL); Extr C 1820-37 (IGI); C 1820-37 (SLC)

SALTASH (Persons who object to be designated) Union Meeting House, Fore
Street [1882 Return]
Cop (Mf) I SLC)

SALTASH (S of F) f by 1696, part of CORNWALL Eastern Division MM; new
meeting house 1732. Transferred to DEVON QM and attached to Plymouth
OR   see also Devon QM and Plymouth MM registers (PRO)

ST SAMPSON or GOLANT St Sampson [Powder Hundred; St Austell Union] [314]
Chapelry in TYWARDREATH. Separate parish 1737 ? Now with TYWARDREATH
OR C 1568-1905 M 1568-1984 B 1568-1974 (CRO)
BT CMB 1678-1735, 1741-72 (CRO); CMB 1609-73, 1737-40, 1773-1841 (DRO)
Cop M 1568-1812 (Ptd Phillimore: 1904); C 1836-75 (CFHS); M 1813-37 (CMI);
    CB 1568-1812 (SG); M 1568-1812 (Boyd); M 1790-1812 (Pallot); B 1813-37
    (CBI)
Cop (Mf) CB 1568-1959 M 1568-1957 (RIC); CMB 1609-1812 (Mf of BT at DRO:
    CRO,CSL); M 1813-1925 (Ross); Extr C 1568-1875 M 1568-98, 1632-1876
    (IGI); C 1568-1875 M 1568-98, 1632-1876 (SLC)
MI (Ptd CFHS)

ST SAMPSON (Wes) Golant, St Sampson [1882 Return]
OR C 1901-89 M 1918-88 (CRO)
Cop C 1901-32 M 1918-37 (CRO,CFHS)

SANCREED St Creden [Penwith Hundred; Penzance Union] [1069] United with
ST JUST IN PENWITH
OR C 1566-1835 M 1559-1966 B 1579-1973 (CRO)
BT CMB 1681-1736, 1741-72 (CRO); CMB 1597-1673, 1737-40, 1773-1812, 1817-36
    (DRO)
Cop M 1559-1812 (Ptd Phillimore: 1903); C 1566-1812 M 1559-1754 B 1579-1812
    (CRO); C 1566-1835 M 1559-1837 B 1636-1854 (Ms RIC); B 1579-1812 (CSL);
    C 1566-1812 B 1579-1812 (Morrab,SG); M 1813-37 (CMI); M 1559-1812
    (Boyd); M 1800-12 (Pallot); B 1813-37 (CBI)
Cop (Mf) C 1566-1959 M 1559-1956 B 1579-1957 (RIC); CMB 1597-1812 (Mf of BT
    at DRO: CRO,CSL); M 1813-1925 (Ross); Extr C 1566-1875 (IGI);
    C 1566-1834 (SLC)
MI (Ptd CFHS)

SANCREED (Wes) Newbridge. Erected 1840 [1882 Return]

SANCREED (Wes) Chapel Place. Erected 1823. fl c.1851

SANCREED (Wes) Court [Kelly 1889]

SANCREED (Bible Christian) Brane Moor. Erected 1845 [1882 Return]

SANCREED (Bible Christian) Church Town [1882 Return]

SANCREED (Bible Christian) Grumbla [Kelly 1889]

SANCREED (Bible Christian) Drift [Kelly 1889]

SANCREED (Bible Christian) Tregerest. Erected 1862
MI (Ptd CFHS)

SANCREED (Prim Meth) Newbridge c.1835. fl c.1851

SANDPLACE   *see* MORVAL

SCARCEWATER   *see* LADOCK

SCILLY ISLES St Mary, St Mary [Isles of Scilly Union] [2465] Church at Old
Town, and later church St Mary 1834-37 at Hugh Town
OR C 1726-1949 M 1726-1940 B 1726-1886 (CRO)
BT None
Cop M 1726-1812 (DCRS/WSL,CSL); M 1813-37 (CMI); C 1726-1889 M 1726-1940
    B 1726-1886 (SG,CFHS); B 1813-37 (CBI)
Cop (Mf) CB 1726-1960 M 1726-1953 (RIC); M 1727-1925 (Ross);
        Extr C 1726-1875 (IGI); C 1726-1875 (SLC)
MI Extr cy 1973 (Ts SG); (CFHS)

SCILLY ISLES St Agnes, St Agnes Erected 1827

SCILLY ISLES All Saints ? Bryher Erected 1742
MI (Ptd CFHS)

SCILLY ISLES St Martin Erected 1822; rebuilt 1867

SCILLY ISLES St Nicholas, Tresco New church 1879

SCILLY ISLES (RC) Our Lady Star of the Sea, Strand, St Mary's f 1930

SCILLY ISLES (Bapt) St Mary. Erected 1823 [*Bapt. Manual* 1850]
OR Z 1819-37 (PRO)
Cop Z 1819-37 (SG)
Cop (Mf) Z 1819-37 (DCRS/WSL,CRO); Extr Z 1819-37 (IGI); Z 1819-37 (SLC)

SCILLY ISLES (Bapt) Bryher. Erected 1877

SCILLY ISLES (Wes) Isles of Scilly Circuit
OR C 1838-1916 (CRO)

SCILLY ISLES (Wes)
OR ZC 1817-37 (PRO)
Cop ZC 1817-37 (SG)
Cop (Mf) ZC 1817-37 (DCRS/WSL); Extr ZC 1817-37 (IGI); ZC 1817-37 (SLC)

SCILLY ISLES (Wes) Holy Vale. Erected 1815. Closed by 1940

SCILLY ISLES (Wes) Hugh Town. Erected pre-1800

SCILLY ISLES (Wes) Old Town. Erected 1819

SCILLY ISLES (Bible Christian) Isles of Scilly Circuit
OR ZC 1823-37 (PRO); C 1840-1907 (CRO)
Cop ZC 1823-37 (SG)
Cop (Mf) ZC 1823-37 (DCRS/WSL); Extr ZC 1823-37 (IGI); ZC 1823-37 (SLC)

SCILLY ISLES (Bible Christian) St Mary. Church Street. Erected c.1830-40

SCILLY ISLES (Bible Christian) St Martin. Erected 1822

SCILLY ISLES (Bible Christian) St Agnes. Erected 1832; now a public hall

SCILLY ISLES (U Meth) Isles of Scilly Circuit
OR C 1907-34 (CRO)

SCLERDER   see TALLAND

SENNEN St Sennen [Penwith Hundred; Penzance Union] [689] Chapelry in
ST BURYAN. Royal Peculiar. Separate parish 1850. Now with ST BURYAN,
ST LEVAN
OR C 1700-1895 M 1700-1966 B 1700-1886 (CRO) No earlier registers noted in
1831. *see* ST BURYAN
BT CMB 1699-1847 (CRO) None at Exeter
Cop M 1699-1812 (Ptd Phillimore: 1903); CMB 1699-1700 from BT; CB 1700-1812
(DCRS/WSL); C 1699-1812 B 1700-1812 (CRO,RIC,SG,Morrab); M 1813-37
(CMI); M 1699-1812 (Boyd); M 1790-1812 (Pallot); M 1876-1900 (CFHS);
B 1813-37 (CBI)
Cop (Mf) CB 1700-1812 (Mf of Ts, RIC); M 1813-75 (Ross); Extr C 1699-1847
M 1699-1812 (IGI); C 1699-1812 (SLC)
MI (Ptd CFHS)

SENNEN (Bapt) [Kelly 1856] [*Bapt.Handbook* 1869] [Kelly 1889]

SENNEN (Wes) Erected 1815 [Kelly 1856]; [1882 Return]

SENNEN (Bible Christian) Escalls. Erected 1832 [1882 Return]
MI (Ptd CFHS)

SENNEN (Prim Meth) [Kelly 1856]

SENNEN (S of F) Land's End. f at Trevescan c.1656; Treeve 1696; closed by
1783. Part of PENZANCE MM
Cop B 1659-1782 in 1828 copy of old register book of Cornwall QM (CRO)

SHEFFIELD   *see* PENZANCE

SHEVIOCK Blessed Virgin Mary [East Hundred; St Germans Union] [453] United
with ANTONY
OR C 1624-1871 M 1570-1840 B 1569-1890 (CRO)
BT CMB 1677-1736, 1741-72 (CRO); CMB 1597-1673, 1737-40, 1773-1812, 1838
(DRO)
Cop M 1570-1812 (Ptd Phillimore: 1903); M 1813-37 (CMI); M 1570-1812 (Boyd);
M 1790-1812 (Pallot); M 1800-12 (Pallot)
Cop (Mf) C 1624-1871 M 1571-1840 B 1569-1900 (RIC); CMB 1597-1812 (Mf of BT
at DRO: CRO,CSL); M 1670-1709 (SG); M 1813-40, 1876-1925;
banns 1841-59 (Ross); Extr C 1624-1871 M 1570-1840 (IGI);
C 1624-1871 M 1570-1709 (SLC)
MI (Ptd CFHS)

SHEVIOCK (Wes) [Kelly 1856]; Crafthole. Erected 1867 [1882 Return]
[Kelly 1889]

SHOP   *see* MORWENSTOW

SHOP CHAPEL   *see* ST COLUMB MINOR

SHORT LANES END   *see* KENWYN

SIMONWARD   *see* ST BREWARD

SITHNEY St Sithney [Kerrier Hundred; Helston Union] [2772] United with
PORTHLEVEN
OR C 1667-1993 M 1664-1981 B 1664-1895 (CRO) Noted in 1831: vol.1 CMB 1623-
1709 imperfect
BT CMB 1674-1736, 1741-72 (CRO); CMB 1608-73, 1737-40, 1773-1812, 1814-21,
1823, 1827-38 (DRO)
Cop M 1614, 1654-1812 (Ptd Phillimore: 1904); C 1608-1858 M 1608-1837
B 1608-1845 (CSL); CMB 1664-1845 (CRO,CFHS); M 1813-37 (CMI);
M 1608-1812 (SG); M 1654-1812 from OR; M 1608-73 from BT (Boyd);
M 1800-12 (Pallot); B 1813-37 (CBI)
Cop (Mf) C 1667-1959 MB 1664-1959 (RIC); CMB 1608-1812 (Mf of BT at DRO:
CRO,CSL); M 1813-1900 (Ross); Extr C 1666-1875 (IGI); C 1666-1875
(SLC)
MI (Ptd CFHS)

SITHNEY St Bartholomew, Porthleven. Parish created 1840 from SITHNEY,
Erected 1842. Now united with SITHNEY
OR C 1846-1950 M 1847-1969 B 1848-1951 (CRO)
Cop C 1846-75 (CFHS)
MI (Ptd CFHS)

SITHNEY (Wes) Erected 1859= ? Church Town [1882 Return]

SITHNEY (Wes) Chynhale. Erected 1879 [Kelly 1889]
OR C 1880-1989 (CRO)
MI (Ptd CFHS)

SITHNEY (Wes) Fore Street, Porthleven. f by 1907

SITHNEY (Wes) Old Chapel, Porthleven [1882 Return]

SITHNEY (Wes) Torleven. Rebuilt 1883 [Kelly 1897]

SITHNEY (Wes) Prospidnick [1882 Return]

SITHNEY (Bible Christian/U Meth) Peverell Road, Porthleven [1882 Return]
OR C 1946-89 M 1974-88 (CRO)

SITHNEY (Bible Christian) Zion, Gwavas [1882 Return] = ? (Free Meth) Gwavas
[Kelly 1889]

SITHNEY (UMFC) Crown Town. Association Chapel owned by William Hendy
[1882 Return]

SITHNEY (UMFC) Tregathenan. Association Chapel [1882 Return]

SKINNERS BOTTOM   *see* ST AGNES

SLADESBRIDGE   *see* EGLOSHAYLE

SOUTH DOWNES   *see* REDRUTH

SOUTH HILL   *see* HILL, SOUTH

SOUTH PETHERWIN   *see* PETHERWIN, SOUTH

STEBB   hamlet in KILKHAMPTON

STENALEES   *see* ST AUSTELL

ST STEPHEN IN BRANNEL St Stephen [Powder Hundred; St Austell Union] [2477]
OR C 1694-1951 M 1694-1924 B 1695-1859 (CRO)
BT CMB 1681-1736, 1741-72 (CRO); CMB 1608-78, 1737-40, 1773-1815, 1817-18, 1820-21, 1828-36 (DRO)
Cop M 1681-1812 (Ptd Phillimore: 1906); CMB 1608-73 (Ts from BT, RIC); M 1608-73 (CSL); M 1813-37 (CMI); C 1694-1839 M 1608-1850 B 1695-1840 (CRO,SG); M 1681-1812 from OR; M 1608-73 from BT (Boyd); M 1800-12 (Pallot); B 1813-37 (CBI)
Cop (Mf) CM 1694-1959 B 1694-1952 (RIC); CMB 1608-1812 (Mf of BT at DRO: CRO,CSL); M 1813-1925 (Ross); Extr C 1681-1875 M 1694-1876 (IGI); C 1681-1875 M 1694-1812 (SLC)
MI (Ptd CFHS)

ST STEPHEN IN BRANNEL St George, Nanpean. Mission church erected 1878
Cop B 1880-1996 in cemetery (CFHS)
MI (Ptd CFHS)

ST STEPHEN IN BRANNEL (Wes) Coombe = ? U Free Meth [1882 Return]; (UMFC) [Kelly 1889]; Meth [Kelly 1835]
OR C 1829-1985 M 1937-61 (CRO)

ST STEPHEN IN BRANNEL (Wes) Nanpean [Kelly 1889, 1935]

ST STEPHEN IN BRANNEL (Bible Christian) [Kelly 1856]

ST STEPHEN IN BRANNEL (Bible Christian/U Meth) Trelyon [1882 Return]; Meth [Kelly 1935]
OR C 1933-58 (CRO)

ST STEPHEN IN BRANNEL (Bible Christian) Trethosa [1882 Return]; Meth [Kelly 1935]

ST STEPHEN IN BRANNEL (Bible Christian) Old Pound [1882 Return]; [Kelly 1935]

ST STEPHEN IN BRANNEL (UMFC/U Meth) Foxhole. Erected 1894
OR C 1885-1947 (CRO)

ST STEPHEN IN BRANNEL (UMFC/U Meth) High Street [1882 Return]; Meth [Kelly 1935]
OR C 1898-1963 (CRO)

ST STEPHEN IN BRANNEL (U Meth) Whitecross
OR C 1914-53 (CRO)

ST STEPHEN IN BRANNEL (U Free Meth) Nanpean f 1873 [1882 Return]

ST STEPHEN IN BRANNEL (Meth) Lanjeth [Kelly 1935]

ST STEPHEN IN BRANNEL (Meth) Treviscoe [Kelly 1935]

ST STEPHEN IN BRANNEL (Meth) Whitemoor [Kelly 1935]

ST STEPHEN IN BRANNEL (Meth) Church Town [Kelly 1935]

ST STEPHEN IN BRANNEL (S of F) Nanpean. f 1730; closed 1787. Part of ST AUSTELL MM

ST STEPHENS BY LAUNCESTON St Stephen [East Hundred; Launceston Union]
[1084 including Borough of Newport] Now with LAUNCESTON
OR C 1568-1909 M 1566-1968 B 1566-1912 (CRO) Noted in 1831: CB deficient
1758-78
BT CMB 1676-1736, 1741-72 (CRO); CMB 1611-73, 1737-40, 1773-1835, 1817-21,
1823-25, 1828-32, 1836-40 (DRO)
Cop M 1566-1812 (Ptd Phillimore: 1915); M 1813-37 (CMI); M 1837-75 (CFHS);
CB 1566-1812 (SG); M 1566-1812 (Boyd); M 1800-12 (Pallot); B 1813-37
(CBI)
Cop (Mf) CMB 1607-1812 (Mf of BT at DRO: CRO,CSL); M 1813-75 (Ross);
Extr C 1568-1812 (IGI); C 1568-1812 (SLC)
MI (Ptd CFHS)

ST STEPHENS BY LAUNCESTON (Ind) Langore f by 1821

ST STEPHENS BY LAUNCESTON (Wes) Newport
MI (Ptd CFHS)

ST STEPHENS BY LAUNCESTON (Bible Christian/Meth) Truscott [1882 Return]
MI (Ptd CFHS)

ST STEPHENS BY SALTASH St Stephen [East Hundred; St Germans Union] [1455]
United with SALTASH
OR C 1545-1973 M 1545-1978 B 1545-1974 (CRO)
BT CMB 1674-1736, 1741-72 (CRO); CMB 1597-1673, 1738, 1773-1823, 1828-40
(DRO)
Cop M 1813-37 (CMI); B 1813-37 (CBI); Extr CMB 1608-73 (SG); M 1599-1673
from BT (Boyd)
Cop (Mf) CMB 1597-1812 (Mf of BT at DRO: CRO,CSL); M 1546-1875 (Ross);
Extr C 1679-1737, 1741-72 from BT (IGI); C 1679-1737, 1741-72
from BT (SLC)
MI Ch (Ptd Jewers 95-124)

ST STEPHENS BY SALTASH (Bapt) Saltash [1882 Return]

ST STEPHENS BY SALTASH (Calv Bapt) Burraton [1882 Return]

ST STEPHENS BY SALTASH (Wes) Trematon [Kelly 1856]; [1882 Return];
closed 1983

ST STEPHENS BY SALTASH (Wes) Forder [1882 Return]

ST STEPHENS BY SALTASH (Wes) Burraton [1882 Return]

ST STEPHENS BY SALTASH (Plymouth Brethren) Burraton [Kelly 1889]

STICKER *see* ST MEWAN

ST STITHIANS St Stythians [Kerrier Hundred; Redruth Union] [1874] United
with PERRANARWORTHAL, GWENNAP
OR C 1656-1983 M 1690-1993 B 1658-1992 (CRO)
BT CMB 1676-1736, 1741-72 (CRO); CMB 1597-1673, 1737-40, 1773-1839 (DRO)
Cop M 1614, 1654-1812 (Ptd Phillimore: 1904); CMB 1614-1751 (CRO);
CMB 1597-1634, 1800-12 from BT; CB 1653-1837 (DCRS/WSL); C 1653-1751
M 1598-1694 (CSL); C 1713-1813 B 1710-1814 (Ts CRO,RIC); M 1813-37
(CMI); M 1598-1812 (SG); M 1654-1812 from OR; M 1598-1673 from BT
(Boyd); M 1800-12 (Pallot)

ST STITHIANS cont.
Cop (Mf) C 1653-1959 MB 1654-1959 (RIC); CMB 1597-1812 (Mf of BT at DRO:
          CRO,CSL); C 1753-1812 (SG); M 1813-1900 (Ross); Extr C 1597-1634,
          1653-1861 M 1655-1750 (IGI); C 1597-1634, 1753-1861 M 1655-1750
          (SLC)
MI (Ptd CFHS)

ST STITHIANS (Wes) 'Stithians in Gwennap' [1882 Return]; [Kelly 1935]
OR C 1844-57 (PRO)
Cop C 1844-57 (SG)
Cop (Mf) Extr C 1844-57 (IGI); C 1844-57 (SLC)

ST STITHIANS (Wes) Foundry Chapel, Velandrocia [1882 Return]

ST STITHIANS (Wes) Penhalvean [Kelly 1889]

ST STITHIANS (UMFC/U Meth) Hendra = ? Wes Hendra. Erected 1814;
Wes [1882 Return]
OR C 1858-1976 M 1947-74 (CRO)

ST STITHIANS (Free Meth) Penmennor. Erected 1866

STOKE CLIMSLAND or STOKECLIMSLAND dedication unknown [East Hundred;
Launceston Union] [1608]
OR C 1548-1975 M 1538-1963 B 1539-1950 (CRO)
BT CMB 1675-1736. 1741-72 (CRO); CMB 1597-1673, 1737-40, 1773-1812, 1814,
   1817-20, 1822, 1824-25, 1829, 1832, 1836-39, 1841-45 (DRO)
Cop MB 1538-1820 (CSL); CMB 1538-1629 (CRO); C 1837-75 M 1876-1900 (CFHS);
    M 1538-1639 (Ms RIC); M 1813-37 (CMI); M 1597-1674 (SG); M 1597-1673
    from BT (Boyd); B 1813-37 (CBI)
Cop (Mf) CMB 1597-1812 (Mf of BT at DRO: CRO,CSL); M 1538-1875 (Ross);
        Extr C 1675-1773 (IGI); C 1675-1773 (SLC)
MI (Ptd CFHS)

STOKE CLIMSLAND (Wes) Luckett [1882 Return]
MI (Ptd CFHS)

STOKE CLIMSLAND (Wes) Venterdon [1882 Return]
MI (Ptd CFHS)

STOKE CLIMSLAND (Wes) Holmbush [Kelly 1889]

STOKE CLIMSLAND (Bible Christian) Brays Shop [1882 Return]
MI (Ptd CFHS)

STOKE CLIMSLAND (Bible Christian) Downgate. Erected 1854 [1882 Return]

STOKE CLIMSLAND (Bible Christian) Cross [Kelly 1889]

STOKE CLIMSLAND (UMFC) Downhouse = ? (Wes Meth Assn) Upsett, formerly
Downhouse. Erected 1850; [1882 Return] new chapel 1885
MI (Ptd CFHS)

STOKE CLIMSLAND (Meth) Kelly Bray. Erected 1908
MI (Ptd CFHS)

STOKE CLIMSLAND (Plymouth Brethren) Hampt. Jehovah Jireh. Erected 1835.
Burial ground [Kelly 1935]
MI (Ptd CFHS)

STOKE CLIMSLAND (S of F) f c.1656. Part of East Cornwall MM. Meetings often held at CALLINGTON. Meeting house 1732
<u>OR</u> B 1663-76 in CORNWALL QM register RG 6/1578 (PRO); Z 1675-1712
   M 1668-1724 B 1663-1722: RG 6/1249; B 1659-89: RG 6/1498 (PRO)
<u>Cop</u> B 'at Stoak burying place' 1663-76 in 1828 copy old register book of
   Cornwall QM (CRO)

STOW ST JAMES   *see* JACOBSTOW

STRATTON St Andrew [Stratton Hundred; Stratton Union] [1613] United with
LAUNCELLS
<u>OR</u> C 1687-1980 M 1687-1989 B 1687-1978 (CRO) Noted in 1831: CB deficient
   1733-51
<u>BT</u> CMB 1674-1735, 1741-72 (CRO); CMB 1611-73, 1737-40, 1773-1836 (DRO)
<u>Cop</u> M 1674-1812 (Ptd Phillimore: 1912); CMB 1611-91 from BT; CMB 1687-1860
   (DCRS/WSL); CMB 1611-1860 (CRO,RIC,SG); M 1813-37 (CMI); M 1674-1812
   from OR; M 1611-73 from BT (Boyd); M 1800-12 (Pallot); M 1876-1900
   (CFHS); B 1813-37 (CBI)
<u>Cop (Mf)</u> CMB 1611-1812 (Mf of BT at DRO: CRO,CSL); M 1813-75 (Ross);
      Extr C 1611-33, 1663-1860 (IGI); C 1611-33, 1663-1860 (SLC)
<u>MI</u> (Ptd CFHS); ch,cy 1977 (Ts SG)

STRATTON St Michael and All Angels, Bude Haven. Erected 1835. Parish created
1836 from STRATTON. Now with MARHAMCHURCH
<u>OR</u> C 1836-1978 M 1849-1970 B 1848-1972 (CRO)
<u>BT</u> None
<u>Cop</u> C 1837-60 M 1849-60 B 1848-60 (Ts RIC, SG); CMB 1843-60 (CRO)
<u>Cop (Mf)</u> M 1849-75 (Ross); Extr C 1843-60 (IGI)
<u>MI</u> (Ptd CFHS); ch,cy (Ts SG)

STRATTON (RC) St Peter, Bude Haven f 1926

STRATTON (Presb) fl 1672-90

STRATTON (Wes) Market Street. Erected 1837 [1882 Return]   [Kelly 1889]

STRATTON (Wes) Bude Circuit
<u>OR</u> C 1894-1935 (Barnstaple Record Office, Devon)

STRATTON (Wes) Bude
<u>OR</u> C 1861-1927 (Barnstaple Record Office, Devon)

STRATTON (Bible Christian/U Meth) Bush. Erected 1869 ? [1882 Return];
Meth [Kelly 1935]
<u>OR</u> M 1854-76 (CRO)

STRATTON (Wes Meth Assn) [Kelly 1856]

STRATTON (UMFC) Stratton [1882 Return] = ? (Free Meth). Erected 1838
[Kelly 1889]

STRATTON (UMFC) Bude [1882 Return]

STREET AN GARROW   *see* ST IVES

SUMMERCOURT   *see* ST ENODER

SUMMERCOURT   *see* ST GLUVIAS

SUNNY CORNER   *see* GWENNAP

TALKARNE   *see* MINSTER

TALLAND St Tallan [West Hundred; Liskeard Union] [841] see also LOOE.
Now with LANSALLOS
OR C 1653-1987 M 1653-1996 B 1653-1978 (CRO) Noted in 1831: up to 1731
"very imperfect and many years illegible"
BT CMB 1680-1736, 1741-72 (CRO); CMB 1617-73, 1737-40, 1773-1812, 1816,
1818, 1827-29, 1831, 1833, 1835-38, 1840-41 (DRO)
Cop CMB 1617-30 from BT; CMB 1653-1837 Banns 1799-1837 (DCRS/WSL);
M 1654-1837 (Ts with index, CRO,RIC); M 1654-1812 (CFHS); M 1617-1837
(CSL); M 1813-37 (CMI); M 1617-74 (SG); M 1617-73 from BT (Boyd);
M 1790-1812 (Pallot); B 1813-37 (CBI)
Cop (Mf) CMB 1607-1811 (Mf of BT at DRO: CRO,CSL); M 1654-1875 (Ross);
Extr CMB 1617-37; CMB 1653-1837 (SG); Extr CM 1617-1837 (IGI);
CM 1617-1837 (SLC)
MI (Ptd CFHS); ch (Ptd J.Parson *A Short History and Description of Talland
Church*: 1920); cy 1959 (Ts SG)

TALLAND St John the Baptist, Polperro. Erected 1837, chapel-of-ease to
Talland

TALLAND (RC) Sclerder, Our Lady of Light erected 1851. Mission moved from
Trelawne, Pelynt, 1860. Carmelite Convent 1864-71, 1981+ (Poor Clares 1965
Directory) Now Carmelite Nuns
OR C 1833+ M 1856+ B 1856+ (Inc)
Cop D 1851-1981 (Catholic FHS)
MI (Ptd CFHS)

TALLAND (Wes) Polperro f 1789 [1882 Return]
OR ZC 1818-37 (PRO); C 1872-89 M 1978-94 (CRO)
Cop ZC 1818-37 (SG)
Cop (Mf) ZC 1818-37 (DCRS/WSL); Extr ZC 1818-37 (IGI); ZC 1818-37 (SLC)

TALLAND (Wes) Pool, Polperro. Erected 1862

TALLAND (Bible Christian) Polperro [Kelly 1889]

TALLAND (Wes Meth Ass/UMFC/U Meth) Central, Polperro [1882 Return]
OR C 1837-1915 (CRO)

TALLAND (Free Meth) Mable Barrow [Kelly 1889]
OR C 1837-1915 (CRO)

TALSKIDDY   *see* ST COLUMB MAJOR

TAMERTON, NORTH St Denis [Part Stratton Hundred (Cornwall), part Roborough
Hundred (Devon); Holsworthy Union] [517] United with BOYTON, and with
Werrington, St Giles in the Heath and Virginstow [Devon]
OR C 1560-1865 M 1560-1962 B 1560-1937 (CRO) Noted in 1831: CMB 1556+;
see DCRS/RIC copy and IGI below: C 1556+ M 1542+ B 1562+
BT CMB 1674-1736, 1741-72 (CRO); CMB 1597-1673, 1737-40, 1773-1814, 1816-37
(DRO)
Cop C 1556-1837 M 1542-1837 B 1562-1837 (DCRS/WSL); M 1813-37 (CMI);
M 1837-97 (CFHS); M 1599-1674 (SG); M 1597-1673 from BT (Boyd);
B 1813-37 (CBI)
Cop (Mf) CMB 1597-1812 (Mf of BT at DRO: CRO,CSL); M 1542-1837 (Ross);
Extr C 1556-1837 M 1542-1837 (IGI); C 1556-1837 M 1542-1837 (SLC)

TAMERTON, NORTH (Meth) [Kelly 1935]

ST TEATH St Teatha [Trigg Hundred; Camelford Union] [1260]
OR C 1558-1993 M 1558-1994 B 1558-1992 (CRO)
BT CMB 1676-1736, 1741-72 (CRO); CMB 1608-70, 1737-40, 1773-1812, 1825,
    1827-49 (DRO)
Cop M 1558-1812 (Ptd Phillimore: 1900); C 1558-1846 M 1558-1837 B 1558-1845
    (Ts RIC,CFHS); CMB 1558-1722 surnames only (CSL); M 1813-37 from BT,
    incomplete (CFHS); M 1813-37 with index (CRO); M 1813-37 (CMI);
    M 1813-37 from BT (CFHS); M 1558-1812 (Boyd); M 1790-1812 (Pallot);
    B 1813-37 (CBI)
Cop (Mf) CMB 1609-1812 (Mf of BT at DRO: CRO,CSL); Extr C 1713-1804
         M 1558-1812 (IGI); C 1713-1804 (SLC)
MI (Ptd CFHS)

ST TEATH St John the Evangelist, Delabole. Erected 1881
OR (CRO)

ST TEATH (Wes) Pengelly. Erected 1806; rebuilt 1869 [1882 Return]
[Kelly 1889]

ST TEATH (Bible Christian) Treligga. Erected 1836 [Kelly 1889]

ST TEATH (Bible Christian) [Kelly 1856]; Church Town [1882 Return]

ST TEATH (Bible Christian) Medrose. Erected 1835; rebuilt 1863 [1882 Return]

ST TEATH (UMFC) [1882 Return]

ST TEATH (Free Meth) Church Town [Kelly 1889]

ST TEATH (Free Meth) Treligga [Kelly 1889]

ST TEATH (Free Meth) Pengelly [Kelly 1889]

ST TEATH (Meth) Erected 1863 [Pevsner]
MI (Ptd CFHS)

TEMPLE St Catherine [Trigg Hundred; Bodmin Union] [29] Church of Knights
Templar ruined by 18th century. Outside episcopal authority until 1774.
Said to have been a 'Gretna Green' for illicit marriages until 1754.
Rebuilt 1883. United 1972 with BLISLAND. Now with BLISLAND, ST BREWARD
OR M 1884-1960 (CRO) and see BLISLAND
BT None
Cop (Mf) M 1884-1960 (Ross)
MI (Ptd CFHS)

TEMPLE (Bible Christian) f c.1879 [Kelly 1897]; =? Meth f c.1875
[Kelly 1935]

TEMPLE   see BLISLAND

TETSON   see MARHAMCHURCH

ST THOMAS BY LAUNCESTON St Thomas the Apostle [East Hundred; Launceston
Union] Former chapelry in LAUNCESTON. Separate parish 1726. United with
LAUNCESTON
OR C 1652-1943 M 1563-1971 B 1595-1890 (CRO) Noted in 1831: CMB 1673+.
    CB deficient 1736-45, 1752-55

ST THOMAS BY LAUNCESTON cont.
BT CMB 1681-1735,1741-72 (CRO); CMB 1623-72, 1737-40, 1773-1839 (DRO)
Cop M 1563-73, 1623-26, 1644, 1652, 1664, 1672-1812 (Ts RIC,CFHS,SG);
   M 1813-37 (CMI); B 1813-37 (CBI); M 1623-72 from BT (Boyd)
Cop (Mf) CMB 1623-1812 (Mf of BT at DRO: CRO,CSL); M 1662-1875 (Ross);
      Extr C 1681-1804 (IGI); C 1681-1804 (SLC)
MI (Ptd CFHS)

ST THOMAS BY LAUNCESTON St Mary, Tregadillett. Mission church erected 1875.
Now Anglican/Methodist

ST THOMAS BY LAUNCESTON (Wes)
OR B 1858-1922 (CRO)

ST THOMAS BY LAUNCESTON (Wes) Tregadillett f 1874 [1882 Return];
Meth [Kelly 1935]
MI (Ptd CFHS)

THREE BURROWS   see ST AGNES

THURDON   see KILKHAMPTON

TIDEFORD   see ST GERMANS

TINTAGEL St Materiana [Lesnewth Hundred; Camelford Union] [1006 including
Borough of Bossiney]
OR C 1569-1980 M 1588-1910 B 1546-1978 (CRO)
BT CMB 1679-1736, 1741-72 (CRO); CMB 1607-74, 1737-40, 1773-1822, 1824-33
   (DRO)
Cop M 1588-1812 (Ptd Phillimore: 1902); M 1558-1812 (CFHS); M 1813-37 (CMI);
   M 1837-75 (CFHS); M 1588-1812 (Boyd); M 1790-1812 (Pallot); B 1813-37
   (CBI)
Cop (Mf) CMB 1607-1812 (Mf of BT at DRO: CRO,CSL); M 1813-75 (Ross);
      Extr C 1678-1804 M 1588-1812 (IGI); C 1678-1804 (SLC)
MI (Ptd CFHS)

TINTAGEL St Piran, Trethevy.15th century chapel, in agricultural usage until
restored for ecclesiastical use in 1940s
OR None

TINTAGEL The Holy Family, Treknow.Mission church erected early 20th century.
OR None

TINTAGEL (RC) St Paul f 1934

TINTAGEL (Bible Christian/U Meth) Trewarmett, Erected 1856 [1882 Return]
OR C 1940-86 (CRO)

TINTAGEL (Bible Christian) Bossinney. Erected 1860 [1882 Return]
[Kelly 1889]

TINTAGEL (Wes Meth Assn) [Kelly 1856]

TINTAGEL (UMFC/U Meth) = ? Trevena. Erected 1838 [Kelly 1889]
OR C 1903-35 (CRO)

TINTAGEL (Meth)
Cop C 1936-91 (CFHS)

TOLSKITHY   *see* ILLOGAN

TOLVERTH   *see* GULVAL

TORLEVEN   *see* SITHNEY

TORPOINT   *see* ANTONY

TOWAN   *see* ST MERRYN

TOWEDNACK or WEDNACK St Tewinock [Penwith Hundred; Penzance Union] [737]
Chapelry in LELANT. Separate parish 1902. Now with ZENNOR
OR C 1676-1983 M 1677-1983 B 1683-1985 (CRO) Noted in 1831: "No.1 contains
    loose Papers of Bap.1676-1706; Bur. 1683-1706, copied from a private
    list of the Parish Clerk; Marr.1677-1705, no Registers till commencement
    of the Book; Bap. Bur.1720-81 Marr.1720-54".
BT CMB 1676-1736, 1741-71 (CRO); CMB 1597-1673, 1737-40, 1773-1837, 1840,
    1842-56 (DRO)
Cop M 1676-1812 (Ptd Phillimore: 1903); CB 1708-20 (Ms RIC); M 1813-37
    (CMI); C 1676-1812 B 1683-1812 (CSL,SG,Morrab); M 1676-1812 from OR;
    M 1597-1674 from BT (Boyd); M 1790-1812 (Pallot); M 1837-75 (CFHS);
    B 1813-37 (CBI)
Cop (Mf) C 1676-1812 B 1683-1812 (Mf of Ts, RIC); CMB 1603-1812 (Mf of BT at
        DRO: CRO,CSL); M 1813-75 (Ross); Extr CM 1676-1812 (IGI);
        C 1676-1812 (SLC)
MI (Ptd CFHS)

TOWEDNACK (Wes) [1882 Return] 4 Wes chapels in Towednack [Kelly 1856]

TOWEDNACK (Wes) Lady Downs [Kelly 1889]

TOWEDNACK (Wes) Nancledra. Erected 1844 [1882 Return]; [Kelly 1935]

TOWEDNACK (Wes) Coldharbour. Erected 1845 [Kelly 1935]

TOWEDNACK (Bible Christian) Lady Downs [1882 Return]

TOWEDNACK (Prim Meth) Nancledra Hill. Erected 1855 [1882 Return]

TOWEDNACK (Bible Christian) Georgia Lane [Kelly 1889]

TOWEDNACK (Prim Meth) Georgia [1882 Return]

TOWEDNACK (Teetotal Meth) [Kelly 1856]

TOWNSEND   *see* FEOCK

TOWNSHEND   *see* CROWAN

TREBARTHA   *see* LEWANNICK

TREBARVAH   *see* CONSTANTINE

TREBUDDANNON   *see* ST COLUMB MAJOR

TREBULLET   *see* LEZANT

TREBURLEY   *see* LEZANT

TRECROGO LANE END	*see* PETHERWIN, NORTH
TREDAVOE	*see* PENZANCE
TREDINNICK	*see* ST NEOT
TREDRIZZICK	*see* ST MINVER
TREECROSS	*see* PETHERWIN, SOUTH
TREEN	*see* ST LEVAN
TREGADA	*see* LAWHITTON
TREGADILLETT	*see* ST THOMAS BY LAUNCESTON
TREGAJORRAN	*see* ILLOGAN
TREGAMINION	*see* TYWARDREATH
TREGANETHA	*see* ST WENN
TREGANGEEVES	*see* ST AUSTELL
TREGARN	*see* ST KEVERNE
TREGATHENAN	*see* SITHNEY
TREGAVARA	*see* MADRON
TREGEARE	*see* LANEAST
TREGEREST	*see* SANCREED
TREGERTHEN	*see* ZENNOR
TREGIDDEN	*see* ST MARTIN IN MENEAGE
TREGISWIN	*see* RUAN LANIHORNE
TREGONA	*see* ST EVAL
TREGONETHA	*see* ST WENN
TREGONNY HILL	*see* MEVAGISSEY
TREGONY	*see* CUBY
TREGOSS	*see* ROCHE
TREGREGHAN MILLS	*see* ST AUSTELL
TREGREHAN	*see* ST BLAZEY
TREGURTHEN	*see* LUDGVAN
TREKNOW	*see* TINTAGEL
TRELAWNE	*see* PELYNT

TRELEIGH   *see* REDRUTH

TRELIGGA   *see* ST TEATH

TRELIGHTS   *see* ST ENDELLION

TRELILL   *see* ST KEW

TELOGUITHACK   *see* WENDRON

TRELOWTH   *see* ST MEWAN

TRELUSWELL   *see* ST GLUVIAS

TRELYON   *see* ST STEPHEN IN BRANNEL

TREMAILL   *see* DAVIDSTOW

TREMAINE St Winwaloe [East Hundred; Launceston Union] [118] Chapelry in
EGLOSKERRY. Separate parish 1719. United with EGLOSKERRY, NORTH PETHERWIN,
TRESMERE
OR CB 1726-1968 M 1726-1925 (CRO) No earlier register noted in 1831.
    see EGLOSKERRY
BT CMB 1674-1736,1741-72 (CRO); CMB 1612-73, 1737-40, 1773-1834 (DRO)
Cop M 1674-1812 (Ptd Phillimore: 1902); M 1813-37 (CMI); M 1612-1812 (SG);
    M 1727-1812 from OR; M 1612-73 from BT (Boyd); M 1790-1812 (Pallot);
    B 1813-37 (CBI)
Cop (Mf) C 1726-1937 M 1726-1913 B 1726-1941 (RIC); CMB 1612-1812 (Mf of BT
         at DRO: CRO,CSL); Extr C 1674-1729 (SG); M 1674-1726, 1817-76,
         1884-1925 (Ross); Extr C 1674-1805, 1813-75 M 1674-76, 1700-1884
         (IGI); C 1674-1805 (SLC)
MI (Ptd CFHS)

TREMAINE (Wes) Erected 1847 [Kelly 1889]
OR C 1945-78 (CRO)

TREMAINE (Wes) Trusell [Kelly 1889]

TREMAINE   *see* EGLOSKERRY

TREMAR   *see* ST CLEER

TREMATON   *see* ST STEPHENS BY SALTASH

TREMEAR   *see* ST TUDY

TREMODRETT   *see* ROCHE

TRENANCE   *see* ST ISSEY

TRENANCE   *see* MAWGAN IN PYDAR

TRENANT   *see* ST NEOT

TRENARREN   *see* ST AUSTELL

TRENCREEK   *see* ST COLUMB MINOR

TRENDRINE   *see* ZENNOR

TRENEGLOS St Gregory [Lesnewth Hundred; Launceston Union] [183] United with
ST GENNYS, JACOBSTOW, WARBSTOW
OR C 1686-1812 M 1695-1838 B 1695-1812 (CRO) Noted in 1831: C deficient
    1686-93
BT CMB 1676-1736, 1741-72 (CRO); CMB 1597-1673, 1737-40, 1773-1836 (DRO)
Cop M 1682, 1687, 1694-1812 (Ptd Phillimore: 1917); M 1813-37 (CMI);
    M 1614-1812 (SG); M 1694-1812 from OR; M 1597-1673 from BT (Boyd);
    M 1790-1812 (Pallot)
Cop (Mf) C 1695-1813 M 1695-1753 B 1695-1812 (RIC); CMB 1598-1812 (Mf of BT
       at DRO: CRO,CSL); M 1813-37 (Ross); Extr C 1676-83, 1686-1813
       M 1682-1804 (IGI); C 1676-83 M 1682-1804 (SLC)
MI (Ptd CFHS)

TRENEGLOS (Bible Christian) Bethel, Goads Green [1882 Return];
(Meth) Bethel [Kelly 1935]

TRENEWAN	*see* LANSALLOS
TRENGROVE	*see* MENHENIOT
TRENOWETH	*see* MABE
TRENOWIN	*see* LUDGVAN
TRENWHEAL	*see* BREAGE
TRENYTHON	*see* TRURO
TREQUITE	*see* ST KEW
TRERUFFE HILL	*see* REDRUTH
TRESAISE	*see* ROCHE
TRESCAW	*see* BREAGE
TRESCO	*see* SCILLY ISLES
TRESILLIAN	*see* MERTHER
TRESILLIAN	*see* PROBUS
TRESKILLARD	*see* ILLOGAN
TRESLOTHAN	*see* CAMBORNE

TRESMERE or **TRESMEER** St Nicholas [East Hundred; Launceston Union] [171]
United with EGLOSKERRY, NORTH PETHERWIN, TREMAINE
OR C 1625-1979 M 1574-1908 B 1673-1979 (CRO) Noted in 1831: "An old Burial
    Register was taken to Launceston Assizes, and proceedings have been
    instituted against the Churchwarden to whose care it was entrusted, to
    compel its restoration."
BT CMB 1679-1736, 1741-72 (CRO); CMB 1597-1673, 1737-40, 1773-1836 (DRO)
Cop M 1597-1673 from BT (Boyd); M 1613-65 (SG); M 1813-37 (CMI); M 1815-35
    (CRO); M 1837-1908 (CFHS); B 1813-37 (CBI)
Cop (Mf) C 1625-1960 M 1574-1952 B 1673-1959 (RIC); CMB 1597-1812 (Mf of BT
       at DRO: CRO,CSL); M 1574-1908 (Ross); Extr C 1625-1875 (IGI);
       C 1625-1875 (SLC)
MI (Ptd CFHS)

TRESMERE (Bible Christian) [Kelly 1856]

TRESPARRETT   *see* ST JULIOT

TRESWITHIAN   *see* CAMBORNE

TRETHEVY   *see* TINTAGEL

TRETHEVEY   *see* ST LEVAN

TRETHOSA   *see* ST STEPHEN IN BRANNEL

TRETHURGY   *see* ST AUSTELL

TRETOIL   *see* LANIVET

TREVADIOCK CROSS *see* LEWANNICK

TREVALGA St Petroc [Lesnewth Hundred; Camelford Union] [192]
see also BOSCASTLE
OR C 1538-1975 M 1539-1933 B 1691-1977 (CRO) Noted in 1831: C deficient
    1589-1691; M 1693+ B 1691+
BT CMB 1685-1736, 1741-72 (CRO); CMB 1611-73, 1737-40, 1773-1846, 1848,
    1850-51 (DRO)
Cop M 1539-1812 (Ptd Phillimore: 1900); C 1538-1845 M 1539-1838 B 1693-1845
    (Ts RIC,CFHS); C 1813-75 M 1876-1900 (CFHS); M 1813-37 (CMI);
    M 1539-1812 (Boyd); M 1790-1812 (Pallot); B 1813-37 (CBI)
Cop (Mf) CMB 1611-1812 (Mf of BT at DRO: CRO,CSL); M 1813-75 (Ross);
        Extr C 1685-1804 M 1539-1670, 1692-1812 (IGI); C 1685-1804
        M 1539-1670 (SLC)
MI (Ptd CFHS)

TREVALGA (Bible Christian) f 1872 [Kelly 1897]; Meth [Kelly 1935]

TREVALGAN   *see* ST IVES

TREVANGER   *see* ST MINVER

TREVARRACK   *see* GULVAL

TREVARTH   *see* GWENNAP

TREVEAN   *see* PERRANUTHNOE

TREVEIGHAN   *see* MICHAELSTOW

TREVELLAS DOWNS   *see* ST AGNES

TREVELMOND   *see* LISKEARD

TREVENSON   *see* ILLOGAN

TREVERBYN   *see* ST AUSTELL

TREVERVA   *see* BUDOCK

TREVETHAN   *see* ST MERRYN

TREVONE   *see* PADSTOW

TREVORED   *see* FORRABURY

TREWALDER   *see* LANTEGLOS BY CAMELFORD

TREWARMETT   *see* TINTAGEL

TREWARTHA   *see* VERYAN

TREWASSA   *see* DAVIDSTOW

TREWELLARD   *see* ST JUST IN PENWITH

TREWEN St Michael [East Hundred; Launceston Union] [213] Chapelry in SOUTH
PETHERWIN. Peculiar of the Bishop of Exeter. United with LEZANT, LAWHITTON,
SOUTH PETHERWIN
OR C 1616-1979 M 1617-1953 B 1616-1979 (CRO) Vol. 1: CB 1616-1812
    M 1617-1761 described in 1831 as "a partial transcript"
BT CMB 1608-1838, 1840 (DRO)
Cop M 1610, 1617-1837 Banns 1754-1837 (Ts RIC,CFHS,SG); M 1813-37 (CMI);
    C 1616-1812 M 1837-75 B 1617-1812 (CFHS); B 1813-37 (CBI); M 1608-75
    from BT (Boyd)
Cop (Mf) M 1617-1825 (Ross); CMB 1608-1812 (Mf of BT at DRO: CRO,CSL)
MI (Ptd CFHS)

TREWEN (Wes) Piper's Pool [1882 Return]; Meth [Kelly 1935]
MI [Ptd CFHS]

TREWENNACK   *see* WENDRON

TREWETHEN   *see* LANEAST

TREWIDLAND   *see* LISKEARD

TREWOON   *see* ST MEWAN

TREWORGY   *see* RUAN LANIHORNE

TREZELAH   *see* MADRON

TRISILLIAN   *see* ST ERME

TRISPEN, TRISPIN *see* ST ERME

TROON   *see* BREAGE

TROON   *see* CAMBORNE

TRURO Cathedral of the Blessed Virgin Mary [Powder Hundred; Truro Union]
[2925] St Mary's parish church 1259, partly incorporated into new Cathedral
of Diocese of Truro 1880-1910
OR C 1597-1946 M 1597-1968 B 1597-1943 (CRO)
BT CMB 1677-1736, 1741-72 (CRO); CMB 1609-72, 1737-40, 1773-1812, 1814-24,
    1836-39, 1841-42, 1847-48 (DRO)
Cop CMB 1597-1837 Banns 1754-1802 (Ptd S.Gay *The register of marriages
    baptisms and burials of the parish of St Mary, Truro*: DCRS: 2 vols:
    1940); CMB 1609-72 from BT (DCRS/WSL); C 1633-1809 M 1597-1838 (CFHS);
    C 1837-75 (CFHS); M 1813-37 (CMI); M 1597-1837 (Boyd); ; M 1790-1812
    (Pallot); B 1813-37 (CBI)

TRURO cont.
Cop (Mf) CMB 1597-1959 (RIC); CMB 1609-1812 (Mf of BT at DRO: CRO,CSL);
     M 1840-1925 (Ross); Extr C 1597-1875 M 1597-1839 (IGI); C 1597-1875
     M 1597-1839 (SLC)
MI (Ptd CFHS)

TRURO St Paul, Agar Road. Erected 1846 as chapel-of-ease to ST CLEMENT.
Parish created 1865. United with ST CLEMENT
OR C 1865-1957 Banns 1880-98 M 1865-1985 (CRO)
Cop C 1865-75 M 1865-1900 (CFHS)
Cop (Mf) M 1865-1900 (Ross)
MI (Ptd CFHS)

TRURO St George, see KENWYN

TRURO St John, see KENWYN

TRURO All Saints, Highertown. see KENWYN

TRURO (RC) Our Lady of the Portal and St Piran f 1885 Dereham Terrace,
Chapel Hill; new church St Austell Street 1973

TRURO (RC) Trenython. Private chapel [Kelly 1889]

TRURO (Bapt) f 1789 First Chapel, Kenwyn Street, later River Street.
Rebuilt 1850 [1882 Return] Now Chapel Hill
OR Z 1760-1837 (PRO); Attendance lists 1829-33 membership list 1844 (CRO)
     None at church
Cop Z 1760-1837 (SG)
Cop (Mf) Z 1760-1837 (DCRS/WSL,CRO); Extr Z 1760-1837 (IGI)

TRURO (Bapt) Second Chapel. Erected 1841 [Bapt. Manual 1850]

TRURO (Presb) f Kenwyn 1672; moved to Truro by 1715. Closed by 1789.
Chapel sold to Bapt.

TRURO (Ind/Cong) f 1761; chapel at Cockpit 1769; Bethesda, River Street
erected 1776 [Cong.Yearbook 1850]; [1882 Return]
OR ZC 1769-1837 (PRO); C 1770-1868 (CRO)
Cop ZC 1769-1837 (SG)
Cop (Mf) ZC 1769-1837 (DCRS/WSL); Extr ZC 1769-1837 (IGI); ZC 1769-1837
          (SLC)

TRURO (Wes) St Mary's Chapel, Union Place, Pydar Street. Erected 1829-30
[1882 Return]
OR C 1810-37 (PRO)
Cop ZC 1810-37 (SG); Newlyn, Truro and St Agnes Methodist baptisms 1837-75
     (CFHS)
Cop (Mf) C 1810-37 (DCRS/WSL); Extr C 1810-37 (IGI); C 1810-37 (SLC)

TRURO (Wes) Lemon, William Street [Kelly 1889]
OR C 1930-61 (CRO)

TRURO (Wes) Merther Lane f by 1900

TRURO (Prim Meth) Kenwyn Street f 1878 [1882 Return]

TRURO (Bible Christian) Circuit. Continued as U Meth, below
OR ZC 1822-37 (PRO); C 1838-1908 (CRO)
Cop ZC 1822-37 (SG)
Cop (Mf) ZC 1822-37 (DCRS/WSL); Extr ZC 1822-37 (IGI); ZC 1822-37 (SLC)

TRURO (Bible Christian) Zelah Lane. Erected 1859 [Kelly 1889]

TRURO (Bible Christian/U Meth) St Clement Street. f c.1814. erected 1834
[1882 Return] Sold 1975
OR M 1950-74 (CRO)

TRURO (UMFC) St George, St George's Road [1882 Return]
OR Members' register c.1910 (CRO)

TRURO (Meth New Conn/U Meth) Ebenezer, Castle Street. Erected 1834.
[1882 Return] Demolished
OR ZC 1832-37 (PRO); C 1887-1906 (CRO)
Cop ZC 1832-37 (PRO)
Cop (Mf) ZC 1832-37 (DCRS/WSL); Extr ZC 1832-37 (IGI); ZC 1832-37 (SLC)

TRURO (Meth New Conn) Circuit
OR None known

TRURO (UMFC/U Meth) St George's Road; erected 1880
OR C 1910-84 (CRO)

TRURO (U Meth) Circuit, formerly Bible Christian
OR C 1909-38 (CRO)

TRURO (Meth) St Mary's Circuit, St Clement Street section
OR C 1948-74 (CRO)

TRURO (Meth) St George Circuit
OR C 1936-86 (CRO)

TRURO (Salvation Army) Kenwyn Street

TRURO (S of F) Truro Vean f c.1658. Part of ST AUSTELL MM. Joined FALMOUTH
MM 1680. Meeting house Paul's Terrace, erected 1825
OR Z 1655-80 M 1659-85 B 1656-87 in CORNWALL QM register RG 6/1578 (PRO);
Z 1658-73 M 1659-78 B 1659-87 in Western Division registers
RG 6/1503,1582 (PRO); B 1814-1907 (CRO); Z note 1838; B notes Kea and
Truro Vean burial ground 1836-60, 1865-1907; M 1839-94 Falmouth, Truro,
Redruth and Penzance; membership list ? 1814-94; B counterfoils 1926-66
(CRO
Cop Z 1659-80 M 1659-85 B 1656-87 in 1828 copy of old register book of
Cornwall QM (CRO); M 1659-78 (CFHS)
Cop (Mf) M 1839-94 ? (Ross)
MI (Ptd CFHS)

TRURO Cemetery
OR B 1929-54 (CRO)
MI (Ptd CFHS)

TRUSCOE   see BREAGE

TRUSCOTT   see ST STEPHENS BY LAUNCESTON

TRUSELL   see TREMAINE

TRYTHALL   see GULVAL

TUCKINGMILL   see CAMBORNE

ST TUDY St Tudy [Trigg Hundred; Bodmin Union] [658] United with ST MABYN,
MICHAELSTOW
OR   C 1559-1865 M 1560-1690, 1696-1963 B 1559-1899 (CRO)
BT   CMB 1682-1736, 1741-72 (CRO); CMB 1608-73, 1737-40, 1773-1812, 1814,
     1817-20, 1822-29, 1835-40 (DRO)
Cop M 1560-1690, 1696-1812 (Ptd Phillimore: 1902); M 1813-37 (CMI);
     C 1559-1729 (CRO); CB 1559-1812 (SG); M 1560-1812 (Boyd); M 1790-1812
     (Pallot); M 1837-76 (CFHS); B 1813-37 (CBI)
Cop (Mf) C 1559-1960 M 1560-1843 B 1559-1899 (RIC); CMB 1608-1812 (Mf of BT
         at DRO: CRO,CSL); M 1813-75 (Ross); Extr C 1559-1875 M 1560-1812
         (IGI); C 1559-1875 (SLC)
MI   (Ptd CFHS); ch,cy (Ptd J.Maclean *Parochial and Family History of the
     Deanery of Trigg Minor*: 1868-79)

ST TUDY (Wes Meth Assn) [Kelly 1856]; Erected 1869 [Kelly 1889]

ST TUDY (Meth) Erected 1889

ST TUDY (S of F) Tremear f c.1659. Part of ST MINVER MM. Joined ST MINVER
c.1685
OR   M 1659-1719 B 1669-1754 in CORNWALL QM register RG 6/1578 (PRO);
     Z 1609-1704 M 1659-85 B 1669-1712 in EAST CORNWALL MM register
     RG 6/1314 (PRO)
Cop Z 1659-1719 B 1669-1754 in 1828 copy of old register book of Cornwall QM
     (CRO); M 1712-63 extracted from MM registers 1838 (CRO)

TYWARDREATH St Andrew [Powder Hundred; St Austell Union] [2288] Now with
ST SAMPSON
OR   C 1642-1967 M 1642-1975 B 1642-1972 (CRO)
BT   CMB 1679-1736, 1741-72 (CRO); CMB 1608-73, 1737-40, 1773-1856, 1858-59
     (DRO)
Cop M 1642-1812 (Ptd Phillimore: 1905); CMB 1608-37 from BT; CB 1642-1837
     (DCRS/WSL); M 1813-37 (CMI); M 1837-50 (CFHS); M 1608-1812 (SG);
     M 1642-1812 from OR; M 1608-73 from BT (Boyd); M 1790-1812 (Pallot);
     B 1813-37 (CBI)
Cop (Mf) CMB 1642-1959 (RIC); CMB 1608-1812 (Mf of BT at DRO: CRO,CSL);
         M 1813-1925 (Ross); Extr C 1608-1875 (IGI); C 1608-1875 (SLC)
MI   (Ptd CFHS); cemetery (CFHS)

TYWARDREATH Tregaminion. Chapel-of-ease erected 1815
OR   None

TYWARDREATH (Wes) Well Street. Erected 1828 [1882 Return]
Cop C 1838-1930 (CFHS)

TYWARDREATH (Wes) Polkerris. Erected 1850 [1882 Return]

TYWARDREATH (Bible Christian/U Meth) Highway. Erected 1841 [1882 Return]
[Kelly 1889]
OR   C 1920-71 (CRO)
Cop C 1923-71 (CFHS)

TYWARDREATH (Bible Christian) Glenview. Erected 1826

TYWARDREATH (Bible Christian) Building in the occupation of Joseph Barron [1882 Return]

TYWARDREATH (Who refuse to be designated) Justice Room, the back of the Porcupine Inn [1882 Return]

UNY LELANT   *see* LELANT

UPSETT   *see* STOKE CLIMSLAND

UPTON CROSS   *see* LINKINHORNE

ST VEEP St Cyriacus and St Julitta [West Hundred; Liskeard Union] [697] United with LOSTWITHIEL, ST WINNOW, ST NECTAN'S CHAPEL, BOCONNOC
OR C 1538-1992 M 1558-1985 B 1558-1992 (CRO) Noted in 1831: B deficient 1647-53, 1693-1722
BT CMB 1676-1736, 1741-72 (CRO); CMB 1611-73, 1737-40, 1773-1812, 1814-17, 1821-28, 1830 (DRO)
Cop M 1558-1837 (Ts CRO,RIC); M 1558-1812 (CFHS); M 1813-37 (CMI); B 1813-37 (CBI); M 1611-73 (SG); M 1611-73 from BT (Boyd)
Cop (Mf) CMB 1611-1812 (Mf of BT at DRO: CRO,CSL); M 1558-1837 (Ross); Extr C 1676-1772 (IGI); C 1676-1772 (SLC)
MI (Ptd CFHS)

ST VEEP (Wes) [Kelly 1856]

ST VEEP (Wes) Lerryn [1882 Return]

VELANDROCIA   *see* ST STITHIANS

VENTERDON   *see* STOKE CLIMSLAND

VENTONLEAGUE   *see* PHILLACK

VERYAN or ELERKY St Symphorian [Powder Hundred; Truro Union] [1525] United with RUAN LANIHORNE
OR C 1683-1966 M 1683-1974 B 1683-1947 (CRO)
BT CMB 1676-1736, 1741-72 (CRO); CMB 1602-73, 1737-40, 1773-1837, 1839-52 (DRO)
Cop M 1676-1812 (Ptd Phillimore: 1915); CMB 1602-82 from BT; CB 1683-1837 (DCRS/WSL); C 1681-1742 M 1602-73 (SG); M 1813-37 (CMI); M 1676-1812 from OR; M 1602-73 from BT (Boyd); M 1800-12 (Pallot); B 1813-37 (CBI)
Cop (Mf) CMB 1602-1959 (RIC); CMB 1602-1812 (Mf of BT at DRO: CRO,CSL); M 1813-1925 (Ross); Extr C 1602-73, 1676-1875 M 1602-73, 1683-1754 (IGI); C 1602-73, 1676-1875 M 1602-73 (SLC)
MI (Ptd CFHS); Ch (Wall,81-83, Ms SG)

VERYAN All Saints, Portloe. Shared church building: Anglican/Methodist

VERYAN (Ind) Zion Chapel, Portloe f 1820. Closed
OR None known

VERYAN (Wes) Trewartha [1882 Return]; one Wes at Veryan [Kelly 1856]

VERYAN (Wes) Port Holland Chapel [1882 Return]

VERYAN (Bible Christian/U Meth) Port Holland [Kelly 1889]

VERYAN (Bible Christian/U Meth) Zion, Portloe [1882 Return]

VERYAN (Bible Christian) Ebenezer, Calendra [1882 Return]

VIRGINSTOW Devon parish in Diocese of Truro. *see* NIPR Devon

VOGUEBELOTH *see* ILLOGAN

WADEBRIDGE [Bodmin Union] Town located in ecclesiastical parishes of
EGLOSHAYLE and ST BREOCK. Civil parish created 1898, *see also* EGLOSHAYLE
St Petrock; St Conan, Washaway; ST BREOCK St Breoke

WADEBRIDGE St Mary's Church Centre, Trevanion Road, Wadebridge.
Erected 1951-52

WADEBRIDGE (RC) St Michael, Trevanson Street f 1948

WADEBRIDGE (Cong) f.1836; rebuilt 1874 [*Cong.Yearbook* 1850]; [1882 Return]
OR C 1843-98, 1901-50 M 1924-51 B 1922-47 (CRO)

WADEBRIDGE (Presb) Wadebridge. Licensed 1672; closed by 1690

WADEBRIDGE (Wes) Camelford Circuit. Wadebridge section
OR C 1884-1914 (CRO)

WADEBRIDGE (Wes) Erected 1879 [Kelly 1889]
OR C 1884-1914 (CRO)

WADEBRIDGE (Bible Christian) f 1852 [1882 Return]; Meth [Kelly 1935]

WADEBRIDGE (Wes Meth Assn/UMFC/U Meth) Egloshayle Road
OR C 1865-84 M 1935-70 (CRO)

WADEBRIDGE (U Meth) Camelford and Wadebridge Circuit
OR C 1925-32 (CRO)

WADEBRIDGE (S of F) Wadebridge f c.1821. Part of ST AUSTELL MM [1882 Return]
Currently [1998] meeting at John Betjeman Centre
OR B notes 1841 (CRO)

WALL *see* GWINEAR

WARBSTOW St Werburgh [Lesnewth Hundred; Launceston Union] [481] Chapelry in
TRENEGLOS. Separate parish 1926. United with ST GENNYS, JACOBSTOW, TRENEGLOS
OR CB 1695-1813 M 1695-1838 (CRO); for M 1745-71 *see* TRENEGLOS
BT CMB 1672-1736, 1741-72 (CRO); CMB 1612-73, 1737-40, 1772-1836 (DRO)
Cop M 1695-1812 (Ptd Phillimore: 1917); M 1813-37 (CMI); M 1612-1812 (SG);
        M 1695-1812 from OR; M 1612-29 from BT (Boyd); M 1790-1812 (Pallot)
Cop (Mf) CMB 1612-1812 (Mf of BT at DRO: CRO,CSL); M 1813-38 (Ross);
        Extr C 1681-1772, 1804-05 M 1681-1759, 1770-72, 1804-05 (IGI);
        C 1681-1772, 1804-05 M 1770-72, 1804-05 (SLC)
MI (Ptd CFHS)

WARBSTOW (Bible Christian) Canworthy Water f 1821 [1882 Return]
OR ZC 1821-24 (PRO)
Cop ZC 1821-24 (SG)
Cop (Mf) ZC 1821-24 (DCRS/WSL); Extr C 1821-24 (IGI); C 1821-24 (SLC)

WARLEGGAN St Bartholomew [West Hundred; Bodmin Union] [274] United with
ST NEOT
OR C 1548-1904 M 1548-1983 B 1548-1778 (CRO) Noted in 1831: CMB 1540+
BT CMB 1682-1735, 1741-72 (CRO); CMB 1614-70, 1737-40, 1773-1834, 1839-42
     (DRO)
Cop M 1547-1718; 1682-1812 (Ptd Phillimore: 2 vols 1904, 1903); CMB 1548-
     1719 (CRO,CFHS); M 1813-37 (CRO); M 1813-37 (CMI); CB 1547-1719 (SG);
     M 1547-1812 (Boyd); M 1790-1812 (Pallot); B 1813-37 (CBI)
Cop (Mf) C 1547-1904 M 1547-1837 B 1547-1960 (RIC); CMB 1614-1812 (Mf of BT
          at DRO: CRO,CSL); M 1813-37 (Ross); Extr C 1548-1875 M 1547-1837
          (IGI); C 1548-1875 M 1547-1837 (SLC)
MI (Ptd CFHS)

WARLEGGAN (Wes) Erected 1821 [Kelly 1889]

WARLEGGAN (Bible Christian) [Kelly 1889]

WASHAWAY   *see* EGLOSHAYLE

WEEK ST MARY St Mary [Stratton Hundred; Stratton Union] [769] United with
POUNDSTOCK, WHITSTONE
OR C 1602-1981 M 1602-1978 B 1602-1982 (CRO) Noted in 1831: CMB defective
     1707-50
BT CMB 1679-1736, 1741-72 (CRO); CMB 1611-73, 1737-40, 1773-1835, 1837-48,
     1850 (DRO)
Cop M 1602-1812 (Ptd Phillimore: 1917; 'hopelessly inaccurate' [Raymond]);
     CMB 1602-19 from BT (DCRS/WSL); M 1813-37 (CMI); M 1602-1812 (Boyd);
     M 1790-1812 (Pallot); M 1876-1900 (CFHS); B 1813-37 (CBI)
Cop (Mf) CMB 1611-1812 (Mf of BT at DRO: CRO,CSL); CB 1620-1812 (DCRS/WSL);
          M 18\;3-75 (Ross); Extr C 1602-1812 M 1679-1805 (IGI); C 1602-1812
          M 1679-1805 (SLC)

WEEK ST MARY (Wes) Erected 1821

WEEK ST MARY (Bible Christian) Circuit
OR C 1838-1934 (CRO)

WEEK ST MARY (Bible Christian) Bakeson Chapel [1882 Return]

WEEK ST MARY (Bible Christian) Zion [1882 Return]

WEEK ST MARY (Wes Meth Assn) [Kelly 1856, 1889]

WEEK ST MARY (U Meth) Circuit
OR C 1901-34 (CRO)

WEEK ST MARY (UMFC) Week Green [1882 Return]

WEEKHAMPTON   *see* KILKHAMPTON

WENDRON St Wendron [Kerrier Hundred; Helston Union] [4780] *see also* HELSTON,
chapelry with which now united
OR C 1560-1917 M 1560-1979 B 1560-1927 (CRO)
BT CMB 1677-1736, 1741-72 (CRO); CMB 1597-1670, 1737-40, 1773-1839, 1843-44
     (DRO) *and see* HELSTON

WENDRON cont
Cop M 1560-1812 (Ptd Phillimore: 1909); C 1562-1866 M 1560-1837 B 1560-1845
(CSL,CFHS); CB 1560-1812 M 1560-1837 (CRO); CMB 1597-1670 from BT;
CB 1560-1837 (DCRS/WSL); C 1562-78 M 1560-1812 (Ms RIC); C 1813-75
M 1876-1909 (CFHS); M 1813-37 (CMI); M 1560-1812 (Boyd); M 1800-12
(Pallot); B 1813-37 (CBI)
Cop (Mf) CMB 1597-1812 (Mf of BT at DRO: CRO,CSL); M 1813-75 (Ross);
Extr C 1562-1837 M 1597-1670 (IGI); C 1562-1837 M 1597-1670 (SLC)
MI (Ptd CFHS)

WENDRON St Decumannus, Merthen. 'Desecrated at the end of the last
century...now a farmyard' [Kelly 1889]

WENDRON Holy Trinity, Carnmenellis. Parish created 1846 from WENDRON.
Erected 1850. Demolished 1970
OR C 1846-1967 M 1851-1965 B 1851-1938 (CRO)
Cop (Mf) M 1851-75 (Ross)
MI (CFHS)

WENDRON St Andrew, Pencoys or Four Lanes. Erected 1880; parish created 1881
from Carnmenellis, to which united 1969. Now with REDRUTH, LANNER, TRELEIGH
OR C 1881-1989 M 1882-1990 B 1884-1990 (CRO)
MI (Ptd CFHS)

WENDRON St Christopher, Porkellis. Mission church erected 19th century.
Now dual purpose, village hall with chapel

WENDRON (Bapt) Lower Town [Kelly 1889]

WENDRON (Ind) Edgcombe f 1813
Cop B 1894-1994 (CFHS)

WENDRON (Ind) Treloguithack f pre-1821

WENDRON (Wes) Burhos or Burras [Kelly 1889] = ? Burrows [1882 Return]
OR C 1941-91 (CRO)

WENDRON (Wes) Manhay [1882 Return]
OR C 1964-69 (CRO)

WENDRON (Wes) Crelly [1882 Return]
OR C 1941-91 (CRO)

WENDRON (Wes) Porkellis [1882 Return]
OR C 1969-94 (CRO)

WENDRON (Wes) Edgcombe [1882 Return]

WENDRON (Wes) Forest [Kelly 1889]

WENDRON (Wes) Penmarth [Kelly 1889]

WENDRON (Wes) Coverackbridges [Kelly 1889]

WENDRON (Bible Christian) Bethel, Boskynwen Down [1882 Return]

WENDRON (Bible Christian) Bethesda, Carnkie Common [1882 Return]

WENDRON (UMFC/UM) Burhos
OR C 1889-96 (CRO)

WENDRON (UMFC/U Meth) Trewennack [1882 Return]
OR C 1969-93 (CRO)

WENDRON (UMFC/U Meth) Four Lanes or Penwys [Kelly 1889]

ST WENN St Wenna [Pydar Hundred; St Columb Major Union] [649] United with
ST COLUMB MAJOR
OR C 1706-1865 M 1706-1968 B 1706-1892 (CRO) No earlier registers noted in
    1831
BT CMB 1678-1736, 1741-72 (CRO); CMB 1609-73, 1737-40, 1773-1834 (DRO)
Cop M 1678-1812 (Ptd Phillimore: 1907); CMB 1608-1706 from BT (CRO);
    M 1813-37 (CMI); M 1609-1812 (SG); M 1678-1812 from OR; M 1609-73
    from BT (Boyd); M 1790-1812 (Pallot); B 1813-37 (CBI)
Cop (Mf) C 1706-1958 MB 1706-1959 (RIC); CMB 1609-1812 (Mf of BT at DRO:
        CRO,CSL); M 1813-1925 (Ross); Extr C 1608-1875 from BT (IGI);
        C 1608-1875 from BT (SLC)
MI (Ptd CFHS)

ST WENN (Wes) Tregonetha
OR C 1946-88 (CRO)
MI (Ptd CFHS)

ST WENN (Wes) Rosenannon [1882 Return]

ST WENN (Bible Christian) Treganetha [1882 Return]

ST WENN (UMFC/U Meth) = ? Demelza [1882 Return]
OR C 1890-1937 (CRO)

WENNACK   *see* TOWEDNACK

WERRINGTON Devon parish in Diocese of Truro. *see* NIPR Devon

WEST LOOE   *see* LOOE

WHEAL ALFRED   *see* PHILLACK

WHEAL BULLER   *see* REDRUTH

WHEAL BUSY   *see* KENWYN

WHEAL FRANCES   *see* PERRANZABULOE

WHITECROSS   *see* ST STEPHEN IN BRANNEL

WHITECROSS   *see* CURY

WHITECROSS   *see* LUDGVAN

WHITEMOOR   *see* ST DENNIS

WHITSTONE St Anne [Stratton Hundred; Stratton Union] [481]
OR C 1663-1981 M 1663-1977 B 1663-1963 (CRO)
BT CMB 1676-1736, 1741-72 (CRO); CMB 1597-1673, 1737-40, 1773-1823, 1825-
40, 1842-46, 1848-54 (DRO)
Cop M 1813-37 (CMI); B 1813-37 (CBI); M 1598-1674 (SG); M 1597-1673 from BT
(Boyd)
Cop (Mf) CMB 1663-1837 (DCRS/WSL); CB 1597-1960 M 1663-1960 (RIC);
CMB 1597-1812 (Mf of BT at DRO: CRO,CSL); M 1663-1925 (Ross);
Extr C 1597-1631, 1663-1875 M 1664-1875 (IGI); C 1597-1631,
1663-1875 M 1664-1837 (SLC)
MI (Ptd CFHS)

WHITSTONE (Bible Christian) [Kelly 1856]; Ebenezer, Boot. Erected 1864;
rebuilt 1885 [1882 Return] [Kelly 1889]

WIDEGATES   see MORVAL

WIDEMOUTH BAY   see POUNDSTOCK

WILCOVE   see ANTONY

WINNINGTON   see GUNWALLOE

ST WINNOW St Winnow [West Hundred; Bodmin Union] [1048] Peculiar of the Dean
and Chapter of Exeter. United with LOSTWITHIEL, ST NECTAN'S CHAPEL, ST VEEP,
BOCONNOC
OR C 1622-1970 M 1622-1947 B 1622-1920 (CRO)
BT CMB 1612-1832 (DRO)
Cop M 1622-1812 (Ptd Phillimore: 1906); CMB 1622-1724 (CRO); M 1813-37
(CMI); CB 1622-1812 M 1612-1812 (SG); M 1622-1812 from OR; M 1611-73
from BT (Boyd); M 1800-12 (Pallot); M 1837-75 (CFHS); B 1813-37 (CBI)
Cop (Mf) CMB 1612-1808 (Mf of BT at DRO: CRO,CSL); M 1813-75 (Ross);
Extr C 1612-19, 1622-1837 (IGI); C 1612-19, 1622-1837 (SLC)
MI (Ptd CFHS)

ST WINNOW St Nectan's Chapel. Medieval chapel, damaged in Civil War. Ruined
by 1947. Closed. Restored 1971
OR None
MI (Ptd CFHS)

ST WINNOW St Saviour, Bridgend, Chapel-of-ease erected 1896-97

ST WINNOW St Faith, Cornwall. House of Mercy Established at Truro 1861.
Erected 1864. Private chapel [Kelly 1897] St Faith's Training Home [Kelly
1935]

ST WINNOW (Presb) Ethy. fl 1672-90

ST WINNOW (Wes) Bofarnel [1882 Return]

ST WINNOW (Prim Meth) Bridgend f 1858 [1882 Return]; Meth [Kelly 1935]

WITHIEL St Clement [Pydar Hundred; Bodmin Union] [406] United with ROCHE
OR C 1567-1879 M 1568-1979 B 1568-1918 (CRO)
BT CMB 1678-1736, 1741-72 (CRO); CMB 1597-1673, 1737-40, 1773-1813, 1815,
1826-31, 1833-71 (DRO)
Cop M 1568-1812 (Ptd Phillimore: 1904); CMB 1597-1740 from BT (DCRS/WSL);
M 1813-37 (CMI); CB 1567-1812 (SG); M 1568-1812 (Boyd); M 1790-1812
(Pallot); M 1851-1925 (CFHS); B 1813-37 (CBI)

WITHIEL cont.
Cop (Mf) C 1786-1959 M 1754-1959 B 1788-1959 (RIC); CMB 1597-1812 (Mf of BT
    at DRO: CRO,CSL); M 1813-1925 (Ross); Extr C 1567-1875 (IGI);
    C 1567-1875 (SLC)
MI (Ptd CFHS)

WITHIEL (Wes) [Kelly 1897]

WITHIEL (Wes) Retire [1882 Return] [Kelly 1935]

WITHIEL (Bible Christian) [Kelly 1897]

WOODFORD   *see* MORWENSTOW

WOOLLEY   *see* MORWENSTOW

ZELAH   *see* ST ALLEN

ZENNOR St Senera [Penwith Hundred; Penzance Union] [811] Now with TOWEDNACK
OR C 1599-1963 M 1617-1977 B c1655-1988 (CRO) Noted in 1831: Vol.1:
    "Bap.Bur.Marr. 1592 or 1593-1713".
BT CMB 1681-1736, 1741-72 (CRO); CMB 1611-73, 1737-40, 1773-1838 (DRO)
Cop M 1617-1812 (Ptd Phillimore: 1906); C 1599-1837 M 1813-37 B 1713-1837
    (DCRS/WSL,RIC,Morrab); C 1599-1837 B 1713-1837 (CSL); C 1599-1600,
    1713-1837 M 1611-1837 (SG); M 1813-37 (CMI); M 1837-75 (CFHS); B 1813-37
    (CBI); M 1617-1812 from OR; M 1611-73 from BT (Boyd); M 1800-12 (Pallot)
Cop (Mf) C 1599-1837 M 1813-37 B 1713-1837 (Mt of Ts, RIC); CMB 1611-1812
    (Mf of BT at DRO: CRO,CSL); M 1813-37 (Ross); Extr C 1599-1608,
    1713-1837 M 1813-37 (IGI); C 1599-1608, 1713-1837 M 1813-37 (SLC)
MI (Ptd CFHS)

ZENNOR (Wes) Church Town. Erected 1809 [Kelly 1889, 1935]

ZENNOR (Wes) Porthmeor. Erected 1839 [1882 Return] [Kelly 1935]

ZENNOR (Wes) Tendrine. Erected 1843 [1882 Return]

ZENNOR (Bible Christian) Bethesda, Tregerthen. Erected 1833 [Kelly 1889]